MW01284255

Multisituated

Multisituated

Ethnography as Diasporic Praxis

———

KAUSHIK SUNDER RAJAN

DUKE UNIVERSITY PRESS *Durham and London* 2021

© 2021 DUKE UNIVERSITY PRESS

All rights reserved

Printed in the United States of America on
acid-free paper ∞

Cover designed by Drew Sisk
Text designed by Aimee C. Harrison
Typeset in Portrait Text Regular and Helvetica Neue
by Westchester Publishing Services

Library of Congress Cataloging-in-Publication Data
Names: Sunder Rajan, Kaushik, [date] author.
Title: Multisituated : ethnography as diasporic praxis /
Kaushik Sunder Rajan.
Description: Durham : Duke University Press, 2021. |
Includes bibliographical references and index.
Identifiers: LCCN 2021003040 (print)
LCCN 2021003041 (ebook)
ISBN 9781478013983 (hardcover)
ISBN 9781478014928 (paperback)
ISBN 9781478022206 (ebook)
Subjects: LCSH: Ethnology—Study and teaching (Higher) |
Anthropology—Methodology. | Decolonization—Study
and teaching (Higher) | Critical pedagogy. | Racism in
higher education. | Education and globalization. |
Culture and globalization. | BISAC: SOCIAL SCIENCE /
Anthropology / Cultural & Social
Classification: LCC GN307.8 .S86 2021 (print) |
LCC GN307.8 (ebook) | DDC 305.80071/1—dc23
LC record available at https://lccn.loc.gov/2021003040
LC ebook record available at https://lccn.loc.gov/2021003041

Cover art: Sujith S.N., *Untitled*, 2014. Watercolor on paper,
34 in. × 71.5 in. Courtesy of the artist and Vadehra Art
Gallery.

For Gayatri di

Contents

———

Acknowledgments ix

INTRODUCTION. A Problem,
a Paradox, a Politics . . . and a Praxis 1

1. Scale 29

2. Comparison 57

3. Encounter 91

4. Dialogue 136

CONCLUSION. Toward a
Diasporic Anthropology 169

Notes 189

References 229

Index 245

Acknowledgments

This book is an homage: to my teachers, to key collaborators and friends, and to my students. I acknowledge how they figure in to my thinking, because they inform the structure of this book and its argument.

My first and biggest acknowledgment is to Michael Fischer and George Marcus. I write this book under the sign of their work, which has been foundational to my even being able to think the research I have done over the past two decades. Fischer, as my dissertation advisor, taught me not just how to do ethnography, but also how to develop an ethnographic sensibility and why I should care to do so. Marcus taught me how to teach ethnography, by teaching alongside me and helping me develop an investment in a pedagogy of ethnography.

A second acknowledgment is to Gayatri Spivak. It was Spivak who brought Derrida to the Anglophone world with her translation of *Of Grammatology* (Derrida [1967] 1976). In significant measure, she also thus brought Derrida to India. This has autobiographical resonance for me, since my mother, Rajeswari Sunder Rajan, was teaching English at Delhi University at the time. Even though I was too young to have any inkling of (let alone inclination toward) the significance of this work, I was old enough to know that something exciting was afoot—not just in the endless confabulations over cups of tea between my mother and her friends in our flat, which would drive me somnolent with boredom, but also in recognizing that these were people who, inspired by scholars such as Spivak and Edward Said, were reformulating the pedagogy of English literature in the university. A certain "decolonizing" moment was actively underway, even if it was not called thus at the time. This was also, in directly entangled ways, an emergent intellectual and political moment in Indian feminism. Years before I had occasion to read Spivak, and well before I thought I would live a life in which I would want to, her immense intellectual and political influence had already imprinted itself upon me. Since becoming an academic myself, her work has become foundational to my thinking. Hence, this book is dedicated to her, for debts that cannot be repaid.

A third set of acknowledgments is to my peers. I obtained my PhD in a small, interdisciplinary program (Science, Technology and Society at the Massachusetts Institute of Technology) and had perforce to develop an intellectual peer group beyond my program. I was lucky to be among a generation of scholars being taught and brought into the emerging field of the anthropology of science, and I developed close and enduring conversations and friendships with a number of them while still a graduate student. Of special personal importance to me was my friendship with Kristin Peterson, a doppelgänger of sorts, in that our dissertation projects paralleled each other in significant methodological ways. Of equal importance to my intellectual growth were Joseph Dumit, another of my PhD advisors; and Kim Fortun, who was in the process of finalizing her extraordinary book *Advocacy after Bhopal* (2001) while I was a PhD student.

What was important about this peer group for me, in ways that endured well beyond my dissertation and common research investments, was their shared and continuing investment in pedagogy. (This indeed was true of my mother's generation and her friends at Delhi University in the 1980s; it is equally true of friends I have made recently in South Africa, who are actively intervening in the "decolonizing" moment in their country through pedagogical and curricular development.) My peers have been at the forefront of developing creative modalities of teaching ethnography, especially in ways that recognize the changing nature of the research university. Thus, they do not merely teach with the assumption that the endgame of pedagogy is disciplinary reproduction in the ivory tower of the metropolitan university; they are actively intervening in a pedagogy *of* the university itself through their teaching of ethnography. Kim Fortun (with Mike Fortun) spent many years teaching ethnographic method in the Science and Technology Studies (STS) Department of an engineering school, where the primary student demographic consisted of engineering students. How to think the stakes of ethnography in such a situation, especially alongside epistemic modalities that emphasize design-based learning? The Fortuns have answered this question through their teaching and also through the expression of that teaching in their own design-based ethnographic experiments, The Asthma Files and their Platform for Experimental Collaborative Ethnography (PECE) (http://theasthmafiles.org/; http://worldpece.org/), and in their respective multisited ethnographic monographs, *Advocacy after Bhopal* (K. Fortun 2001) and *Promising Genomics* (M. Fortun 2008). Joseph Dumit developed his "implosions project," initially, as an explanation of Donna Haraway's research method, articulating her pedagogy and praxis of vigilant curiosity (Dumit 2014). It has become part of a methods pedagogy toolkit in a number of anthropological graduate student teaching situations. Dumit has since proceeded to develop pedagogical articulations between anthropology, STS, and performance studies, developing a consideration of ethnography as bodily practice, with attention to both improvisation and fascia work (http://dumit.net/embodying-improvisation/; http://dumit .net/fascia-lab/). His exploration of the bodily work of ethnographic praxis is undertaken in pedagogical contexts where the terms under question (such as "improvisation") mean very different things depending on what any particular student is training to be (an anthropologist or dancer, for instance). Dumit develops these pedagogies through theoretical engagements with contemporary Black radical thought and feminist conceptualizations of practices of bodily relationality. Kristin Peterson joined the University of California at Irvine just as George Marcus and I had developed our initial iterations of the "Methods" pedagogy there. She developed our curriculum along more elaborated and systemic lines with Valerie Olson, producing a syllabus and curricular structure that I have borrowed from extensively myself while developing my "Methods" pedagogy at Chicago. Peterson and Olson are currently writing a book that will elaborate some of their key pedagogical concepts. Irvine has more generally been a forging ground for this book. I am grateful to have had an opportunity to present an initial series of lectures at the Critical Theory Institute there in 2018, which provided the first occasion for me to even think of my investments in ethnography as a book. I was subsequently invited to present chapter 3 of this book at Irvine's Center for Ethnography in early 2019. George Marcus, Kim Fortun, Mike Fortun, Kris Peterson, and Gabriele Schwab were gracious hosts and extraordinary interlocutors on both occasions.

Additionally, this book owes a debt of gratitude to Timothy Choy, Emilia Sanabria, and Kelly Gillespie, as well as to George Marcus, James Faubion, and Dominic Boyer, as the editors of the collection *Theory Can Be More Than It Used to Be*. I have largely learned to read the work of Marilyn Strathern, which is integral to my argument in chapter 2, in conversation with Choy (initially) and Sanabria (subsequently). Both Choy and Sanabria have read and commented on this manuscript in detail at different stages of its production. Choy organized a conversation with Kris Peterson at the University of California at Davis in February 2019, at which I received invaluable feedback: I am grateful to him and to members of the Anthropology and STS Departments there for their generous engagement. Sanabria spent days of her time in patient reading of and conversation with this work, especially consequent to readers' comments on a first draft of this manuscript, pushing hard at its lacunae and pulling forward its most generative threads. Gillespie's invitation to present chapter 2 at the "African Ethnographies" conference she co-organized at the University of the Western Cape was essential to the last stages of its conceptualization, especially in a postcolonial locale where questions of pedagogy and of the university are urgent and acutely political. Conversations with her at and beyond that conference have been both inspirational and sustaining. Meanwhile, an earlier version of my research on the Translational Health Science and Technology Institute of India (THSTI), elaborated in chapter 4, appeared in a different form and context in the aforementioned collection by Boyer, Faubion, and Marcus, and my initial capacity to think through that unpublished research owes greatly to my conversations with, and the editorial input of, the coeditors.

A final set of collaborators are my students. Not just those who have been subjected to my "Methods" pedagogy over the years (for which, a special debt of gratitude is owed to those in my initial "Methods" classes at Irvine with George Marcus, above all those who have continued conversations with me in years since in ways that constantly push me to think my stakes. Thank you, Janet Alexanian, Asya Anderson, Andrea Ballestero, Cristina Bejarano, Allison Fish, Philip Grant, Alexandra Lippmann, Marisa Menna, Joanne Nucho, Seo-Young Park, and Robert Werth). Thanks also to those who were members of the seminar I taught at Chicago in the winter of 2018 on the topic "Multi-si(gh)ted," which became the forging ground of and inspiration for this book. Thank you, Winston Berg, Ji Yea Hong, Rachel Howard, Melissa Itzkowitz, Alexandra Kaul, Jeanne Lieberman, Nida Paracha, Ellen Richmond, Jill J. Tan, Shruti Vaidya, and Emily Wilson.

Many thanks to Ken Wissoker for believing in and supporting this project and for his editorial stewardship. I am grateful to Kate Herman, Ryan Kendall, Liz Smith, and Christine Dahlin for their support and assistance through the review and production process; to Sujith S.N. for allowing me to use his painting (*Untitled*) on the cover and to Drew Sisk for his cover design; and to the generous reading by two anonymous reviewers for Duke University Press. Finally, a debt of gratitude to my mother, Rajeswari Sunder Rajan, who has taught me what it means to be a postcolonial scholar.

Introduction

A Problem, a Paradox,
a Politics . . . and a Praxis

This book stems from a problem, a paradox, and a politics.

The problem is this: ethnography is a practice that is suited to intimate, experience-proximal observation and interpretation, yet it increasingly tackles and theorizes problems of global scale and complexity. How does a method that in its very conception is oriented toward the local, the particular, and the contingent draw conclusions that are at scale, generalizable, and structural and systemic?

The paradox is this: anthropology as a discipline still largely presumes the metropolitan university as the locale, and disciplinary reproduction as the purpose, of graduate pedagogy. Yet diasporic students, who have accountabilities to multiple communities of practice, such that disciplinary reproduction is not the only stake for many emergent practitioners in the field, increasingly inhabit metropolitan anthropology departments. There is also increasing discordance between a pedagogical aspiration to disciplinary reproduction and the grim realities of metropolitan academic job markets.

The politics is this: over the past decades, anthropologists have explicitly disavowed their discipline's colonial inheritances; yet ethnography remains a knowledge practice based on the epistemic objectification of the native informant, which is at the heart of colonial reason. Thus, the intentional disavowal of a colonial desire to know the Other does not necessarily nullify modes of knowing that are objectifying in ways that are of colonial provenance and colonizing consequence.

I argue that this knotting of problem, paradox, and politics brings up questions for contemporary ethnographic method. In addition, it presents problems for pedagogy in relation to the discipline (and disciplining) of anthropology, at least as it is currently taught in the metropolitan research university. This book reflects on these intercalations of method, pedagogy, and institution through considering ethnography as *multisituated*. It espouses an idea and ideal of ethnography as a *sensibility*: a mode of attunement and orientation to the stuff of the world under question, one simultaneously curious and vigilant, open and sensitive, whose potential and ambit go beyond a formally articulated set of methodological techniques and institutional concerns with disciplinary reproduction. It situates such an expansive, experimental, and ethical ethnographic sensibility out of the arc of the epistemic critiques of the 1980s.

The 1980s saw the "crisis of representation" ripple through the human sciences. Forty years later, we seem to be facing another generational inflection point. Old disciplinary norms still endure. They presume intimate experience-proximity as the sine qua non, methodologically and ethically, of the ethnographic encounter. They implicitly center the metropolitan university. They depend on the epistemic objectification of the native informant. At the same time, anthropology concerns itself increasingly with questions concerning global political economy, becomes avowedly postcolonial or decolonizing, and questions the modes of epistemic constitution of the native informant. In other words, there is a disjuncture between the ideological inheritances of anthropology as a discipline, with its established norms and forms of ethnographic practice, and its emergent aspirations.

Ethnography is an example of what Michael Fischer has called an "emergent form of life" (Fischer 2003), a sociality of action, forged within and outside the walls of the university, whose practices are, in Fischer's rendering of the term, "outrunning the pedagogies in which we were trained" (37). What kinds of pedagogy would be adequate to our times—times that see the forging of new configurations of and challenges for the research university even as they see a diversification of the "we" who practice ethnography? How do our inheritances structure our practices in both enabling and constraining ways? This book thus concerns itself with, in Raymond Williams's formulation, the *residual, dominant, and emergent* formations and horizons of ethnography, as constituted within and out of the metropolitan academy (Williams 1978).

This disjuncture between ethnography's ideological inheritances and emergent aspirations points to a *postcolonial* paradox. A strongly diasporic graduate student population in many American anthropology departments intensifies the paradox. This process of the formation of an anthropology that is postcolonial not just in sentiment but also in its demographics started decades ago. Then, however, such students would have likely come to a university such as the University of Chicago, where I currently teach, to study their native country, given the well-consolidated history of area studies in the metropolitan university. Consider, for instance, the Kannada short story "Annayya's Anthropology" by A. K. Ramanujan, who had himself taught at the University of Chicago's South Asian Studies Department for many years. In this story, the protagonist Annayya, who has come to America for higher studies, marvels at the knowledge the American anthropologist has of his Brahminical ritual practices, knowledge that he himself did not possess growing up in India. The purpose of going to America was to know one's culture and civilization better: "You want self-knowledge? You should come to America. Just as the Mahatma had to go to jail and sit behind bars to write his autobiography. Or as Nehru had to go to England to discover India. Things are clear only when looked at from a distance" (Ramanujan 1973).

While browsing in the university library, Annayya comes upon a recently published monograph on Hindu customs and rituals. He reads the book's description of funereal and cremation rituals in detail, fascinated, only to learn that the cremation that the book describes is that of his father, of whose death he had not yet been informed. It was only from the ethnography—and the familiar photographs of his neighbors' house and of his cousin Sundararaya performing the ceremony—that Annayya finds out.

"Annayya's Anthropology" speaks to the disfigurations of the relationship between knowing subject (the ethnographer) and the object of knowledge (the "society" being described) when the university becomes increasingly diasporic. It speaks not just to ethnography as an epistemic problem-space but also to the structure of metropolitan pedagogy, which welcomes the student from elsewhere, knowing fully well that her "elsewhere" is here; but it (still) educates her within a disciplinary genealogy that assumes the metropolitan ethnographer to be "here" and the social object of ethnography to be "elsewhere." If, as is often pronounced, anthropology is about making the familiar strange and the strange familiar, then the diasporic practitioner invariably has to code-switch between the disjunctures of "familiarity" and "strangeness" that often exist between her own personal, intellectual, and political biographies and that of a metropolitan disciplinary history that is professionalizing her.

The postcolonial conjuncture of anthropological knowledge production thus poses some notable pedagogical problems.[1] The diasporic question concerns not just the anthropologist's *identity* but also her *addressee*. By addressee, I do not mean audience, which is a reductive, instrumental idea of the market for one's work. Rather I mean the multiple communities of practice to which the ethnographer feels herself accountable, including those who remain outside the calculable metrics of the professionalized metropolitan academe. This is especially so in the context of the politicized and changing nature of the research university around the world. I think, for instance, of friends in South Africa who did PhDs in the United States and went back to South Africa to teach even as student movements to decolonize the university erupted there over the past few years; alternatively, of transformations in the Indian university today, such that students coming to the United States from India travel from a milieu that sees new forms of radicalism (for instance, of the Dalit Left) emerging in the context of an authoritarian attack on the university itself by the Narendra Modi government; of Korean students who come out of the praxis of pro-democracy student movements there; or of Iranian student activists I have encountered, especially while teaching at the University of California at Irvine, who were active in the pro-democracy Million Signatures Campaign, itself a diasporically situated political movement.

Therefore, we can no longer assume that the *epistemic* consequences of what it means to be a diasporic student in the metropolitan university sit comfortably within area studies paradigms. These students bring with them accountabilities to communities of practice elsewhere in the context of changing mores of disciplinary conversation and what it even means to be (in) a research university in transforming (xenophobic, authoritarian, decolonizing) times. Resonances of this constantly emerge (and sometimes erupt) in the classroom, not just in relation to postcolonial diasporic questions but also very much in relation to racial, indigenous, and feminist politics. At stake here is not just the practice of ethnography but its *praxis*: how to think this diasporic conjuncture within the context of metropolitan disciplinary pedagogy? What does it mean to develop ethnographic sensibilities and attunements in such a context?

This diasporic question is not just about students who have traveled from one country to another: it speaks to all manner of intersectional intellectual, political, and biographical trajectories, and it calls for a "decolonization" of method and discipline. In other words, the politics of a disciplinary disavowal of its colonial inheritance encounters an actual, demographic trend toward decolonization by its diasporic practitioners. These encounters are rarely seamless and on the contrary are often conflictual. This *de*colonizing moment exists in a potentially antagonistic relationship not just with explicitly colonial genealogies of anthropology from the late nineteenth and early twentieth centuries, but also a more proximal generational sensibility, harkening back to the 1980s, which we might call *post*colonial. This latter sensibility maintains a vigilant, even we might say adversarial, relationship to Europe (as place, imaginary, and forging ground for epistemic assumptions about how we know the world), without quite rejecting its intellectual and political inheritance. Student movements for decolonization, most dramatically in South Africa, are in part a rejection of this colonial inheritance that the "post" of postcolonialism necessarily acknowledges and lives with (however critically or uncomfortably). A radical repudiation of white heteronormative masculinity, which entails asserting a certain radical identitarian difference, is thus potentially at odds with a postcolonial sensibility. Meanwhile, virulent and energized right-wing, xenophobic, and autocratic views attack any humanistic investment in difference altogether.

This book argues that a multisited sensibility provides better descriptions of the world we live in and the stuff of the world our research projects interrogate. Further, a multisited sensibility can and should be postcolonial and feminist in its ethos (hence my shift in nomenclature to "multisituated"). I emphasize not just the importance of multiple objects of research or of following objects to multiple places (speaking to a literalist conception of multisitedness). I am invested instead in what Donna Haraway (1988) would call the multiple and multiply situated perspectives (including of individual ethnographers in their variously and variably diasporic personae) that are brought to bear in such an ethnographic sensibility. Thus, this book considers the 1980s as a seminal moment that articulated a set of promissory agendas for anthropology through calls for multisited or multilocale ethnography, even as it saw critical conceptual, methodological, and pedagogical developments in postcolonial and feminist studies.

At its core, this is a reading of George Marcus and Michael Fischer's *Anthropology as Cultural Critique* (1986), alongside and through feminism and postcolonial studies. Marcus and Fischer share two allied concerns as they develop their epistemic critiques of representation and their calls for novel kinds of humanistic inquiry. One is structural, systemic, and global in its scope: how might we understand contemporary political economies of global capitalism? The other is intimate, psychobiographical, and concerned with personhood. Considering ethnography in terms of the former requires attending to its scalar and comparative dimensions. In terms of the latter, it requires consideration of ethnography as a practice of and attention to encounter and dialogue.

All ethnography is inherently comparative, even if our "sites" are "single," because the generation of ethnographic knowledge is based on what we as ethnographers already know, how we assume what we know, and the background assumptions that ground our observations. Encounter is not just about proximity or participation: it is about the qualities of relationships and intimacies that develop in the process of responsible commitment and accountability to others, whom we as ethnographers constitute and draw upon as native informants. This cannot be reduced to a formal procedural ethics, such as of informed consent, as enshrined in institutional review boards. By definition, all encounter contains within itself the possibility of violence. It is risky. Understanding and negotiating this is at the heart of developing a feminist practice of ethnography. Hence, praxis: there is a politics to comparison and to encounter, to the work of scalar attentiveness, scale making and dialogic interlocution, such that ethnography is not just a question of doing but of the stakes involved in its practice. Why and how do we encounter others, the Other, and in what ways do we objectify the subjects of our research, and why does it matter? These concerns with ethnography as an encounter and comparative, scalar and dialogic, are at the heart of all ethnographic projects, "multisited" or not: but they are highlighted and exacerbated in a multisituated problem-space, as I hope this book will explain.

....

Why multisituated, why now, and why from here? This question speaks to the place of a set of practices (ethnography) in relation to a discipline (anthropology), at a moment when disciplinarity cannot contain these practices that define it. The relationship between ethnographic practice and the disciplinary history of anthropology calls for a deconstruction and decentering of the project of disciplinary reproduction, even as these times call for an investment in, and a preservation of, the discipline of anthropology as a humanistic social science that contains within itself some of the best aspirations of both scientific and avant-garde experimental practice. Such "preservation" must involve a rejuvenation of its core method, ethnography, through an elaboration and multiplication of its norms and forms.

What is at stake is a relationship of method to discipline, but also of discipline to the metropolitan university, and the vexed place of disciplinary reproduction in anthropology's raison d'être, at odds with other investments that ethnographers might have, especially those with variously diasporic trajectories. Hence, this becomes a question of the nature of the metropolitan research university, at a historical moment of its corporatization and financialization, a moment that is also one of xenophobic and authoritarian attack on the university itself, such that it becomes an essential institution to fight for and preserve. The place of the American university, at once the quintessence of a globalizing, imperialist, and corporate institutional form, but also a relatively safe space that preserves and articulates an ethic of the Enlightenment when it is societally under attack, is especially vexed. Thus, the university has come to be recognized as the site of the expression both of the most virulent elements of contemporary capitalism (neoliberal, corporate, financialized, imperialist) and of a vibrant ethic of cosmopolitanism and struggle for decolonization.[2] This entwining, to reiterate, materializes in the articulations between ethnography as *practice*, anthropology as *discipline*, and the university as *institution*, between the *doing* and *teaching* of ethnography.

The question of situation is one of time, place, and inheritance.[3] It is a question, respectively, of conjuncture; of locale, event, and the mise-en-scène of the ethnographic encounter; and of autobiography and intellectual genealogy. There are multiple lineages out of which situation has been thought as a structuring methodological principle of analysis. Gregory Bateson, for instance, demonstrated the analytic potential of ethnographic situation in his account of the Naven (Bateson [1936] 1958), using it as a device of comparison and juxtaposition to generate an account of society and culture from multiple actors' perspectives. Another possibility is to use situation as the ground from which politics can be theorized. Situated analysis of this sort is central to Karl Marx's historical writings, such as *The Eighteenth Brumaire of Louis Bonaparte* ([1852] 1977) and *The Civil War in France* ([1871] 2009), and to Antonio Gramsci's accounts of contemporary Italian politics in the 1920s, such as on "the Southern Question" (Gramsci [1926] 2000). A third analytic modality is provided by John Dewey's situational theory, articulated especially in his treatise *Logic, the Theory of Inquiry* ([1938] 2007), which arguably breaks new ground in analytic philosophy in the way in which it articulates the importance of situation as something beyond mere context. Dewey thereby moves analytic philosophy beyond the realm of a formalist logic toward something akin to anthropology, even as it articulates a logical mode of inquiry. It is perhaps telling that Bateson, Gramsci, and Dewey, themselves writing out of such different situations, were doing so in the interwar years, a transformational moment in world history with resonances of the kinds of global trends one sees today. This time period simultaneously witnessed world-historical movements toward authoritarianism and fascism alongside aspirations toward new forms of collectivity. What is the epistemic milieu this signifies for social thought? What kinds of social thought emerge out of such a milieu?[4]

These elaborations of a situated methodology speak to the comparative, historical, and philosophical-anthropological dimensions contained in this spatiotemporal concept. Of even more importance to the argument of this book is the explicitly feminist ethos that animates situation, as articulated by Donna Haraway in her essay "Situated Knowledges" (1988), which in many ways structures its argument writ large. In this essay, Haraway refutes the idea and ideal of objectivity as a "view . . . from nowhere" (589). This is an epistemic refusal, an insistence on other and Other ways of knowing that do not purport to a disembodied Cartesian rationality. Haraway's call for situated knowledges is resolutely not a relativist repudiation of fact per se. Rather, it is a development of a critical stance regarding the scopic privilege of heteropatriarchal modes of objectifying the world in order to know it in possessive ways. It is an espousal of an ethics of the Enlightenment, even as it is a refusal of its most appropriative elements. Thus, it provokes us to think about other, less possessive ways of knowing. There is another call alongside, a haunting one that animates the text, at the moment she asks "with whose blood were my eyes crafted" (585)? This is a reflexive, autobiographical, and transferential question, a question of *inheritance*. Thus, situation for Haraway is inherently a partial perspective, a function of where one comes from. It is not just a question then of time or place, or mode of logical inquiry or sociocultural understandings of personhood (all dimensions of situation given to us by the methods of Marx, Gramsci, Bateson, or Dewey), but also one of what can any one person say about this? The answer to this latter question is a function of one's biography and itinerary.

By following the epistemic ethos that Haraway calls for, what I will say about ethnography in this book is necessarily provisional and partial, a function of my biography and itinerary, both personal and intellectual. This is not just an epistemic limit of this analysis but also its explicit politics. This book is resolutely not an overview of the field of anthropology or a comprehensive review of the large oeuvre of ethnographic work that reflects a multisituated ethos and method. There are many critical, exemplary works that would belong in such a review, which I do not reference or account for. I will instead speak to the genealogies out of which I am thinking the problem-space of ethnography, which is in part the genealogy in which I was taught and the genealogy that I teach. Nor does this book provide or insist on a "correct" definition of multisituated ethnography, in some programmatic sense. Rather, it is about the *idea* and *ideal* of certain sensibilities and modalities of ethnographic practice, which are necessarily personal and autobiographical. It does not describe "how to do," but why we might care. This is a question of stakes, of what kind of work one wants to make and, again, is at least in part a function of where one comes from. I argue both that ethnography itself is a situated practice and that my own argument about ethnography as practice is a situated one. So it is not an objective declamation about what ethnography *is*, in some absolute sense, but a situated reflection of what ethnography has come to mean for me in the course of my research and pedagogical dialogues and itineraries.

The genealogy that is most directly explicated traces back to *Anthropology as Cultural Critique*. In this, Marcus and Fischer call for what they refer to as a multilocale ethnography. Marcus subsequently reframed this as a call for multisited ethnography in his seminal essay "Ethnography in/of the World System: The Emergence of Multi-sited Ethnography" (1995). Both the essay and the term have become canonical points of reference in anthropology, especially in the articulation of a certain kind of research method and agenda that performs a complex or systemic ethnographic analysis involving more than one field site. "Multisituated" is an obvious play with and extension of these notions of multisited or multilocale ethnography, which both decentered and expanded ideas of ethnographic site and location that occupied a hitherto privileged place in the anthropological canon, especially in its Malinowskian ideas and ideals of fieldwork.[5] This was happening at a time when the notion of "the field" was more broadly being brought into question in the discipline, for instance, in Akhil Gupta and James Ferguson's *Anthropological Locations* (1998). It was also a time that saw an explicit disciplinary and methodological turn toward anthropologies of globalization and modernity, for example, in the "Alternative Modernities" and "Late Editions" conversations of the 1990s and in the establishment of journals such as *Public Culture* and *Cultural Anthropology* as central to the discipline, at a fin de siècle moment of reflection upon and invigoration of the objects and projects of ethnographic analysis.

The notion of a multisituated ethnography *supplements* that of multisited or multilocale ethnography. Jacques Derrida developed the idea of the supplement as something that is allegedly secondary to the "original" but comes to aid it (Derrida [1967] 1976). Thus, "multisituated" takes faithfully and inhabits the genealogies out of which ideas and ideals of multisited and multilocale ethnography were developed, out of the milieu of epistemic critiques of the 1980s that participated in articulating and responding to the "crisis of representation" in the human sciences.

In foregrounding questions of conjuncture, location, and inheritance, a "multisituated" perspective draws attention to two things. First, there is the situation of ethnography itself, in relation both to the discipline of anthropology and the institution of the research university. This is a question of the place of method and practice: how is the method of ethnography taught, and the practice of ethnography disciplined, by anthropological histories as they materialize in contemporary institutions that are meant at once to teach students and to reproduce these disciplines? How does the practice of ethnography also, in both its aspirations and its epistemic potential, *exceed* the constraints of both disciplinary history and institutional rationality? These are questions of pedagogy: how do we teach and learn the practice of ethnography within disciplinary and institutional constraints and confines, in ways that take seriously the value of disciplinary genealogies and inheritances and the institutional affordances of the research university, while also seeking to exceed—and specifically decolonize—these structures and inheritances?

Second, being "multisituated" highlights the situation of ethnographic practitioners, who are increasingly diasporic across multiple axes. What would it mean to take into account the necessary excess, dislocation, and decentering that stem from the diasporic embodiments of ethnographers? How does one create the disciplinary space and institutional affordance for the expression of the multiplicity of aspirations and investments of these practitioners, such that they (we, for I myself am one) benefit from an acknowledgment of the genealogies from which their (our) stakes derive, but also such that they (we) are not forced to constantly justify themselves (ourselves) in relation to disciplinary and institutional norms that are grounded in colonial, masculinist histories? This is an especially important question at a moment of financialized, neoliberal resource constraint in the metropolitan university, such that work that is coded as nonnormative, even if deemed acceptable, is imagined and internalized as professionally risky, especially by graduate students navigating increasingly precarious job markets. In other words, the conversation about decolonization that is being had, in vibrant and transformative ways in universities across the world, emerges in the context of these structural, political economic cross-currents that place a burden of risk upon diasporic, decentering, nonnormative, excessive, but also potentially experimental, feminist, and decolonizing modalities of ethnographic practice (unless they can be rendered legible to disciplinary and institutional expectations whose provenance is often at odds with these very kinds of transformative projects). I articulate my sense of, and case for, a multisituated ethnography out of such a conjuncture, marked both by epistemic affordances and structural constraints and by the double binds of a moment that is at once neoliberal and authoritarian and radically decolonizing.

....

The stakes that I articulate in this book are pedagogical. The form of the book is the *seminar*.

The form of the seminar is reflected in this book in three ways. First, it is a set of actual lectures that I wrote and delivered, initially in a graduate seminar called "Multi-si(gh)ted" at the University of Chicago in the winter of 2018 and subsequently as a series of mini-seminars at the University of California at Irvine.[6]

The second element to the seminar is the syllabus. The syllabus for me is one of the most difficult parts of designing a seminar, because the argument of a seminar is contained in its syllabus. One of my PhD advisors, Joseph Dumit, would often set this as an exercise for me when I was a student. He would ask me, if you want to articulate the knowledge of a field of study, how would you do so as an annotated syllabus? It proved to be an enlightening exercise for me, as it would force me to imagine and distill what I would ask a hypothetical set of students to read in the course of ten to fourteen weeks, and to justify the selection of certain readings rather than others. This book is, in its essence, an annotated syllabus. The pedagogical imperative of the syllabus, in the way I teach, is that it must serve as an articulation of how one wants to make an argument. Even as the syllabus reflects my very particular investments, however, I do not wish it to be simply a regurgitation of the particular kinds of work that I myself do. Hence this book engages with a number of ethnographic, theoretical, and meta-methodological works that inspire me and in which I have invested. Yet many of the exemplary ethnographies that I discuss adopt very different ethnographic modalities to those that I myself adopt in the course of my own research. I do not want the space of the seminar to be one where my students learn to reproduce what I *do*. I wish rather for it to be a space for the articulation of possible ethnographic norms and forms that reflect a *politics* of ethnography. This politics is one that deconstructs, decenters, and repudiates the positivist, objectivist, masculinist colonial gaze of ethnography, what Jacques Derrida (1978) has called phallogocentrism. While an anti-phallogocentric politics is unconditional to the argument and ethos of this book, I nonetheless insist upon and attempt to show a range of possible approaches to realizing such a politics. During the course of the seminar, different readings resonated with different students in differential ways. There are tensions, methodological and political, between various texts that I discuss, and I do not expect consensus or an equally enthusiastic embrace of all the ethnographic modalities that I teach and discuss during the course of the seminar. I do not expect that of the readers of this book either: there are bound to be different bodies of work that resonate in different ways with different readers, no doubt a function of your own varied biographies, itineraries, investments, and locations. This is as it should be.

The third element of a seminar is that it is dialogic. What begins as a monologue gets interrupted. Once students start responding to texts and lectures, one's own sense of the argument as a teacher changes. This book reflects the ways in which my lectures in the seminar came to be interrupted by students' own reading of various texts. In writing this book, I have gone back repeatedly to the postings that students wrote in response to each of the readings we did in the class. At various points, I draw upon and cite these interventions. Thus, in addition to being a meta-methodological enunciation, this book also implicitly (and unintentionally has come to be) an ethnography of the class in which its ideas were dialogically developed. The citational form that I adopt at various points in the book is an attempt to preserve and expand the sensibility and ethos of this dialogue, of this book itself as an emergent form of life and a sociality of pedagogical action and response. Thus if one important sense of situatedness that structures this book concerns its time and place (and the time of and for a multisituated ethnographic sensibility), another speaks to a set of partial perspectives that emerged dialogically out of a pedagogical space. It did so in an experimental manner, speaking to a notion of "experiment" articulated by Hans-Jörg Rheinberger (1997), as a structured set of practices with a certain open-endedness built into them, such that the potential always exists for the conversations and arguments to end up somewhere else, other than or beyond where they began, exceeding their initial structuring.

I initially designed my "Multi-si(gh)ted" graduate seminar to take stock of some of the theoretical genealogies that feed into my investments in multisited ethnography. The seminar, however, turned into a charged, intimate pedagogical space. Importantly, it turned into an explicitly feminist space. Some of this was undoubtedly because the class was constituted almost exclusively of women (except for a male political science PhD student and myself); yet also, the epistemic investments and sensibilities that were articulated had to do with more than just demographic identity. The students in this class educated me, in generative and generous ways, to see some of the feminist stakes and investments of what I was trying to get across about ethnography. They were always kind, often patient, and relentlessly probing and questioning: they offered and modeled the best kind of dialogic and pedagogical political praxis. These students also engaged, in their own lives, with other forms of creative practice: there were writers, poets, photographers, and artists in the room, all of whom were also training to be ethnographers. There were moments of searing autobiographical implosion of intellectual and biographical trajectories in our classroom conversations, in ways that not just reflected the stakes of a discipline or a practice in some abstract and abstracted sense, but also responded directly to the dark, masculinist, and racist times we currently live in. There was no moment in the class when we did not consider ethnography as praxis, and no moment when its praxis was taken for granted, romanticized, or unreflexively celebrated.

Thus, this book deliberately falls between genres. It is neither a research monograph nor a review of literature. It is personal and situated. I leave it to the reader to see whether it nevertheless succeeds, even provisionally, in speaking to the serious methodological and pedagogical challenges of the day.

....

My investment in writing this book has emerged from my own academic trajectory and teaching practice. I initially trained as a biologist, but I left science because I hated laboratory work. I did my PhD in science and technology studies (STS), working on the political economy of biotechnology for my dissertation and then on global pharmaceuticals for my second project. My work has been situated between India and the United States, initially studying the global political economy of genome science as constituted between the two countries, and subsequently following the global political economy of drug development, clinical trials, and access to medicines as seen from India (K. Sunder Rajan 2006, 2017).

I am from India. Not only was I not trained in anthropology, I had never trained in the United States when I moved here for my PhD. It has been an extraordinary boon and privilege to study in the United States, because it has given me a training that I am sure I would never have received anywhere else. Yet it means that I come to my investments in anthropology and ethnography as a diasporic intellectual. I do not—indeed cannot—fully inhabit the metropolitan disciplinary and institutional investments that I find in America. I have a set of interlocutors elsewhere to whom I want to be accountable—especially those working in an activist context in India and globally—and that drives me more than professional metropolitan academic concerns.

Therefore, I am concerned with the double agency problem in academic and especially anthropological work: how do we activate, animate, and maintain accountabilities to the communities of practice with whom we inhabit our practice, whatever they may be, in ways that do not have to be reduced to corridor talk and side labor? There is a way in which American academe professionalizes us toward ivory-tower concerns such that other (more activist or worldly) concerns are kept in their place. Yet a lot of what shapes us as ethnographers involves accountabilities to these other communities of practice, often nonacademic and sometimes nonmetropolitan, which means that we often inhabit multiple worlds at once and often live two lives, both of which take up enormous time and labor. Usually, only the former is going to be legible on a professional résumé. That second life is one that is not often legible in America. When such nonacademic, nonmetropolitan investments do come to count as professionally legible, they are increasingly couched in terms of "benefits to society" metrics—a reduction of complex political stakes, dialogues, and investments to top-down, measurable audit culture imaginaries.

I am not arguing for some kind of zero-sum game between being an "academic" or an "activist." Rather, I am wrestling with the fact that our academic work is worlded differently in other situations in which we might be intimately invested. I care about cultivating a stance or disposition that allows for, and building institutional arrangements that foster, a fuller expression and inhabitation of these multiple investments. This differential accountability to different communities of practice, especially including those that operate outside metropolitan and academic circles, is a central stake and question for this more expansive idea and ideal of ethnography, as "multisituated," that I wish to explore in this book. This requires not just looking back at the disciplinary history of anthropology in order to reproduce it, but also looking outward and beyond the purely disciplinary confines of anthropology to learn from ethnographic practitioners in other fields and domains. Hence, even as I am concerned with a certain disciplinary history of anthropology, I seek to go beyond it. A number of conceptual resources I draw on in developing my argument are from outside the discipline. Furthermore, a number of exemplary ethnographies I cite are not by anthropologists, even as some are.

This is because, quite simply, the practice of ethnography exceeds the discipline of anthropology. A range of academic disciplines or interdisciplines uses ethnography as a core or ancillary method—from oral history, to qualitative sociology or political science, to literary studies, to creative arts, to critical legal studies, to the interdiscipline in which I trained, STS, to name but some. Ethnography is also practiced outside academe.[7] Ethnographers also collaborate with practitioners in other fields and domains in order to generate ethnographically rich knowledge that may not take the form of the conventional anthropological monograph.[8] To be sure, different standards may obtain as to what constitutes "good" ethnography in these other disciplines and domains, and part of a disciplinary function is the imposition of rigor, ethics, and reflexivity into its core methodological practices. Yet it is also the case that some of the practices at the frontiers of methodological development in ethnography, developing new norms, forms, and praxiological orientations, are occurring outside disciplinary anthropological spaces.

This speaks to the risk that disciplines might fetter or constrain modalities of practice or at least generate disciplinary anxieties about non-normative practice that might constrain experimentation with, or fuller exploration of, the potential of a method. Learning ethnography in an STS department, I did not experience a set of predominantly Malinowskian disciplinary anxieties that I have commonly found among anthropology graduate students that I have subsequently taught (as I will elaborate). This is not to make some kind of adjudication about the relative possibilities or impossibilities of certain kinds of ethnographic work within or outside anthropology, but simply to say that a lot can be learned by staying attentive to the ways in which ethnography as a practice exceeds disciplinary boundaries, not least about how one might conceptualize, elaborate, and decenter some of its norms and forms in salutary ways. Certainly, even as many of the ethnographers who have most inspired me are anthropologists, many others who have done so are not.[9]

There is a diasporic politics to my insistence in thinking ethnography beyond anthropology in this book, even as it is concerned as well with disciplinary inheritance and reproduction. This is a xenophilic cosmopolitanism that, I feel, should attend any community of thought and action: disciplines ought to behave no differently than nations in welcoming and learning from those outside their boundaries, especially disciplines such as anthropology that now base themselves in an inclusive, antiracist politics. A drawing of boundaries against and lack of receptiveness to nondisciplinary influences of method at the altar of a closed, internalist reproduction of norms and forms is dangerous. This does not preclude rigor or disciplinary standards and does not require uncritical acceptance of every modality of ethnographic practice; it does, however, behoove an openness to other norms and forms, even (indeed necessarily) to the point of putting one's own at risk. If decolonization entails learning from diasporic, nonmetropolitan practitioners of ethnography, so too does it require learning from diasporic, nondisciplinary practitioners.

My investment therefore is to think about ethnography as providing a capacious set of resources to engage the world through a multiplicity of stakes, which go beyond the goals of disciplinary reproduction. The question of developing stakes is also a question of developing one's ethnographic voice. Here, questions of diasporic biographies, of race, of gender, of disciplinary backgrounds and investments, matter in ways that are not simply epiphenomenal.

....

I have taught some version of an "anthropological fieldwork methods" class now, by myself or with others, for over a decade, first at the University of California at Irvine with George Marcus and then at the University of Chicago, where I have been developing a "Methods" curriculum with my colleagues Julie Chu and Michael Fisch. "Methods" in both departments occupies a similar place in the graduate curriculum. It is compulsory for second-year PhD students, and it follows theory-heavy first-year core courses (called the "Pro-Seminar" at Irvine and "Systems" at Chicago). Both departments are similarly oriented, with a strong research emphasis on political economic issues broadly conceived. Both are also in some ways anachronistic, being elite top-tier universities (one public, one private), primarily training their students for disciplinary academic positions. They do so in an increasingly precarious academic labor market.

When I teach my "Methods" class at Chicago, I base it on an argument about ethnography that consists of the following four parts. As I have stated it in my syllabus:

- The aim of this class is not to tell you how to do fieldwork in a narrowly mechanical sense: how to interview or transcribe or code, how to do surveys, how to do participant observation, how to get access, what questions to ask and so on. No doubt, all of these things are important in the course of research projects, but they are also things that are best done by figuring out. No predetermined template or formula for how to do these things will be adequate for the messy encounters with the stuff of the world that ethnography in fact involves.
- Instead, the fundamental problem of fieldwork involves the *cultivation of attentiveness*. Ethnographers rarely know things that their interlocutors do not. What makes good ethnography work—as surprising, insightful, novel, useful, meaningful—is the fact that the ethnographer is capable of attending to things that her interlocutors might attend to differently (ignore, naturalize, fetishize, valorize, take for granted, etc.).
- Attentiveness is always cultivated, and there are many different *modes* of attentiveness. One can learn to slow down, listen deeply, listen further, converse, elicit, observe nuance, piece things together, interpret, map, connect dots, situate, historicize, contextualize, improvise, in order to shift perspective and move beyond constrained modes of attentiveness toward more expansive and self-reflexive ones. Some projects lend themselves better to certain modes of attentiveness. Some people are better at being attentive

in certain ways rather than others. The nature of the ethnographic encounter—who one's interlocutors are, in what contexts and circumstances relationships get made and forged, and so on—can help us re-cultivate or expand our modes of attentiveness in different ways. This is why the norms and forms of ethnographic practice and narration are not singular or uniform. This is a major strength of ethnography.

  - All of these questions of the cultivation of ethnographic attention are never purely concerns of fieldwork; they are always, simultaneously, acts of conceptualization. Hence, "theory" is never ideally done just after the act (and fact) of fieldwork; it is always enmeshed in every aspect of fieldwork, from identifying research objects and projects, to engaging in ethnographic encounters before, within, and beyond "the field." Rather than think about a binary of fieldwork and theory/narration, I wish to think about the deeply imbricated actions of fieldwork and *concept work*—the active labor of conceptualizing the stuff of the world that ethnographers constantly engage in.[10]

Fieldwork is a technical activity, even as it is about figuring things out in contingent fashion "in the field." In my "Methods" pedagogy, I attempt to articulate an expansive conceptualization of technique. I argue for a mode of movement and engagement that is not about a mechanistic performance of method, as something reduced to formulaic or programmatic practices. Rather, there is an active relationship between the performance of method and the conceptualization of project design, one that is iterative, recursive, and ongoing, even (especially) through the process of fieldwork. It is important to embed methods in project design, which requires concomitant concept work.

Hence, technique is essential but cannot be merely instrumental (how to do interviews, how to transcribe, how to code, etc.). Providing some kind of mechanical formula for participant observation in the classroom will not magically produce ethnography. Furthermore, a narrow and instrumentalist conception of technique is phallogocentric, because it is predicated upon a gendered separation of intellectual and manual labor, relegating methods to a mere "doing," privileging "Theory" as intellectual labor performed before and after fieldwork, through an acquaintance with the relevant literature and some kind of post facto conceptual synthesis. I push for an idea and ideal of technique that refuses this kind of temporality and purification. Thus, my pedagogy is not a refutation of technique, but its expansive rearticulation. This epistemological and political insistence lay behind Chu's, Fisch's, and my decision to rename the "Methods" class at the University of Chicago "Modes of Inquiry." This suggests that the conceptual development of a research project—which, for ethnography, must perforce be empirically driven and accountable—is at the heart of ethnographic technique. Technique is inextricably linked with project development and with the concomitant identification of suitable ethnographic objects of study.[11]

My "Methods" pedagogy is located within three genealogies. The first concerns the reformulation of the norms and forms of ethnographic practice, especially as they emerged out of the mid-1980s and the "Writing Culture" moment" (Clifford and Marcus 1986), which was also the moment of publication of *Anthropology as Cultural Critique* (Marcus and Fischer 1986). The kinds of reflections upon ethnography generated at this time have seen serious conversations with STS over the past three decades in the process of the development of anthropologies of science and technology that have drawn on and gone beyond the foundational impulses of both fields of inquiry. In significant measure, therefore, this genealogy operates at STS/anthropology interfaces.[12]

The field of postcolonial studies was in formation at the very same time as the *"Writing Culture"* moment. Meanwhile, feminism that was also exploring epistemological issues came into its own. The critiques of representation of the 1980s did not have a single voice, but they did share an ethos. These critiques have to some extent been internalized and regurgitated into the disciplinary anthropological canon as it has since developed; but these were never just negative critiques (as I am afraid they are too often misread as being) and contained within them a promissory call that has not necessarily been responded to. This call asks, once one has acknowledged the epistemic violence of the colonial, patriarchal representational gaze and its objectification/textualization of the primitive, raced, sexed, gendered, colonized "Other," then what? How, now, do the *norms and forms of ethnographic practice themselves come to be at stake?*

A third personal genealogy is the most speculative and experimental, and it is borne of a deepening photographic practice over the past few years. As I have done so, I have asked myself what it means that when making photos, the world looks different. This is not just a representational question (does the photograph document the world as is?) but also a creative and evocative one (of being able to see the world differently, and the possibilities and potentialities of being able to do so). This speaks to a broader emergent genealogy of relationships between ethnography and the creative arts, which is a lively subject of debate and practice in anthropology today.

These genealogies, in related but distinct ways, constitute epistemological problem-spaces for the conceptualization, practice, and, importantly, teaching of ethnography. The space of the classroom, however, is not just one of the transparent reflection of a teacher's intellectual inheritance. It is also an immediately institutional space, one that reflects both the specific ethos of particular departments at moments in time and the affordances, constraints, expectations, and ideologies that structure and animate the contemporary research university itself.

My own pedagogical investments seek to teach a rigorous ethnographic research practice that is feminist and decolonizing in its ethos, that addresses global, systemic complexities through an ethnographic practice that focuses on the situated and the particular in ways that are open to the creative and evocative potentials of humanistic and artistic ways of knowing and doing. How one does that in relation to a phallogocentric epistemic history is a methodological question that is not reducible to a technical one. Thus, my interest in teaching "method" is praxiological. It does not concern how one "does" ethnography in any programmatic sense; it is concerned with the praxis of ethnography, one that is always both practical and ethical—not ethical in the liberal, instrumental sense of informed consent that institutional review boards concern themselves with, but by being accountable to the stuff of the world under question within our research projects, including the insistence on certain kinds of refusals.[13] It would also simultaneously encourage the proliferation of ethnographic modalities.

In privileging the teaching of a multisituated research sensibility, I found two things about how Marcus and Fischer's call for a multisited or multilocale ethnography was internalized or responded to. The first was an anxiety among students about the feasibility of multisited research projects, especially at the dissertation stage: an anxiety that I suspect is not entirely self-generated but instilled by disciplinary norms and forms as they reproduce themselves pedagogically. The second was a proliferation of actual dissertation research projects that nonetheless proposed or promised to do multisited work, albeit often conceptualized and articulated in formulaic, reductive, and technical ways ("I will go to so many places . . . ," etc.). What idea of multisitedness has led to this contradictory anxiety toward multisited work alongside a formulaic investment in it, I wondered? From what ideas (and ideals) of ethnography does this stem from? How is it suited, or not, to the realities and challenges of contemporary ethnographic research projects, especially at the dissertation stage? Yet even within the context of these resistances and anxieties, I found, over the years, a certain kind of student finding her (yes, it is usually, though not exclusively, her) voice within this pedagogical environment—with a certain kind of project. These tend to be students with diasporic trajectories of various kinds (not just cross-national) and feminist and anticolonial investments in ethnographic work, wishing to explore multimodal ways of doing ethnography.[14]

What was happening via these dialogues with institutional transformations and constraints on the one hand and student desires and resistances on the other was a personal and pedagogical investment on my part in ethnography. This book offers me a chance to take stock: what are my own stakes in method, such that they have formed a constitutive part of my own pedagogy for so long? Why am I so invested in arguing not just for the feasibility but also for the desirability and necessity of multisited projects? What are the implications for adopting a multisited sensibility for research design, in the process of conceptualizing projects across site and scale; for developing multimodal pedagogical offerings, as arguments for proliferating the norms and forms of ethnographic practice; for arguing for a multisituated praxis?

....

Given this biographical itinerary and intellectual trajectory, the situated perspective this book provides is written not from the margins of ethnographic practice but from its various *borders*.

My own research and teaching is located at, and constituted by, national, disciplinary, and praxiological borders (India/United States; anthropology/STS; academe/activism). This book, therefore, does not take the form of speaking *to* the discipline from a marked subject position, as some very important meta-methodological critiques have done.[15] Rather, it inhabits that awkward diasporic space that shuttles back and forth between different locales and commitments. It is inspired by the practice of scholars such as Marilyn Strathern, who articulates her own awkward relationship between anthropology and feminism, and Gayatri Spivak, who attends to and writes from her diasporic location as a postcolonial, South Asian feminist scholar and teacher of the humanities within the elite metropolitan university, "outside in the teaching machine" (Strathern 1987a; Spivak 1993). It contains situated perspectives that are hybrid, embodying forms of what Homi Bhabha, following histories of Black radical thought from W. E. B. Du Bois to Frantz Fanon, has called double consciousness (Bhabha 1994).[16]

This has consequences for the kind of book this can be and for the kinds of spaces it can claim to speak from. Mine is an elite trajectory: I am an upper-caste, middle-class, Hindu male from a caste-ridden, patriarchal, increasingly majoritarian society, who is a tenured professor in an elite, private American university, in a department that has long been central to the discipline of anthropology. It is also a trajectory that has some sense of what it means to be caught within the folds of empire, folds that at different times and in different ways both provide refuge and suffocate. The sense of alienation that I, like so many others, still feel while passing through immigration checkpoints at Euro-American ports of entry, even as my mobility reflects a privileged itinerary, is mirrored by the alienation that the discipline of anthropology sometimes thrusts upon me, especially at moments when it parses center and periphery onto its objects and subjects of research in ways still deeply marked by its colonial inheritances. It is further mirrored in the sense of alienation that the American university sometimes thrusts upon me, as it does upon so many others when it fails to attend to the subjective experience of those who might inhabit it from elsewhere, even as it provides an Enlightenment sanctuary and physical safe haven.

Gloria Anzaldúa's *Borderlands/La Frontera* ([1987] 2012) and Sandro Mezzadra and Brett Nielsen's *Border as Method* (2013) are works that inspire this understanding of the "border." These important works teach us that "the border" is not just an object but also a method. By paying attention to what constitutes a border, to the work done by such constitutions, one can understand something significant about contemporary global capitalism: in this instance, about the epistemology and ethics of ethnographic research, and the ethics and labor of a pedagogy of ethnography, conducted within capitalized worlds and institutions. This involves being attentive to the border not just as something that excludes but also as something that creates new and differential forms of inclusion, which can be as productive and as violent as exclusion. What is at stake here is an attention to the translations that attend the production of a diasporic ethnography in metropolitan institutions and disciplines with colonial inheritances, with all the impossibilities and infidelities that translation necessarily entails.[17] At stake in writing (and teaching) from the borders is, necessarily, a consideration and reimagination of norms and forms of ethnographic practice, in order to decenter the colonial inheritances of anthropology that separate center from periphery, inside from outside, self from other, ethnographer from native.

Simply put, as a book written from the borders, this is—perforce, must be—an anti-Malinowskian book. It writes against an ideal of the romantic Malinowskian fieldworker (always, implicitly, "from here") who was "there" and in the process could generate an authoritative account of the authentic Other, by becoming Other—an act that can only be one of appropriation and possession. My attempt to think ethnography otherwise and Otherwise, from the borders, as a diasporic practice, is not a polemic against fieldwork. On the contrary, it is a provocation to rethink the pedagogy of fieldwork without reproducing the phallogocentrism of its Malinowskian ideology. This ideology is not just colonial in the way in which it presumes an inscription of center and periphery; it is also deeply masculine in its imagination of how the fieldworker is embodied.[18]

The answer to the question that I am asking—is it possible to have a decolonial, non-phallogocentric ethnographic practice?—is yes, if it is multisituated in its ethos. This ethos, as already mentioned, is a sensibility, a mode of bodily attunement to the stuff of the world under question. However, that attunement alone can never suffice unless it destabilizes and reinvigorates pedagogical modalities of teaching research design in ways that institutionally interrogate the metropolitan research university and reorient it toward postcolonial and decolonizing praxis.

I do not have programmatic answers to how this might be achieved. I do not want to suggest a formalizing or totalizing "manifesto" for anthropology. Rather I attempt to puzzle through the epistemic, ethical, and political problems these questions pose, especially to the imaginary of ethnographic research design and pedagogy. Answers do exist, however, in the form both of exemplary ethnographies that have performed, and of meta-methodological reflections that have conceptualized, non-phallogocentric modes of fieldwork and analysis—including, importantly, from within the metropolitan university. This book provides a reading of works that chart some such avenues. These do not articulate a singular method that is reducible to a technical formula. One does not achieve a decolonial practice by following a fixed path or program, but by proliferating possibilities—many of them partial, provisional, and frictioned with respect to one another—and by thinking ethnography otherwise and Otherwise.

Nor does one do so, simply, by rejecting "white male" anthropology. We have to live with and learn from our inheritances in order to be able to deconstruct, subvert, or torque them. My argument for decolonizing ethnography is resolutely not one that refuses a white male intellectual lineage: it is not an idea of "decolonization" based in identitarianism.[19] At its core, I argue for an imagination of the fundamental method of ethnography as *being something other or more than participant observation*, at least as constructed in its colonial, masculinist, Malinowskian guise. I wish to signal and develop non-Malinowskian approaches to the practice of ethnographic fieldwork: not just by exploding understandings of what constitutes locality, but also by dispensing at a deeper intellectual and political or ethical level with wanting to position ethnography as comprehensive knowledge of alterity. This involves questioning the status of the native informant in ethnographic practice, reorienting the spatial imaginations of ethnographic practice beyond those of core and periphery, and considering the obligations of ethnographic encounter.

This book consists of four chapters, each of them searching for forms of praxis that deal with the problem, paradox, and politics with which this book is wrestling. How to study complex systems and structures using experience-proximal practices? How to do so at a moment of the becoming-diasporic of the discipline and the metropolitan university? How to decolonize a practice that is dependent on the native informant, who is fundamentally constituted through colonial epistemic genealogies? The book considers these questions through the problem-spaces of scale, comparison, encounter, and dialogue.

Each of these problem-spaces exceeds participant observation. One cannot scale an analysis simply by expanding one's presence beyond the local: other conceptual maneuvers beyond authorial presence are required. Comparison can be effected physically, but it is also an epistemic practice, a function of how one constitutes figure and ground: a constitution that never simply occurs "in the field" but begins as a set of structuring, often implicit assumptions, about what, where, and who is central and which peripheral. Encounter and dialogue are, by definition, about twos (and threes, as I will argue), not about the solitary fieldworker. Fieldwork is at the heart of the problem-space of each chapter, but the romantic, authorial presence of the fieldworker, an ideological inheritance that is both colonial in provenance and masculinist in its ideal-typification of the ethnographer, is deconstructed.

Chapter 1, "Scale," elaborates an idea and ideal of multisituated ethnography as conceptual topology rather than literalist methodology. It is, in significant measure, an engagement with chapters 3 and 4 of *Anthropology as Cultural Critique*. I think through potential modes of feasible operationalization of a multisituated sensibility without reducing it to a formalist program, considering exemplary works that attend to global political economic structures and systems on the one hand and personhood, biography, and subjectivity on the other. I suggest how the two are imbricated with one another in a multisituated sensibility, including very different modalities of ethnographic research design and practice. Thus, I build discussion of fieldwork about, and in the age of, globalization beyond early multisited concerns with how to "follow" objects and processes across multiple sites and locales.

Chapter 2, "Comparison," considers how we might compare otherwise and Otherwise, in ways that do not reproduce colonial, masculinist center-periphery assumptions. This chapter sees the beginning of a sustained engagement with Spivak's work, here in part through a dialogue with Clifford Geertz's considerations of experience-proximity and experience-distance in relation to an ethnographic articulation of "the native's point of view" and with Marilyn Strathern's *Partial Connections* (Geertz 1974; Strathern 1991). I question the status of the native informant in ethnographic practice and as a basis for anthropological comparison, as I consider how to cultivate an openness to others that would recognize not just their answers to comparative human questions, but also the different questions, and thus comparisons, those others might enunciate in the first place.

Chapter 3, "Encounter," considers ethnography through an engagement with Lauren Berlant's conceptions of intimacy and with theorizations of literature and photography, especially those of Gabriele Schwab and Roland Barthes, respectively (Barthes 1980; Berlant 1998; Schwab 2012). I am specifically interested here in the relationship between representation and evocation, as well as the ways in which modes of attentiveness and attunement to the world can be made ethnographically resonant in multisituated ways. I am grasping here for an idea(l) of multisituatedness that is accountable rather than innocent, that is cognizant of the constitutive risk of encounter, with all of its potential for appropriation and violence. I am also arguing for a sense of ethnographic ethics that is not just about abstinence from acts that might harm one's interlocutors, but is rather a more positive socialization of the research process itself, one that fully explores the creative and humanistic potentials of ethnography, which can never escape the unanticipated third entity (reader/viewer) who is constitutive to the praxis of ethnography (and literature and photography).

Chapter 4, "Dialogue," is an elaboration of Douglas Holmes and George Marcus's call for para-ethnography (Holmes and Marcus 2005). Drawing in part on some of my own para-ethnographic work studying the establishment of India's first biomedical translational research institute, I elaborate how the activation and inhabitation of what Michael Fischer calls "third spaces" are vital to a multisituated sensibility, specifically in the ways in which they can reconfigure relationships with native informants away from masculinist, colonizing ones toward ways that are more dialogic (Fischer 2003). I consider the epistemic and political consequences of this rescripting and realignment of the ethnographer–native informant relationship, which is necessarily also a reimagination of the forms and spaces of ethnographic encounter. In contrast to the Malinowskian understanding of a field site as an already existing object that the fieldworker must come to know and be able to represent, I think of para-sites as designed from the start as dialogical spaces where interlocutors develop questions and answers instead of providing raw material. The conceptualization of fieldwork here is as conference rather than interview.

Scale, comparison, encounter, and dialogue are all elements of ethnographic practice. The relationship between these elements, and the conversations between the chapters, is not seamless. The trajectory of the argument across these chapters is not synthetic: there is not a *solution* to phallogocentrism to be found at the end of it all, just different modalities of working against, working around, and working through the difficult inheritances of ethnography. These modalities are often in tension with one another. For example, I presented a version of chapter 2, on comparison, at the conference "African Ethnographies" at the University of the Western Cape (UWC).[20] The conjuncture of this conference is inseparable from that of a continuing conversation about decolonizing the discipline and the university in South Africa in the burning embers of the #FeesMustFall student movement. In such a site, I encountered important questions about why I remained invested in the project of comparison itself, a project that, as my interlocutors pointed out, is of colonial provenance. There was a sense there that one should think scale *instead* of comparison as the means to thinking decolonization.[21] Yet there remains an important postcolonial and feminist function to rescripting comparison, as I argue through the works of Spivak and Strathern. Similarly, chapter 3 is in part an engagement with certain trajectories of psychoanalytic thought, a consideration of questions of encounter through questions of transference and affect as articulated, for instance, in the works of Schwab and Berlant. Yet if one reads these genealogies through Strathern, one would be forced to decenter the very notion of personhood that is at the heart of psychoanalytic reasoning, as a quintessential Western construct.[22]

Thus, all of these modes of analysis—scalar, comparative, encountering, dialogic—provide ways of thinking ethnography beyond Malinowskian phallogocentrism. None of them provides, in any simple way, an escape from the colonial and patriarchal inheritances of ethnographic practice. Deconstruction is not absolution, which does not make it any the less important. Even if there is no synthesis to be found in this book, there *is* a trajectory. The book begins with this question: how does an ethnographer make a structural analysis of systemic complexity while decentering the romantic authorship of the social analyst, which depends on both her grounding epistemic assumptions and the native informant? This is a deconstructive move, one that the ethnographies I describe in chapter 1, Marcus and Fischer in *Anthropology as Cultural Critique*, and scholars such as Geertz, Strathern, and Spivak whom I engage with in chapter 2, all engage in, in different ways. Nonetheless, this deconstructive project retains the form of the monologue, as the form of the production of social theory. Theory making, as the labor of the conceptualization of the stuff of the world that we live in, as articulated by the theorist, is at the heart of the endeavor—as, indeed, it is for this book. This speaks, in some sense, to the *sociological* functions of ethnography.

When I move to chapters 3 and 4, I move resolutely to the dialogic dimensions of ethnography, not just as a means to a monologic authorial end, but potentially as an end in itself. I further consider it as a *trialogic* practice, one that operates between the ethnographer, her interlocutors in "the field," and an unintended subsequent third entity, the reader of the (usually) monologue that is generated through the fieldwork encounter. This draws upon Schwab's argument of ethnography as a form of *literary* knowledge, wherein the function of literature involves the transferential relationships established by the unintended and subsequent third, the reader of the novel. This triad is about much more than production, consumption, and reception constituting a communicative idea of readership. It is about responsibility, about the work of ethnography in a world full of appropriative and overdetermined discursive spaces. The relationship between ethnographer, her interlocutors (native informants, brought into decentered relationships or not), and the unintended, subsequent third reader is both noninnocent and politically vital. This speaks to the *evocative* function of ethnography, one that is about more and other than its aesthetic function. It shares skin not just with the epistemology of literature, but also with the praxis of photography, which I explore alongside in chapter 3, as I consider the simultaneous violence and transformative potential of both writing and seeing. What other ethnographic norms and forms does this give rise to, and how might those be scripted through reconceptualizations of both research design and the means and ends of ethnography? I ask this in chapter 4, through an exploration of para-ethnographic possibilities and experiments.

Ultimately, what is at stake is a question of ethnography as what the organizers of the "African Ethnographies" conference at UWC called a *difficult* practice, one that is difficult to perform and that constitutively occupies a politically difficult space.[23] It is alongside this a question about the place of ethnographic knowledge today: about, if you like, the *ends* of ethnography (its ultimate objectives; the points at which its practices and explanations run out; whether, in fact, it has exhausted itself in times that are both financialized and decolonizing).[24] What kind of knowing is this, especially as its colonial and heteropatriarchal inheritances are acknowledged and decentered? Why is it important? What are the grounds upon which one can simultaneously be committed to it while remaining ambivalent about so many of its genealogies, to the point even of loathing some of its histories? Through what emergent norms and forms can one recommit to its most radical potentials, in ways that cannot deny or excise its painful histories but that can potentially script them toward Other futures? These are the questions for this book. They are praxiological questions, at once epistemological, pedagogical, and institutional.

1

Scale

In my application to PhD programs, I proposed a project that would study the life sciences in India. I knew about India, having grown up there; I knew about the life sciences because I had trained as a biologist; and, as an undergraduate, I had been active in politics around intellectual property rights, as India was becoming a signatory to the Trade Related Intellectual Property Rights (TRIPS) agreement, which would have particular impact on pharmaceuticals. My proposal reflected trajectories with which I was already familiar.

The dissertation that I ended up doing was on the life sciences, and I did situate some of my work out of India. The trajectory that took me there, as with all ethnographic projects, was serendipitous. It started with my PhD advisor, Michael Fischer, suggesting I spend some time in a lab, any lab, as an observer. I got in touch with some people I knew at the National

Institutes of Health from my days as a biologist, who let me spend time at their lab. There, I happened to meet a bioinformaticist, Mark Boguski, who had read Paul Rabinow's *Making PCR* (1995) and therefore decided "he knew exactly why I was there" (something I had no idea myself). It so happened that Boguski was one of the organizers of the Cold Spring Harbor Genome Meetings that year. That year, 1999, happened to be the year when the so-called race to sequence the human genome had begun in earnest because of the challenge presented by a private genome company, Celera Genomics, to the public genome project. I subsequently followed genomics into its corporate sites, which resulted in a significant period of fieldwork in Silicon Valley at the height of the dot.com boom. By the time I gathered with my committee for my oral examinations, I had already spent a few months doing research in California. I was assuming that the United States had emerged as the locale for my dissertation, and that interests with India would have to be deferred to postdoctoral work. Yet the unanimous—indeed, only—question at my exam from my committee was, when are you going to India? Not knowing any better, and because my teachers told me to, I went. Thus, I ended up doing a multisited dissertation located out of the United States and India, which was subsequently published as my first book, *Biocapital* (2006).

Going to India was essential for my dissertation. Specifically, it enabled two things that I could not have realized had I stayed put in the United States. First, it afforded me a different perspective *on* Silicon Valley and more generally on the biomedical developments that I was following in the United States. This is the classic perspectival shift afforded by projects of what Fischer and George Marcus have called "cultural critique" (Marcus and Fischer 1986). India was not just an empirical site in itself; it helped me dis-locate the research I had done in the United States in productive ways. Second, I was able to trace all sorts of actual networks and connections between Silicon Valley and India, and I saw at the time what aspects of Indian genome science these networks activated and which they did not. In other words, mapping the specificities of global interconnections became part of the empirical task of the project.

These reflect two of the oldest strengths of the anthropological discipline: the ability to compare, and the ability to track relationships. Yet nearly two decades after I located my dissertation research in two countries, the dominant assumption in anthropology still seems to be that such projects are "unfeasible," certainly at the dissertation stage. At the same time, the theoretical aspirations of anthropology are resolutely not restricted to single sites anymore. Indeed, the objects of theory tend to be things like "global capital" or "financialization" or "human rights" or "governmentality"—things that are abstract and operate across sites and scales. In other words, there seems to be a disjuncture between the theoretical aspirations of anthropology that demand conceptualization across site and scale, and the actual norms and forms of ethnographic fieldwork and narration that are valorized in anthropological research projects, especially at the dissertation stage. This disjuncture speaks to Marcus and Fischer's provocation to study global political economic structures and systems using a method (ethnography) that depends on experience-proximal interactions. Thus, even as my own initial understanding and performance of multisited ethnographic work were primarily oriented around the literal multiplication of ethnographic sites and cross-national comparison, something more significant concerning project conceptualization was at stake.

....

There is a working idea(l) of multisited ethnography as doing fieldwork in more than one space or place. So, it is fieldwork with multiple communities, or with communities in multiple places, such that the ethnographer has to move around to more than one geographical location. I want to think with and beyond this idea(l)—one that has become almost paradigmatic in the ways in which multisited ethnography is referenced, for instance, in graduate student dissertation proposals and grant applications. I elaborate this literalist conception of multisitedness into an idea and ideal of multisituatedness, as a stance rather than a formal methodological program; as a certain disposition of epistemic openness (K. Fortun 2006); as a conceptual topology. I begin with Marcus's more literalist conception of multisited ethnography as articulated in his seminal review essay "Ethnography in/of the World System: The Emergence of Multi-sited Ethnography" (1995).[1] I will read this against the problem-space of generating an ethnographic understanding of global political economic systems on the one hand, and of personhood and subjectivity on the other, as posed by Marcus and Fischer previously in *Anthropology as Cultural Critique* (1986).

The impulse for multisited projects, Marcus says in "Ethnography in/of the World System," comes from "following the thread of cultural process" (1995: 97). As method, this means potentially following people, objects, metaphors, plots/stories/allegories, biographies, and conflicts into the multiple sites of their social life. Indeed, the second part of Marcus's piece precisely consolidates the call for multisitedness into these potential, tangible, methodological strategies of "quite literally following connections" (97). These are extremely useful, and, arguably, no actual multisited research project can avoid engaging at least some of these strategies some of the time. However, what interests me most about Marcus's piece is the long conceptual and praxiological preamble to this program, which brings up questions of epistemology, disposition, and politics, without a sense of which the program itself risks being understood or followed reductively. For it is in these prior questions through which Marcus sets the stage for his program that he articulates kinship with a feminist and postcolonial epistemological sensibility that, as I hope to argue through this book, is the most necessary and valuable inheritance of a multisited sensibility, as "multisituated."

In setting the stage for his programmatic articulation of a multisited research strategy, Marcus points to three "methodological anxieties" that arise in relation to multisited projects. The first has to do with "testing the limits of ethnography" (99). This speaks to the tension between doing an ethnography of communities and groups who live within and are impacted by global political economic systems, and an ethnography of "the system" itself. The second has to do with "attenuating the power of fieldwork" (100), that is, anxieties about the feasibility or practicality of multisited projects. The third has to do with "the loss of the subaltern" (101), an anxiety about an anthropological ethos that is concerned with the recuperation of the subaltern voice and how that might be put at stake in multisited projects of systemic analysis.

This book is relentlessly concerned with the first and third anxieties. I think through the question of doing systemic analysis using a method (ethnography) that privileges intimate, small-scale encounters, which returns to the Geertzian problematic of experience-proximity and experience-distance (Geertz 1974). The key point of reference for me here is chapter 4 of *Anthropology as Cultural Critique*, which calls for an ethnography of political economic systems and structures. I then want to think about the representational politics of multisited ethnography, which derives in significant measure from concerns with the role of ethnography in articulating the voices of marginalized, subaltern peoples and cultures, but which also directly recognizes the necessity of the native informant for ethnographic authority. This immediately implicates the romantic ethos of subaltern recuperation within the history of anthropology as a colonial discipline; it forces the question of the relationship between a multisited ethnographic sensibility and a decolonizing ethnographic praxis. I consider this in relation to chapter 3 of *Anthropology of Cultural Critique*, concerning an ethnographic elucidation of personhood and subjectivity.

Before I proceed, I want to mention Marcus's second anxiety, because I consistently encounter it while teaching anthropology graduate students who worry about the "feasibility" of multisited projects (or perhaps have those worries articulated to them). These are anxieties that we ethnographically oriented science and technology studies (STS) students never had (and perhaps were never taught to have). This is grounded in a Malinowskian ideology of fieldwork whose residues are thickly sedimented in the disciplinary formation of anthropological pedagogy, which suggests that ethnographic legitimacy comes from a certain kind of embodied presence "in the field," a romantic authority borne of having "been there." If one thinks this against Marcus's formulation of the term, the tension is evident.[2] How might one do that without compromising rigor, if in fact a proper and authoritative ethnographic account requires a certain kind of authorial presence in the "site" over time? Thinking beyond this zero-sum conundrum requires conceptualizing multisitedness through other registers and modalities of scaling and perception, in ways that potentially recalibrate the norms and forms of ethnographic practice and narration.

....

There are a number of passages in *Anthropology as Cultural Critique* that I return to often, as promissory provocations that provide guidelines for thinking about how to do and teach ethnography. I quote some here (from both the first and second editions) to provide a flavor of the book's line of argument but also of its multisited (or, as the authors called it therein, "multi-locale") sensibility:

> First, the ethnographer might try to represent in a single text, by sequential narrative and the effect of simultaneity, multiple, blindly interdependent locales, each explored ethnographically and mutually linked by the intended and unintended consequences of activities and orientations within them. . . . the point of this kind of project would be to start with some prior view of a macrosystem or institution, and to provide an ethnographic account of it, by showing the forms of local life that the system encompasses, and then proposing novel or revised views of the nature of the system itself, translating its abstract qualities in more fully human terms. (Marcus and Fischer 1986: 91–92)

These [new] forms [of anthropological authority in line with reconfiguration of knowledge in other disciplines] will depend on the articulation of new norms and regulative ideals of ethnographic practice, in which collaboration and dialogue are no longer just theories and sentiments of ethnographic writing nor the revealed essence of what anthropologists have been doing all along, but become the starting points for novel research landscapes, agendas, and relationships stimulated by the equally new objects of study that anthropologists pose for themselves and for the general public. (Marcus and Fischer 1999: xxii)

How much more interesting, instead, to retain the different perspectives on cultural reality, to turn the ethnographic text into a kind of display and interaction among perspectives. Once this is done—either in terms of the direct inclusion of material authored by others, or in more sociological terms of the description of the idioms of different classes or interest groups—the text becomes more accessible to readerships other than the usually targeted professional one. (Marcus and Fischer 1986: 71)

No longer, then, is the project of anthropology the simple discovery of new worlds, and the translation of the exotic into the familiar, or the defamiliarization of the exotic. It is increasingly the discovery of worlds that are familiar or fully understood by no one, and that all are in search of puzzling out. (Marcus and Fischer 1999: xvii)

Anthropology as Cultural Critique is a disciplinary text. In it, Marcus and Fischer periodize the discipline of anthropology twice. The first periodization concerns the shift in the stakes of the discipline, from its nineteenth-century guise as a "science of man" toward its twentieth-century one as a fundamentally descriptive practice. With this shift, ethnography, itself a semiliterary genre, became the signature feature and form of anthropological research. In this guise, anthropology refused a certain Galilean "scientific" aspiration, without quite abandoning the objectifying and textualizing aspirations—themselves often positivist—of a descriptive enterprise that claimed knowledge of the other. Therefore, these were not the aspirations of a unificatory synthetic theory (even as both structuralist and functionalist theories skirted and flirted with comprehensive and programmatic claims), but nonetheless the aspirations of description as a means to knowledge, to a certain kind of comprehension that would allow claims to be made—claims about other cultures, about others, about the Other. This is the tense position of anthropology within the human sciences.

Marcus and Fischer posit this as a productive tension, one that highlights the humanistic sensibility of anthropology (for which its "semiliterary" genre form and modalities of representation, and the question of ethnographic writing, become very important) while refusing to abandon a certain kind of "scientific" aspiration. The question of how to straddle these two at times antithetical aspirations is a vital methodological and conceptual—meta-methodological—one that is at the heart of their text. Indeed, it is at the heart of their book's subtitle, *An Experimental Moment in the Human Sciences*. "Experimental" here has a dual meaning (the significance of which is acknowledged in the preface to the second edition of the book more than it was at the time of its original publication). On the one hand, it suggests the avant-garde, speaking to the investments of anthropology in the literary and the artistic. On the other hand, it references a certain rigorous practice of validation as it operates in the sciences. Ethnography straddles the tension between these two ideas and ideals of experiment.[3]

The second periodization that Marcus and Fischer make concerns the post-1960s shift in anthropology from description to interpretation. How do we place this second split, as descriptive realism is taken over by the interpretive turn, within this straddle between the humanistic/avant-garde aspirations of ethnography that the authors clearly want to push to the limit, and a certain history of science within which ethnography must be situated? What kind of research endeavor is ethnography, if thought within this straddle? This is after all not an innocent straddle, for at its limit the avant-garde aspirations of ethnography could come to be directly at odds with the aims of descriptive realism.

The interpretive turn of the 1960s, especially if pushed to the limit of its avant-garde imagination, is the other of science, if we consider science in its positivist, synthetic, Galilean guise.[4] At the same time, this turn remains scientific, if we think of the sciences themselves not as singular (or singularly positivist) but as itself constituted by a diverse set of practices, including some that are resolutely interpretive. (How can one be a biomedical scientist today, in an era of functional genomics and epigenetics, for instance, without in some significant measure being an interpretivist?) In other words, it is not so much an opposition between ethnography as "scientific" and "literary" that is at the heart of the matter: the strength of ethnography comes from the fact that it manages (must manage) to contain the ethos of both. Rather, it is that ethnography as practice contains within itself descriptive realist, interpretive, and creative elements, which often operate in epistemic tension with each other. Ethnographic voice emerges not through some kind of consensual resolution of these tensions but through the particular, situated ways in which ethnographers conceptualize and activate their own stakes in the matter, in order to animate these tensions through rigorous and differential expressions of each of these elements.

At issue, here, is the question of the relationship between two kinds of stakes. One concerns the stakes of ethnography as a fundamentally humanistic practice (and, therefore, especially in these times, concerns the stakes of the humanities itself). The other concerns the stakes of interpretive practice across multiple modes of inquiry, including scientific inquiry (especially in these times, the interpretive turn of certain sciences, especially those dealing with complex systems such as the biological, ecological, and informatic sciences, at a historic moment when scientific rationality itself is under fresh and virulent political attack). If the former insists upon articulating the unique and vital modalities of humanistic knowledge, the latter insists upon fighting for more interpretive rather than reductionist versions of science. These contending stakes materialize around ethnography's signature mode of producing knowledge—which uses the descriptive, the particular, and the exemplary in order to produce generalized or systemic understandings. The central challenge of multisited ethnography is *how* to do so, given the global interconnectedness and hypercomplexity of the systems and structures of our political economy.[5]

Alongside the dialectic between humanistic/literary and "scientific" aspirations of an interpretivist ethnography, where the scientific itself is full of interpretive possibilities, is another dialectic that is at the heart of *Anthropology as Cultural Critique*, concerning ethnography as an intimate, experience-proximal practice that has the potential to shed light on global political economic structures. Perhaps the most central provocation of the book in this regard, one that I return to constantly, is this: "What we have in mind is a text that takes as its subject not a concentrated group of people in a community affected in one way or another by political economic forces, but 'the system' itself—the political and economic processes spanning different locales or even different continents. Ethnographically, these processes are registered in the activities of dispersed groups or individuals whose actions have mutual, often unintended, consequences for each other, as they are connected by markets and other major institutions that make the world a system" (Marcus and Fischer 1986: 91).

For students of Marcus and Fischer, this paragraph is indelibly important.[6] For my purposes, this is where the stakes of multisitedness are particularly explicit. It gets to the heart of the problematic of their chapter 4, which is "how to represent the embedding of richly described local cultural worlds in larger impersonal systems of political economy" (1986: 77). This opens up a number of meta-methodological questions concerning antithetical aspirations that must be held in tension, for instance, as follows:

- The relationship between micro and macro, that is, a question of scale. How to scale out the particular, contingent encounters that one has as an ethnographer into a systemic and structural claim? In other words, how to make a claim that goes beyond just "I happened to see this"?
- The relationship between experience-near and experience-distant, or the relationship between what one is learning or hearing from one's interlocutors in their own terms, and things that an ethnographer can claim in other terms that can be intelligible to some kind of systemic analysis (the relationship, in other words, between the -emic and the -etic, between actors' categories and analysts' categories). How does one tack back and forth between actors' and analysts' categories, in ways that have to be constantly accountable to the former but that cannot be reduced to them?
- The relationship between the "visible" and the "invisible," or between the material and the abstract. Between something that one can see (practices, rituals, events) and the abstraction of systems, which are not tangible or visible "things" in themselves but nonetheless have tangible and visible effects.

The call to multisitedness is a call to translate between these constitutive and antithetical scales, perspectives, and (in)tangibilities. Ethnography is constantly translating from there to here, between micro and macro, particular and universal, experience-near and experience-far, -emic and -etic, invisible and visible, material and abstract, and, vitally, the subjective and the systemic. These translations do not pose a dilemma for ethnography; they are *constitutive* to ethnographic practice, in ways that break these putative binaries apart. For an ethnography to be meaningful, it has to straddle these tensions, simultaneously inhabiting and deconstructing them. How to do so becomes a vital methodological question, one that is not reducible to a purely mechanistic idea of technique, one that is immediately conceptual and meta-methodological. Indeed, this is a question for any kind of interpretive ethnography, multisited or otherwise. What the multisited problematic makes explicit is its taking of systemic hypercomplexity as a given, as a constitutive part of the problematic of research design that has to be factored in and figured out from the outset. It is not just something that can be articulated upward and subsequently from more "basic" building blocks (such as Durkheim's [(1912) 2008] "elementary forms" or Lévi-Strauss's [1974] "structure," etc.). What the multisituated problematic further insists upon is the imperative to engage in these hypercomplex studies in nonobjectifying, non-phallogocentric ways.

How to proliferate possibilities for straddling these tensions? One possible strategy for designing multisited research is to construct an ethnography in which one goes to two, three, five, eight, or however many places. Anna Tsing's *The Mushroom at the End of the World* (2015) is an exemplary ethnography in this vein, one that literally follows the matsutake mushroom to the ends of the world in a rigorously multisited fashion.[7] This does potentially raise Malinowskian anxieties about "feasibility," as already discussed, especially at the dissertation stage. Therefore, while recognizing that *Mushroom*, perhaps, is the quintessential example of a multisited ethnographic work that follows the object, I wish to discuss six other exemplary works that provide other kinds of multisituated research design and sensibility.

The first three ethnographies that I discuss—João Biehl's *Vita* (2005), Angela Garcia's *The Pastoral Clinic* (2010), and Jonny Steinberg's *A Man of Good Hope* (2016a, with allusions to Steinberg's earlier *Three-Letter Plague* [2008])—are ethnographies of personhood that demonstrate the promissory call of chapter 3 of *Anthropology as Cultural Critique*. Yet even as each traces, in substantial or exclusive measure, the life history of a single individual, it also provides an analysis of a global economic system and structure. The next three that I discuss—Winnie Wong's *Van Gogh on Demand* (2013), Kristin Peterson's *Speculative Markets* (2014), and Kim Fortun's *Advocacy after Bhopal* (2001)—are exemplary demonstrations of systemic, structural political economic analyses of contemporary globalization, demonstrating the promissory call of *Anthropology as Cultural Critique*'s chapter 4. Yet even as these are macro-structural ethnographies that operate up to and up from institutional scales of analysis, they each serve as a conceptual elucidation of subjectivity. Thus, thinking with these six texts also enables a dialogue between the two seminal reflections, on ethnographies of personhood and political economy, respectively, that form the heart of *Anthropology as Cultural Critique*.

In selecting these six texts, I am not making some representative claim for what is adequate multisituated ethnography and what is not; rather, I elucidate some of my own stakes and inspirations, from different stages of my intellectual formation as an ethnographer. I purposely selected texts published after 2000, reflecting the arc of my own career, since when I was a graduate student first learning about ethnography to now, when I am teaching and writing about it.[8] The latter three that I discuss more closely mirror the kind of work that I myself do, while the former three come out of very different genealogies and operationalize different ethnographic styles and stakes.

I also selected texts that were published at different stages of my career. Biehl and Fortun published their ethnographies during the very early stages of my career, Fortun when I was still a PhD student, Biehl shortly after I began my first teaching job at the University of California (UC) at Irvine. Both *Advocacy after Bhopal* and *Vita* came immediately to be recognized as contemporary classics in the field. Garcia and Peterson published their books at around the time I received my tenure. In many ways, these books were influenced by their predecessors', Biehl's and Fortun's, respectively. Steinberg and Wong are scholars whose works I have encountered later in my career, and neither is located directly within the American networks of disciplinary anthropology like the other four scholars I discuss here are. (Steinberg is in the African Studies Department at Oxford, while Wong is an art historian who does ethnographic work.) All six have inspired me in my research and my teaching of ethnographic praxis.

....

João Biehl's account of a single woman, Catarina, is at the heart of his classic ethnography *Vita*, which is about a "zone of social abandonment" in Brazil where the extremely sick, indigent, or mentally ill are left to die. In that vein but with different articulations and resonances is Angela Garcia's account of Alma, a heroin addict in New Mexico, whom Garcia engaged with as both ethnographer and attendant, in *The Pastoral Clinic*.[9] Alongside these well-known medical anthropological accounts coming out of the American university, I consider two life histories written by the South African ethnographer Jonny Steinberg. One, *Three-Letter Plague*, is an account of Sizwe, a man whom Steinberg followed in the rural Eastern

Cape, and this man's refusal to get tested for HIV in spite of being an obvious candidate for it. The second, *A Man of Good Hope*, follows the "forced" migration of a Somali man, Asad, through a series of constrained decisions and movements that he made, eventually ending up in South Africa and finally in the United States.[10]

Biehl's and Garcia's work follows a tradition of medical anthropology influenced by Arthur Kleinman, Byron Good, and Mary-Jo DelVecchio Good and their emphasis on the illness narrative in developing a subjective account of the experiential dimensions of the medical encounter (Kleinman 1989; B. Good 1994, 2012; Good and Good 2000; Biehl, Good, and Kleinman 2007). Nancy Scheper-Hughes's phenomenological accounts of the body, hunger, and medicine (for example, Scheper-Hughes 1992) and Veena Das's anthropology of "everyday" forms of life through the development of a hermeneutic methodology indebted to Ludwig Wittgenstein and Stanley Cavell (for example, Das 2006, 2015) are equally important inspirations. These scholars were central to the development of a conversation and method around social suffering in the 1990s (Kleinman, Das, and Lock 1997).

Steinberg's life histories are not located in this trajectory. Thus, even as *Three-Letter Plague* could be considered a work of medical anthropology, it is not located out of the same disciplinary genealogies as Biehl's and Garcia's work. Instead, it comes out of a career trajectory spent writing about South Africa's transition to democracy after apartheid. Sizwe, the protagonist of the work, is a high-risk candidate for HIV, but he refuses to get tested. Steinberg conducted the fieldwork for the book in the early 2000s, at the height of the politicization of access to antiretrovirals and Thabo Mbeki's AIDS denialism. Steinberg's animating question is why Sizwe does not get tested. Further, how to work against the answer provided by humanitarian biomedicine, which can only understand such refusal in the midst of an epidemic as irrational? Steinberg is instead interested in understanding Sizwe's rationality: his is an attempt to elucidate a situated perspective. Thus, Steinberg's life history is from the beginning animated by an epistemic question, a different order of inquiry from one that seeks to write the narrative of the suffering subject.

How to write an account of the (individual/suffering) subject in ways that do not objectify? This is the question to be asked of this tradition, and Biehl, Garcia, and Steinberg answer it in multisituated ways. All three authors situate the individual in some way in relation to the institutional. There is no nonsituated life historical narrative per se in any of these works. The situated perspective of the individuals concerned is always in tension with the situated perspectives of institutions that script their particular desires for a life. Elucidating the former, therefore, sheds light not just on the contingent rationality of particular, or particularly interesting, individuals, but also on the institutions that provide affordances and constraints for the trajectories of their lives. *Vita* tells us something vital about the exclusionary institutional practices of zones of social abandonment, which articulate in important ways to the institutionalized accounting practices of Brazilian public health initiatives, including importantly its "model" intervention into AIDS treatment.[11] *Pastoral Clinic* provides an institutional analysis of de-addiction in New Mexico. *Three-Letter Plague*, as already indicated, describes the institutional rationality of global humanitarian biomedicine amid the South African AIDS crisis, as it conflicts with Mbeki's state rationality. *A Man of Good Hope* tells us something about the institutional rationality of global migration, with its xenophobic overtones in South Africa and the United States alike. Steinberg also, across his work, helps us conceptualize the actuarial logics and calculative rationalities that script commonsense liberal assumptions of what a "rational life" means, in ways that we modern, liberal, middle-class subjects internalize and normalize within our desires for a life.

The institutional situation of individual life histories in these works explicitly intercalates the concerns of chapters 3 and 4 of *Anthropology as Cultural Critique*, concerning personhood and political economy, respectively. What is different in approach here, compared to the exemplary multisituated works that concern global political economy that I will subsequently discuss, is the relative foregrounding of the individual life history. In doing so, Biehl, Garcia, and Steinberg engage in a praxis that insists not just upon institutional situation, but also on the ways in which lives, and desires for lives, exceed the institutional. In showing how this excess is contained, constrained, or violated, Biehl, Garcia, and Steinberg in different ways highlight the violence of institutional rationalities. They do so not by the structural elucidation of this violence as much as by ethnographically showing the disjunctures between the institutional scripting of lives and the individual desires for lives that exceed those scripts.

All three authors—especially Biehl and Garcia—produce ethnographic works that are works of mourning. Some of this is explicit: by the time their works were written, both Catarina and Alma had died. What is the multisituated disposition of these works that makes them works of mourning and not romantic, objectifying works of salvage? The answer to this question involves addressing the question of agency in these works and how it is articulated in dialogic ways that are not about the romantic anthropological salvage of the suffering subject. To put it otherwise, the multisituated challenge of these works is to elucidate agency without "giving voice," the act of romantic subaltern recuperation that Marcus wishes to go beyond in his articulation of multisited ethnography.[12] The answer to this lies in attending to how these authors (in different ways and to different degrees) displace their own romantic, Malinowskian authorship in order to attend to the singularities of their encounters with their interlocutors. Even as these ethnographies ultimately take the form of the monograph, there is a crucial dialogic element to the modality of the constitution of life history, which goes beyond the ethnographer "getting" the story of another in an act of appropriation.[13]

Of the works under discussion here, *Vita* is the most masculinist. There is no disguising Biehl's presence as author at the scene of his encounters with Catarina. Garcia's ethnographic relationship with Alma is entangled with the labor of care that she is also simultaneously performing as a social worker helping to treat her addiction; there is constant discomfort, even apology, in the way she writes "about" Alma. Steinberg's accounts of Sizwe and Asad are less explicitly apologetic, but there is a homosocial politics of friendship that develops (albeit across marked class hierarchies) that renders the relationships, if not innocent, then at least differentially loaded. The axes of differentiation in Biehl's relationship with Catarina offer no such possibility of innocence or apology. There is certainly care; there is even the development of a certain sort of friendship over the course of the ethnographic relationship. Yet Biehl's labor is not the institutionalized labor of care that Garcia performs (the various attendants at Vita perform that labor). The friendship that he develops with Catarina cannot but be inscribed across hierarchies of class, gender, and the ill-defined and all-pervasive category of "mental illness" that Catarina is subjected to, which constitutes the very grounds of her abandonment by her family in the first place. In such a situation, there is no escaping the possibility of the objectifying, textualizing gaze, as defining the very condition of the ethnographic relationship. Indeed, there are moments in *Vita* when Biehl almost seems to be psychoanalyzing Catarina. How then to think an ethnographic account of agency and subjectivity otherwise, of a multisituated sensibility and disposition, in such a radically asymmetric encounter?

This is where Catarina's "dictionary" comes to matter. Catarina calls it thus: a notebook that she keeps, which is filled with words, sometimes isolated, sometimes strung together, and sometimes articulated as sentences or thoughts. This dictionary is clearly of great importance to Catarina; it is something she treasures, adds to, works on, shows to, and shares with the ethnographer. It is clearly of great importance to Biehl too: it is something he wants to understand, not in a positivist sense of finding the "real meanings" of the words that Catarina writes, but rather in the sense of understanding the desire for a life that is inscribed in her writing. A hermeneutics of the Other, which does not seek to reductively understand something as deterministic as "motivation," but that engages in a constant and progressively dialogic act of mutual interpretation of Catarina's desire for a life *as* manifested in her writing, in her act of writing. By reproducing the dictionary, Biehl is giving an account not merely of a suffering subject, but of a writing subject.

Catarina's dictionary is as much the ethnographic object of *Vita* as Catarina the individual. One never reduces to the other: Catarina is not just her dictionary, and the dictionary can never fully represent Catarina. Biehl refuses to fully explain, appropriate, or reduce the "meaning" of the dictionary to voice, intention, madness, or pain. The dictionary is not merely an instrumental means to the end of "understanding" Catarina, the way in which the Nambikwara chief's "writing" is instrumentalized to "understand" his motivations by Claude Lévi-Strauss in *Tristes Tropiques* ([1955] 1992). The scene of writing, instead of being the scene of phallogocentric epistemic violence as Lévi-Strauss renders it, becomes the scene of a politics of friendship; it becomes the scene, already and well before Catarina's death, of the work of mourning.[14]

Thus, Biehl does not merely foreground an individual life history to provide an institutional account that exceeds the constraints and scripts of institutional rationality. By attending to the dictionary, he also simultaneously provides a life history that goes beyond the story of the individual, even beyond the story of her institutional situation, to articulate, in some partial and dialogic way, an Other's desire for a life.[15] This is the multisituated work of *Vita*, the manner in which Catarina is situated in something beyond herself, even beyond the zone of social abandonment where she is left to die. Catarina's subjectivity, in some crucial way, remains analytically ungraspable.

....

How did Catarina, Alma, Sizwe, and Asad become key native informants for their anthropologists? How would an ethnographer find someone like each of these individuals: singular enough to become the object of ethnographic attention, yet not reduced to an exception, a curiosity, an object of the voyeuristic gaze of the ethnographer and subsequent reader? How would an ethnographer with a multisituated disposition know when such an informant has been "found," in ways that do not reproduce colonialist tropes of the discovery of a curious "native" subject? Are these singular figures interchangeable with any other native informant in similar situations and settings? Clearly, the answer to this last question is no; these are four people whose stories matter in themselves, as themselves. There is something significant about the intimacies developed between the ethnographers and their singular informants. What so captivated Biehl about Catarina that provided the foundations and conditions of possibility for their ethnographic intimacy?

What stood out for Biehl about Catarina, what he states at the outset of his ethnography, was that *she was in motion*. He first saw her cycling. This was in stark contrast to everyone else at Vita, who seemed listless, despairing, and destitute. Why was Catarina cycling when she had nowhere to go, when the very purpose of a place such as Vita was to render her actions purposeless? The apparent "irrationality" of her mobility was precisely the agency that first caught Biehl's attention. The motion continues through her work of writing her dictionary, again apparently "irrational," but also an exercise, as Biehl figures out over time, in herself trying to figure out her own being in motion. Contra Lévi-Strauss's "writing lesson" in *Tristes Tropiques*, this is not a case of the anthropologist teaching the illiterate to write; it is Catarina teaching the anthropologist to read, to read her dictionary and also her own interpretive exercises. Thus, the scene of the encounter becomes a scene of dialogue rather than merely diagnosis. To reiterate, Biehl never tells us what the "truth" of the dictionary "really" is: it remains an open subject, for both the ethnographer and the reader (and, indeed, for Catarina herself) to speculate on.[16] In this ethnographic refusal, and the openness it engenders, political work is performed, of an order quite different to that of voyeurism or salvage.

Steinberg's captivation with the forced migrant Asad in *A Man of Good Hope* is also because he is in motion, in ways that defy "common sense." Indeed, Asad makes a whole series of decisions that would seem risky or dangerous in our everyday rationalities, for example, taking on the restrictions of national-state borders but also refusing to settle down in situations in which it would have seemed sensible for him to have done so. In the process, he even gives up what was a happily married life, as his wife decides not to follow his decisions and instead to go back to Hargeisa. Yet, on Asad travels, eventually to the United States via an extended sojourn in different parts of South Africa, often performing precarious work and inhabiting precarious life. Asad's motion resists the inscription of frameworks and lives he has been institutionally given, leading us to ask what *is* the "forced" of forced migration, when it is his desire to move that is constantly institutionally constrained and curtailed? It also articulates a certain idea of freedom, one that is different from the "freedom" that is assumed to derive from "rational" (as in actuarial) choice.

For Garcia, Alma's motion—her constant desire to "get clean"—is not entirely singular. Others who are in de-addiction have similar desires. Yet it articulates to other kinds of motion and emotion, including Alma's joining an evangelical church and searching for relief through religion. It also articulates to the singular friendship that developed between Alma and Garcia. Both Alma's attempts to escape what E. Summerson Carr (2010) has called the scripts of addiction and her friendship with the ethnographer are haunted by another kind of (almost preordained) movement, that of return: a return to drugs, a return to addiction, a return to the custody of the de-addiction center.

For all three authors, motion is a sign of agency, and each attends to the singular person who keeps moving when conditions are not conducive to movement. What captivates these ethnographers is their native informants' refusal of abjection in spaces that guarantee it. *That* is what they mean by agency. The insistence on *a* life, a desire for a life, a refusal to reduce their own life to what Giorgio Agamben has called "bare life" (Agamben 1998). Precisely because of this refusal, the ethnographic encounter is not one of the ethnographer giving voice to the abject/subaltern. This refusal provides the condition of possibility for something dialogic. The multisituated disposition is not the ethnographer's own authorial or ethical "choice"; it is forced on them by the agency of their native informant; it is in attending to those who articulate such agency *as* their native informant that the ethnographer displays their own multisituated sensibility.

This does not mean that motion allows them to "break free" of the structures that bind them. The informants' refusal of abjection is in tension with the institutional common sense that demands it. The liberal condition of possibility for Asad to be able to live his dream of eventually migrating to the United States, one that today clamors for leniency toward refugees and protests family separations at the American border, is that he be an abject subject, a Somali refugee who has been forced to flee his country. (Under Trump, of course, even this was not allowed.) In the account that Garcia provides, there is not one institutional common sense that drives toward abjectivity, but two. One is biomedical and the other juridical, both holding someone like Alma within their clutches but also pulling in opposite directions, drawing and quartering her. Yet these individuals refused to stop moving, even when institutional common sense is all about holding them still.

Alongside the question of movement is the question of *return*. I have already pointed to the centrality of return to Garcia's account of Alma: how its inevitability is already inscribed in Alma's biography, in spite of Alma's desires to live otherwise. The only condition under which Alma will not return to the de-addiction center is when she dies. Alma knows that, and so does Garcia. Yet it is not just the informant who keeps returning. What makes Biehl keep returning to Catarina? Biehl recounts Catarina's invariably parting words each time he finishes a visit with her: "will you come back tomorrow?" His return is a function of his curiosity, but it is also his obligation; it is part of the ethical and affective terrain of their friendship. The asymmetry is figured here: the return of the anthropologist under conditions when he can choose when to go back and when not to. There is no such choice for Alma, each time she returns to the de-addiction center. Asad's story is marked by his willful decision *not* to return: not to return to Hargeisa, not to return to his wife and family, whom he loves; he has agency and freedom, marked and haunted by violent rupture and not by the fullness of choice. In Steinberg's story, therefore, there is again the figure who returns: Asad's wife, who makes the "sensible" choice by going back and taking no further part in Asad's risky itinerary. Steinberg traces how Asad's wife emerges as such a figure of ambivalence for Asad: how even as he lives his desire to stay in motion and to go to America, he knows full well the Faustian bargains he is having to make, a knowledge that can come to him only because of his own marital and familial entanglements (entanglements that Catarina, perforce, had been stripped of). The institution of family haunts these accounts as strongly as the institution of the state.

Biehl, Garcia, and Steinberg all insist on a certain kind of humanism, an ethical insistence on a common humanity, one that cannot eradicate the objectification that occurs at the scene of encounter and writing across radically different subject positions, but that can nonetheless engage in a politics of friendship.[17] In their shared insistence on the singularity of "a life" that is not reducible to the sacralized, onto-theological notion of a Foucauldian "life itself," they also have something to say about praxis, even as they construct a conceptual topology alongside and through ethnographic description.

....

I turn next to three ethnographies that are explicitly structural and systemic, Wong's *Van Gogh on Demand*, Peterson's *Speculative Markets*, and Fortun's *Advocacy after Bhopal*, which elucidate global political economies out of tightly located ethnographies.

Van Gogh on Demand is an ethnography of Dafen, a village in southern China where most of the world's art copies are painted. On the face of it, this is traditional village ethnography, based on long-term and extensive participant observation in a local site. Wong's focus is not, however, on Dafen itself as much as it is about the interventions of the world into Dafen. Therefore, it is fundamentally a theorization of globalization and world making through the focus on an extremely local site that is deeply embedded in national, regional, and global relations of power and production. In the process, Wong highlights how Dafen speaks to the "growing perplexity of Sino-Western cultural relations" (5). Wong is working against the typical figuration of Dafen's artists as simply assembly-line painters, which is how Western discussions tend to depict them. In rendering this critique, Wong is working against the totalizing social imaginaries that pervade Western discussions both of China and of originality and labor in art.

Wong achieves this dual move—of locating a village in the context of its worldly relations, and of critiquing Western social imaginaries of such a village and the work that happens there—by tracking global distribution chains, not just in objects but also in imaginaries. Wong shows that the work of art "copying" in Dafen is about not just the fabrication of originals, but also the fabrication of origin stories. Many of these are individual and individualistic stories of local entrepreneurial pioneers. Wong historicizes these origin stories in the context of the globalized painting trade in southern China and its location in regional subcontracting networks. She further traces the urbanization of this trade as it moves to South China at a moment of the area's rapid capitalization.

This opens us up to a stunning theorization of contemporary global capitalism, one that manages a structural analysis while avoiding a simplistic or uniform picture. Wong achieves this in the first instance through a focus on labor practices, particularly the tensions between the work of painting and the performance of the painters in Dafen. What *is* the labor of these assembly-line painters, Wong asks? In what ways are they "skilled" and what does their skill consist of? This involves an exploration of how skills come to be conceptualized, acquired, and practiced both in Chinese labor markets and in Western art markets, which Wong undertakes through life stories of three different sets of painters in Dafen. There is a strong focus in these accounts on pedagogy and training and on the gendered dimensions of these labor practices and formations. The second dimension through which global capitalism is theorized is through a focus on the politics of the copy. This attends to how paintings in Dafen circulate as "copies" in the global market in ways that have consequences for the attribution of authorship and creativity (always to the Western artist, either the painter of the original or the contemporary Western artist who stages Dafen within their conceptual art).[18]

Van Gogh on Demand is centered and located in the best sense of the ethnographic tradition, but it is also multisituated, moving across locales to examine and analyze regional, national, and global connections. It is work that is conducted among multiple communities—not just the artists in Dafen, but also foreign artists, buyers, traders, and government city-level officials—and Wong herself adopts a number of roles in addition to that of the observer, such as a consumer, interpreter, and consultant for the city of Shenzhen at Shanghai's world expo. This allows Wong to undertake her analysis at multiple levels and scales, giving her narrative a texture that only a multiplicity of situated perspectives can afford. The result is an ethnography that is as breathtaking in its scope and detail as it is illuminating in its empirical complexity.

Peterson's *Speculative Markets* is a study of pharmaceutical circulation and access and of the politics attendant to these processes in contemporary Nigeria. It is also a study of a political economic system, such that "Nigeria" can never be bounded in space, and "the contemporary" has to be thoroughly historicized. It thus provides a salutary example of how experience-proximal ethnographic interactions can be fruitfully used to elucidate macro-structural processes and formations whose contours are often abstract and difficult to discern. In the process, even while resolutely grounded in very particular events and concerns in Nigeria, the book manages to be a tour-de-force exemplar of multisituated ethnography.

The grounding is strongest and most explicit in Idumota, one of the largest wholesale drug markets in the world, located on the Lagos Peninsula. The mise-en-scène that serves as the ethnographic entry point for

Peterson in *Speculative Markets* is the market in all its bustling, overwhelming complexity of everyday exchange practices; another entry point is the problem of fake and counterfeit drugs in Nigeria. The immediate question seems to be, how do spaces of exchange such as the market—one of the quintessential sites for observing experience-proximal interactions in the history of economic anthropology—serve as a venue for the creation of an illicit drug economy? What Peterson immediately does, however, is historicize the illicit. The question shifts: what is at stake is not "where do these illicit drugs come from?"—a question that demands "following the drug." Rather, it concerns the conditions of possibility that allow markets such as Idumota to become sites of illicit economies, even as they also remain sites for the distribution of noncounterfeit drugs. The brilliance of Peterson's book lies in forcing us into that analytic frame shift, to locating the problem in conditions of possibility, therefore confronting us immediately with a structural problem to resolve. Here, it turns out that "the markets" that need to be understood are rather different ones and have to do with the Nigerian drug market as a national drug market on the one hand and the "global market" in pharmaceuticals on the other.

The frameshift is therefore a scale shift. Idumota is not just a space of exchange but a space of world making, a space in which other kinds of world making implode, in order to constitute not just a crisis of fake drugs, but also a crisis of a lack of essential medication and public health infrastructure, and a crisis of accountabilities of various sorts across a range of actors. These crises are not just diagnostic of some constitutive "Third World" condition: they are produced systematically and systemically (for instance, through World Bank–imposed structural adjustment policies, or global aid policies such as the Bush administration's PEPFAR AIDS relief program). In the process, particular kinds of pharmaceutical subjects are also produced in Nigeria: ones that are medicated, but not in the regulated fashion that would ensure treatment; ones that are marginalized from certain global market imaginaries even as they are included in them as recipients of humanitarian aid; and ones that live at the intersections of competing political economies of scale and substance.

The nub of the problem in both these books is not "how am I going to get to *x* number of places in order to successfully pull off a multisited project?," but rather to figure out what one's ethnographic *object* is. This is especially vital when ethnographic projects concern more abstract problem-spaces that have to do with systems and structures that are intangible and operate across scale. *That* is the fundamental problem of doing systemic analysis: because it is nonobvious to think about site and project, the question of what emerges as the ethnographic object that mediates the various connections to trace becomes an utterly nontrivial one. If the question of elucidating agency and subjectivity in nonobjectifying ways was the multisituated provocation of the three ethnographies of personhood that I have discussed, then the challenge of identifying, recognizing, and working with appropriate ethnographic objects of analysis is the analogous provocation for multisituated ethnographies of hypercomplex, global political economic structures and systems.

....

Before turning to *Advocacy after Bhopal*, I want to mark some epistemic moves that help straddle the various scalar and conceptual transitions that *Van Gogh on Demand* and *Speculative Markets* need to make, at the heart of which is the problem of attending to the ethnographic object of study. Wong and Peterson develop modalities of situating ethnographies in ways that allow for the development of a multisited sensibility out of discrete and located "sites." In *Van Gogh*, the modality developed is one of *tracking* (how to track the ways in which the art world touches down into Dafen, and how Dafen moves out into the art world?); in *Speculative Markets*, it is of *implosion* (how to attend to the ways in which national, regional, and global drug markets are imploded in to Idumota?).

Philosopher of science James Griesemer has suggested that there are certain sciences—ecological sciences being exemplary—in which a central mode of knowledge production involves tracking (Griesemer 2011). The end game here is not theory (or Theory with a capital *T*, if you like) as a definitive knowledge statement, but rather as a process of constant inference and interpretation.[19] If we acknowledge our practice as ethnographers to be one that is fundamentally constituted by tracking, then three things emerge:

- That the ethnographic imaginary is constitutively multisited in its scope and potential, because tracking by definition is a process of "following"; it is a method that "moves" along with its object, that changes scale by zooming in and out, that compresses and expands, that speeds up and slows down.
- That the cultivation of attention is central to any tracking project. One can be following things that constitutively surround us, but one has to learn to be perceptive to those things in very specific

ways. *How* one attends—how one learns to attend and is taught to attend—is therefore deeply consequential and political. The question of how ecologists learn to see and infer from the clues that they discern (one that is equally relevant to physicians, psychoanalysts, art experts, detectives, and ethnographers) centrally concerns pedagogy and training—how can we train ethnographers to be attentive to what they track? Attention is not just some ethical virtue; it is central to ethnography as practice and as vocation.

- The critical praxiological question then concerns the position of the ethnographer in relation to her interlocutors and to the structures and systems that are being tracked (which are not the same thing). If an earlier epistemic mode that presumed culture or society as "objects" to be "known" has been discredited in anthropology's current postcolonial sensibilities, it was too readily replaced by reflexivity—a suggestion that if somehow the intellectual was *aware* of her objectifying gaze, all would be well (self-knowledge as epistemic absolution). This is not good enough, because it does not fundamentally alter the way in which the object of ethnography is constituted. Unless that object is somehow productively deconstructed, re-situated, dis-located, one cannot, I believe, adequately construct a multisituated project. Because the radical potential of multisituated ethnography is not that we do more or follow further, but that we actually shift frames, undo figure and ground, subject and object, inside and outside.

Before reconstituting the ethnographic object, however, it is essential to know what one's object is. This is a nontrivial task, especially because it can too easily be confused with one's research topic. A topic speaks to the "big picture" question that one is asking in one's research. It often concerns systems and abstractions and, when framed well, articulates as what Aihwa Ong and Stephen Collier have called "anthropological problems": "domains in which the forms and values of individual and collective existence are problematized or at stake, in the sense that they are subject to technological, political, and ethical reflection and intervention" (2005: 4).[20] On the other hand, objects speak to the contingent "stuff of the world" that we actually study in our ethnographic projects, which are themselves material and abstract and often enmeshed across various scales.[21] Joseph Dumit (2014) developed an "implosion" project meant to stimulate a rigorous analysis of one's research object. In this exercise, students explore how their ethnographic object exists in the world and how the world is imploded into their object. They do so by answering a series of algorithmic questions that explore various material, semiotic, and abstract dimensions of the object's existence and relations. One of the functions of this project is to reveal those moments when an ethnographic object is not robust enough: if one cannot ask a series of rigorous preliminary questions about it, it is unlikely to be a good object of long-term ethnographic analysis across dissertations or book projects.

....

Wong and Peterson provide one alternative to a literalist operationalization of multisited ethnography, by developing a deeply situated account of *locales* out of which ethnographic objects are tracked and within which they are imploded. I next consider Fortun's *Advocacy after Bhopal*, which operationalizes a multisituated sensibility by situating toxicity. As an anthropological problem, toxicity implodes the biomedical with the environmental, the deeply individual with the planetary.[22] Thereby, as an ethnographic object, it traverses domains of knowledge and practice, even as it operates across (and constitutes) scales. A global political economy is thus also a political ecology: the ecological dimensions of *Advocacy* itself put "global" systematicity under question. The scaling that Fortun achieves is conceptual, not literal.

Advocacy is a book about the 1984 Bhopal gas disaster, caused by the leak of methyl isocyanate from a Union Carbide chemical plant and which is arguably the worst industrial disaster in world history. Fortun, in grappling with the impossibility of writing the disaster (disaster, by definition, being something that exceeds language), comes to terms with it through an ethnographic modality that is at once systemic and deconstructive.[23] She both situates and looks elsewhere. She situates the disaster in its time, through a stunning opening prologue that looks at the conjuncture of 1984, simultaneously, from the lens of a moment in Indian history and politics and a moment of global politics (including global environmental politics) underwritten in significant measure by Reagan's anti-environmentalism in the United States. This simultaneous consideration, at once scalar (local to national to global) and comparative (developments in India next to those in the United States), is literally run alongside one another, in parallel columns that mimic the form of the newspaper. She looks elsewhere by looking, also and always, at American environmentalism, now itself inscribed under the shadow of Bhopal, haunted by the possibility of another Bhopal happening "here." Thus, there are the actual geopolitical interconnections between an "American" multinational corporation, Union Carbide, and an Indian location, Bhopal, mediated by the Indian and American state and by civil society actors in both locales.

In the process, Fortun's ethnographic object is displaced. It is not the suffering subject of the Bhopal gas disaster, as Fortun consciously refuses the mode of subjective ethnography that Biehl, Garcia, or Steinberg adopt. Instead, it is *advocacy* itself, as enacted and globally articulated. As with the latter trio's, there is something crucial about mobility in Fortun's research design. Fortun moves within and across sites that some of her activist gas victim interlocutors in Bhopal cannot easily access, including notably to Union Carbide in America, which she accesses by becoming a shareholder and attending shareholder meetings. The sites that are traversed in America are not, however, just those of power and privilege, as Fortun conceptually and politically links Bhopal to the chemical corridor of the US Gulf Coast in ways that put conventional "center-periphery" cartographies of industrial capitalism and imperialism into question. She performs what Jean Comaroff and John Comaroff (2012) would subsequently call a "theory from the South" in both registers: powerfully mapping the reiteration of rather old and persistent models of imperial violation ("First World" corporations polluting "Third World" people), but also showing the inscription of center-periphery structures in the landscape of industrial America.[24]

Throughout *Advocacy*, Fortun insists on and performs the political work of ethnography, in ways that refuse simple binaries that might designate the work as either simply "academic" or "activist." Thus, there is an enmeshing of ethnography, hypercomplexity, and praxis, as constituting the conceptual topology of the work. The systemic and structural question—what kind of a world are we living in?—is necessarily, simultaneously, descriptive and political. For Fortun, advocacy is *not* simply resistance: it is about scaling, about making connections, and is fraught with the constant possibility and reality of failure. Fortun shows that advocacy builds worlds; but the world building is not a simple outcome of a romantic resistant subjectivity on the part of the violated, elsewhere, who will take care of giving us our hope in the metropole here.[25] The task of ethnography, Fortun insists through her praxis, is to provide ways of knowing and making sense of complexity, not just establishing it, and certainly not to salvage a "resistance" that is yearned for, predefined, and then "found" by the metropolitan ethnographer. This is the non-phallogocentric, multisituated sensibility of *Advocacy*.

What does this mean, in terms of actual lessons for the operationalization of multisituated ethnographic research design of the sort that elucidates global political economic structures and systems? First, that context *is* ethnographic, not mere background to ethnography. Thus a rigorous elucidation of (historical, locational, situational) context is vital to multisituated work. Second, the work of multisituated ethnography lies not just in *tracing* connections but also in *making* them. The power of multinational industrial capital lies precisely in its ability to territorialize worlds in ways that occlude or prevent connections from being seen: such as, for instance, the shared (albeit differential) violations of chemical industrial workers and residents of the US Gulf Coast and slum dwellers of Bhopal. In articulating the structural relations across these locales, Fortun is opening up spaces to conceptualize political solidarities of the kind that corporate capitalism negates.

Third, particular kinds of narrative work in *Advocacy* themselves engage in conceptual and political work (such as the columnar situation of "1984" in time and across scale and place that I have alluded to). One of Fortun's key concepts in the book is that of "enunciatory communities." Fortun develops this concept as a critique of, and an alternative to, the notion of the "stakeholder," which dominates discussions of interested parties in the aftermath of disaster in ways that reduce these parties purely to rational, transactional, equally situated actors who have similar articulatory capacity. Yet she does not provide a simple definition of what an enunciatory community is. Instead, she engages in conceptual labor, elaborating the idea of an enunciatory community as something that is "like a global disaster" (14). This juxtaposition, in the words of my student Jill J. Tan, "[set] up the contours for her conceptual terminology as distinct from stakeholder analysis, while imploding global disasters."[26]

In the process of these moves, Fortun generates a multisituated conceptual topology that is not just a description of objects, practices, and phenomena in and across different sites, but becomes a question of the question itself. What *is* the anthropological problem of advocacy, of global environmentalism, of disaster, of late industrialism, of their contemporary intercalations across site and scale? What is the discursive terrain, with attendant discursive gaps and discursive risks, which constitutes these problems?[27]

In *Advocacy*, Fortun situates her work in sites of what Rob Nixon has called "slow violence" (Nixon 2011). Her ethnography performs translational work, across scales, locales, and domains. She attends to the corporation, not simply as a site to be "accessed" in a Malinowskian, penetrative sense, but as an institutional form, with discursive, juridical, and appropriative presence in the world. She attends to the erasures that are performed when disaster mutates into slow violence in scenes of enduring corporate unaccountability, thus asking whether and how ethnography can call institutions of power to account by rigorously tracing the structural and systemic terrains that they operate upon and help build. The haunting political question that one is left with concerns the relationship between planetary violence and the (im?)possibilities of planetary collectivity, given the structural difficulties of forging solidarity between victims of the Bhopal gas disaster and residents of the Gulf Coast chemical corridor who depend on companies such as Union Carbide, BASF, or Dow Chemicals for their livelihood.[28] This politics is very different from one that hierarchizes suffering and victimhood. All of this is only possible because Fortun focuses on the practice of advocacy and its relationships to the corporate form as her ethnographic object, rather than remaining bound to the "site" of disaster and suffering.

....

In this chapter, I made four arguments. First, we need a proliferation of the norms and forms of ethnographic practice and narration in ways that are adequate for our contemporary theoretical aspirations. I believe that such proliferation has already taken place but has not been conceptualized into graduate pedagogy about fieldwork method or research design as much as it might. Second, such proliferation would necessarily include thinking about multisituated ethnography not in terms of whether projects are feasible or unfeasible, but, rather, given the constitutive importance of a multisituated sensibility to realizing our theoretical aspirations, how projects might be conceptualized across site and scale in ways that do not compromise rigor and depth. Third, doing so requires thinking of multisituated ethnography not as a literalist methodology, but rather as a *conceptual topology*. In other words, what is at stake is not just a technical formula that "follows" x, y, or z (objects, people, money, etc.) from one site to another, but rather the very consideration of the relationship between the stuff of the world we wish to empirically describe and the stuff of the world we wish to conceptualize. Fourth, there is a politics at stake in these kinds of multisituated conceptualizations. I discussed some exemplary ethnographies that have operationalized these sensibilities and aspirations in different ways, even as I suggested conceptual modalities of engagement and positionality that provide alternatives to a Malinowskian romantic authorship. Nonetheless, the question of the epistemic place of the native informant in a multisituated approach remains unanswered. It is this that I turn to next, in considering the comparative praxis of multisituated ethnography.

2

Comparison

In this chapter, I argue that the development of a multisituated disposition involves thinking the potential for comparison in non-phallogocentric ways: a conceptualization of other (and Other) kinds of comparison. This cannot be based simply in a process of symmetrical accounting in which "dependent" and "independent" variables are established in advance and parsed with respect to one another. Such a symmetrical process presumes figure and ground, the terms of comparison and the nature of the compared entities, in advance. Phallogocentrism lies in those invariably Eurocentric and masculinist presumptions. A comparison Otherwise would seek epistemic unsettlement by holding open the terms, entities, and grounds of comparison, in order to see whether different anthropological problems might emerge to those normally presumed. It would thus seek to deconstruct, and possibly invert, logocentric and patriarchal center-periphery assumptions that structure the terms of dominant comparative modalities.

I do not conceptualize comparison as a formal technical program; it stems from modes of attentiveness and attunement to the stuff of the world under question. When I was a graduate student, Sharon Traweek told me a story of the research trajectory that led to her *Beamtimes and Lifetimes* (1988), a comparative ethnography of high-energy physicists in Japan and at Stanford. On the face of it, this takes the form of a symmetrical comparative project that attends to cultural and organizational differences in the structure and practice of laboratory hierarchy and work in the two locales (American labs exhibiting "sports team" cultures, compared to the more traditional hierarchies and deference of Japanese labs, for instance). Yet Traweek was apparently planning a research project located at the Stanford Linear Accelerator Center, and her teacher Gregory Bateson advised her to undertake fieldwork in Japan first. This was in order for her to develop an attentiveness that would enable her encounters with American cultures, which she was already acquainted with as a function of her biography, to be denaturalized. Thus, Traweek's ethnographic attentiveness toward American physics cultures is marked by a nonparochial sensitivity.

I was myself taught to think comparatively by my teacher Sheila Jasanoff, one of the premier comparativists in science and technology studies (STS). She has told me of her own origin story as a nonsymmetrical comparativist, which emerged from an early research project, conducted in the 1980s, which set out to compare environmental regulations in the United States and Britain. Such projects were relatively rare at the time; what struck Jasanoff on her arrival in the United Kingdom, however, was that the term "carcinogen," ubiquitous in the American regulatory lexicon, was entirely absent in the British one. Thus what came immediately to be at stake was not just a question of the differential content of regulations, but the very conditions of possibility that allowed for fundamentally different framings of environmental risk and toxicity. In other words, it was a question not of social or organizational cultures, as with Traweek, but of political cultures. This attentiveness toward differential political cultures has extended throughout Jasanoff's work, and it is most programmatically articulated in *Designs on Nature* (Jasanoff 2005), a comparison of biotechnology regulation in the United States, the United Kingdom, and Germany.

As described in chapter 1, comparison has remained important to me ever since I was gently but firmly instructed by my PhD advisors (including

Jasanoff) to do fieldwork in India after I had completed dissertation field research in California, a goading that proved crucial to the argument of *Biocapital* (K. Sunder Rajan 2006). The comparative sensibility that I developed then has carried forward throughout my work; it structures the design for my new research project on the articulations of health and law in South Africa and India. This will in some way draw on an empirical consideration of the sometimes similar, sometimes very different, sometimes deeply related, constitutional genealogies and judicial cultures through which health has come to be a matter of legal concern in post-Independence India, both because my interests in health and the law were forged out of earlier work that encountered these interactions in an Indian context, and because South African and Indian judicial cultures themselves often refer to one another in matters of socioeconomic rights and public interest.[1]

The comparative methods that Traweek, Jasanoff, and I employ privilege a certain kind of comparison whose research design is driven by the ethnographer's analytic agenda, even as it is responsive and responsible to the empirics of the "fields" it studies. Comparison in *Beamtimes and Lifetimes, Designs on Nature*, and *Biocapital* is situated across ethnographic focus: what does the ethnographer *choose* to compare, and how? A certain notion of site (in these three cases, all nationally bounded) becomes important to the materialization of that focus and its expression across place. These are thus examples of analyst-driven comparisons. They are ethnographically rigorous in not imposing the terms of comparison in advance (as "variables," dependent or independent), in allowing them to emerge from the sites under study. Nonetheless, they do articulate the *sites* of comparison in advance, as part and principle of research design. This reflects George Marcus's conception of multisited ethnography as "following the thing" (Marcus 1995)—the ethnographers elaborating this, in their respective project conceptualizations, by further asking "to where," and incorporating the answer to that question into their project design from the outset. Though important, this is not the only epistemic modality by which to compare otherwise. As this chapter progresses, I will also elaborate strategies that attend to incommensurability and incongruent juxtaposition in order to allow more actor-driven expressions of non-phallogocentric comparative method.

....

My stakes in articulating an-Other kind of comparison as central to a multisituated praxis are twofold. On the one hand, comparison generates better descriptions. On the other hand, and more radically, comparison can help elucidate structures and operations of *power*, both descriptively and epistemologically, especially if we attend to who gets to compare, on what bases, upon what grounds, which elements of a comparison are deemed normative and which others exceptional. Thus, comparison has both a conceptual and a political function. An-Other kind of comparison, such as I argue for it, is one that is invested in underlining the political function of the comparative epistemological project of a multisituated ethnographic disposition.

One kind of political function is the project of *cultural critique*. What does it mean to study the Other in order to understand "oneself" or "our own society"? In some ways, this was the animating sensibility of the first edition of *Anthropology as Cultural Critique*. The exemplary work in this vein is Margaret Mead's *Coming of Age in Samoa* ([1928] 2017), which describes sexual life among Samoan teenagers in order to understand "our own." This is the sensibility behind Traweek's going to Japan in order to help her "see" Stanford ethnographically. What does this mean, however, when it is not clear that "our" society is Western? In other words, what does this mean for the diasporic anthropologist? The notion of repatriation that lies at the heart of this sensibility, and which was central to the first edition of *Anthropology as Cultural Critique*, is already less relevant by the time of the publication of the second edition.[2]

The first conjuncture that I wish to mark in terms of the contemporary problem-space of comparison for a multisituated ethnographic disposition, therefore, is the "becoming-diasporic" of the metropolitan university writ large, and of the anthropological discipline specifically, in ways that differentiate and put the "universality" of knowledge into question, not just by opposing it to particularity but also by situating what universality looks like, from differently positioned perspectives. As a diasporic ethnographer myself, going to India helped me situate the dissertation research I had already done in California for *Biocapital*. Yet California, not India, was the strange and exotic place for me. Thus like Traweek, I ended up going to a place that was more culturally familiar to me after I had done research in a strange land; but it was in the metropole that true strangeness occurred. This meant that there was a dual comparative edge to my attunements. For example, as part of my work, I was studying the establishment of a "culture of innovation" in Hyderabad, modeled on Silicon Valley and driven in part by expatriate networks. I observed the establishment of venture capital–driven biotechnology in a country where postcolonial science since Independence had largely been a state socialist endeavor. The discourse suggested mimesis, with emergent Indian tech cultures imitating more established and now-successful Northern Californian ones. Yet I found great incongruence in the meaning of venture capital as it was being established in Hyderabad-based initiatives such as "Genome Valley," as so much of the investment was in fact driven by state subsidies for high tech, calling themselves "venture capital," from the government of Andhra Pradesh.

To the extent that a normative definition of venture capital as operational in California was the basis for comparison, its manifestation in Hyderabad was peculiar and different. At the same time, for someone who studied to be a biologist in India, under a postcolonial ethos that adhered to Mertonian scientific norms (Merton 1942), it was Californian venture science that felt nonnormative relative to the scientific and governance ideals I had grown up with. At stake for me was not repatriation, but rather what Marilyn Strathern calls "dual relativization" (Strathern 1991). If I could only understand the emergent culture of innovation in India relative to that established in California, I could also only understand the emergent culture of neoliberalizing science in California relative to that which I was taught to be normative in India. The critical point is that those who inhabit diasporic trajectories often *constitute Otherness otherwise* to metropolitan constitutions of Otherness.

The second kind of political function of the comparative epistemological project of a multisituated ethnographic disposition concerns questions of globalization/modernity/liberalism and its others. This stems on the one hand from the many important diagnoses and critiques of neoliberalism from the past two decades.[3] On the other hand, it continues a series of debates around the question of modernity, ranging from anthropological critiques *of* modernity as part of a project of salvaging "tradition" or "indigeneity," to various forms of "postmodern" anthropology, to diagnoses of "nonmodernity" such as Bruno Latour's (Latour 1993), to the "Alternative Modernities" conversations of the 1990s (Gaonkar 2001). There are many intellectual and political positions, from many standpoints, reflected in these genealogies. Yet, today, there feels to be a dominant sentiment of anomie toward liberal political modernity itself, one that manifests not just in progressive, leftist politics but that is also strongly articulated in various strengthening right-wing xenophobic and authoritarian politics movements around the world. If the latter bridles against values of equality or Enlightenment rationality that are espoused by political liberalism, then the former tends to see liberal political modernity as itself a hegemonic/racist/imperialist project.[4] This reflects a certain praxis of the comparative project as itself oriented toward either a diasporic diagnosis *of* the imperialism of liberal political modernity, or a reflexive metropolitan critical *self*-diagnosis of the violence of liberal modernity. Once this diagnosis is made, then what?

One possible move is to study alterity not as an objectifying end in itself but as a critical elucidation of power. This involves, in part, a reflexive attention to the epistemic violence involved in such a study itself, in understanding the very parameters through, and assumptions against, which "difference" can be imagined, constituted, and/or (not) lived in the first place. This is the move of anthropologists such as Strathern, who has perhaps done more than most to conceptualize comparison Otherwise, as I will elaborate through the course of this chapter. A second possible move would be to study the constitutions and institutions of liberal modernity, as an ethnographic object of analysis, in order to understand it as itself something striated, differentiated, and nonsingular. This is Jasanoff's project in *Designs on Nature* and is my own aspiration in *Pharmocracy*, which simultaneously elucidates the structural logics of global capital while unpacking the hierarchies and contestations between different kinds of global capitalisms (such as of the multinational, Euro-American pharmaceutical industry and the Indian industry, respectively) (Jasanoff 2005; K. Sunder Rajan 2017). Both these moves—diagnosing the underlying power structures (colonial, masculinist, racial, classed) that hierarchically constitute difference *as* inequality on the one hand, and empirically elucidating the striations, differentiations, and contradictions *within* such power structures—are at the heart of a multisituated disposition that seeks an-Other kind of comparison.

If the praxiological stakes of generating an-Other kind of comparison involve the elucidation of power through the study of alterity (while always attending to the diasporic question, alterity for *who*?) and the study of the intricacies of the operations of those structures themselves, then a comparative project must attend to two things. First is the question of the Other that one generates knowledge of or from, speaking to the constitutive place of the *native informant* in ethnographic knowledge production; second is the question of difference, which involves both a description of the alterity of the Other and an understanding of the epistemic basis by which such a description can be understood as being one of alterity. This attaches to questions of *commensuration and incommensurability* in the work of ethnography. I consider the question of the native informant first.

....

In his essay "From the Native's Point of View" (1974), Clifford Geertz explicates the problematic of experience-proximity and experience-distance.[5] This conceptual problem constitutes ethnography, which seeks to make rigorous generalized claims from particular, contingent encounters. Further, it is doing so from encounters *with another*, with the Other. The tensions that ethnography must straddle, between particular/general, micro/macro, material/abstract, -emic/-etic, are necessarily mediated by the native informant, and the epistemological claims that ethnography can make are imbricated with the kind of subject/object relationship that is established, and out of which knowledge claims are made, between ethnographer and native informant. This has historically been a phallogocentric relationship. The meta-methodological questions concerning an-Other kind of comparison are epistemological, ethical, and political questions concerning the relationship between the ethnographer and the native informant.

On the one hand, the problem of experience-proximity and -distance is a straightforward methodological one. Geertz tells us that any ethnography that simply documents experience-proximal ideas and concepts is not adequate as ethnography. At the other end of the spectrum, simply generalizing is also not good ethnography—ethnography needs to get specific, to stay with the trouble of particularity in its entire messy and equivocal contingency. A good ethnography, almost by definition, has to tack back and forth. In articulating the tension between experience-proximity and -distance as constitutive and defining of ethnographic work, Geertz is doing something more than just articulating a technical dictum. He pushes back against an idea and ideal of ethnography as "becoming native," as reducible to transcultural identification with the Other. For Geertz, ethnography is instead about looking over the shoulder of the native and piecing things together. This is where the possibility of a postcolonial politics—the possibility of a relational epistemology that goes beyond phallogocentrism—emerges.

To summarize, the terms of the problem here are that ethnography at its core is a practice that gets knowledge from and makes knowledge through a relation with the Other, a practice in which the ethnographer is both saying something *about* the Other but also saying something about something else, often more abstract and generalizable, *through* the Other. In other words, ethnography must contend with the obligatory place of the Other not just as someone(s) to be ethically accountable to, but also as the source through which to make any claims to knowledge about the general, the structural, and the systemic. This means that the question of how we as ethnographers claim an *epistemic* relationship to the Other— whether the Other is in a position of radical subjective alterity or is someone much more proximal to our various raced, classed, and gendered subject positions—becomes critical. Geertz is provoking us to ask how we know that the claims that we make as ethnographers, which in an obligatory way depend upon the native informant, are rigorous and valid ones: the problem of interpretation, but also of authority. In chapter 1, I focused on the question of the claims themselves, of how to generate a research design and conceptual topology that can straddle the constitutive tensions of scale, perspective, and (in)tangibility required to make robust theoretical claims out of a multisituated ethnographic practice. As I move forward, I want to shift focus to the implicit part of this provocation concerning the epistemological question of claims making, which concerns the place of the native informant in this relational knowledge-making practice. For without the native informant, there is no ethnography.

This move imbricates the ethical with the epistemological. But ethics here cannot simply be about whether we are nice or proper toward our informants—it cannot be reduced to the procedural valences of informed consent and good ethnographic practice as enshrined by institutional review boards, which is a watered-down and proceduralized sense of ethics. Rather, this is a question of ethics and politics at the level of making claims: what claims are being made about a generalized phenomenon based on an essential relationship with an other, with others, with the Other, that is in fact validating the ethnographer as the authorial producer of knowledge?[6]

Geertz says something significant toward the end of "From the Native's Point of View": "understanding the form and pressure of . . . natives' inner lives is more like . . . reading a poem than it is like achieving communion" (45). The stakes of this shift in analogy are high. This is resolutely *not* Geertz saying (as he is too often reductively misread) that cultures are texts. Rather, he is formulating an epistemic interpretive practice that refuses a transcultural identification that validates ethnographic authority, as found, for instance, in Sherry Ortner's "minimal definition of ethnography," which has continued to operate as an ideological backdrop for ethnography: "Ethnography of course means many things. Minimally, however, it has always meant the attempt to understand another life world using the self—as much of it as possible—as the instrument of knowing. . . . Classically, this kind of understanding has been closely linked with field work, in which the whole self physically and in every other way enters the space of the world the researcher seeks to understand" (Ortner 1995: 173).

Ortner's formulation prevents the imagination of a truly postcolonial and decolonizing ethnographic praxis. It remains wedded to a "becoming other" that can only ever be ideological, only ever be an expression and measure of intellectual desire, and only ever be penetrative and appropriative when the ultimate cause it serves is to validate the authorship and the authority of the ethnographer.

Geertz himself does not go all the way in undoing ideologies of ethnographic authority—ultimately, his accounts of Java, Bali, and Morocco are resolutely *his* accounts, and something like the famous story of the Balinese cockfight that got Geertz "in with the natives" is a quintessentially phallogocentric access story, even as his conceptual aspirations for an interpretive anthropology assume fairly fixed identities and practices (the white male ethnographer as the expert of Balinese ritual, who has the last word in articulating what the practice is about) (Geertz 1973). He is not thinking of the kinds of dialogic ethnography that Marcus and Fischer call for in *Anthropology as Cultural Critique.* Nonetheless, his call to read natives' inner lives as poetry (*not* culture as text—natives' inner lives as poetry) rather than communion is an argument for being able to make claims through the natives' point of view, knowing that one *cannot* know or understand it. This is an impossibility that has nothing to do with how radically Other the native might be. Epistemologically, this is a humble, demystifying, and de-romanticizing move. It refuses the ability of the anthropologist to say, "I can tell you about them because I have gone native and therefore I can understand them, and my claim to authority is that I have gone native." Geertz is saying no, you cannot. The best that one can do is interpret, and how one interprets matters. How one renders the subject of interpretation—is the native's inner life an object or a poem?—matters.

As ethnographers, we do not get to make generalized claims because we have understood the other's subjectivity. We get to make generalized claims because the other leaves *traces* that the ethnographer can piece together, or that can be translated, or that can serve as a basis for tracking connections, or that can establish transferential relationships with the ethnographers' own modes of knowing and being. Geertz's own alternative to "becoming native" is an interpretive one that involves cultural translation, suggesting the tight interrelationship between interpretation and translation.[7] Yet translation necessarily involves acts of commensuration that are themselves epistemic and political. How to think about the epistemology and politics of commensurating an account of the Other? This involves asking, first, with respect to what is the Other being commensurated? (i.e., a question of figure and ground). Second, what would it mean to generate a commensurable account of alterity and difference (one that thus constitutes a comparison) when one is dealing with people, societies, processes, or structures that are incommensurable? To address these questions as the next element of articulating the problem-space of an-Other kind of comparison, I turn to Marilyn Strathern.

....

In *Partial Connections*, Marilyn Strathern makes three definitions of comparison: (1) as a practice of generalizing from cases; (2) as an indication of interesting points of difference; and (3) as offering higher- or lower-order propositions about the material (1991: xvi–xvii). What is vital, across these different aims of comparison, is the disproportion that is necessarily at the heart of comparative observations. This could be a function of differential concerns that are central to the domains being analyzed. More radically, it could also be a function of either incongruence (the appearance of similar values and features in different societies at different levels) or incommensurability (a more radical incompatibility between the figuration and grounding of values and features themselves, across societies). The first and third definitions above directly concern the Geertzian problem-space of experience-proximity and -distance. The second squarely places it within a concern with *difference*. Where the difference that ethnography seeks to elucidate is not just about the content of kinship, or property, or personhood across different societies, but about the very foundations of conceptual generation across epistemologies, cosmologies, and ontologies. Comparison for Strathern is thus an act of "dual relativization": the relativizing of one's own society through a relativist understanding of others. There is something akin to the sensibility of cultural critique in this move.[8]

The fundamental question of *kinship* lies at the heart of Strathern's method, where kinship is not a thing-in-itself (kinship as "objective fact" about the Other, where the social structure of the Other *is* the object) but a mode of elucidating relations. The ethnographic task therefore is not to define what kinship really is: indeed, to demolish any approach that would begin thus. Rather, it is to elucidate the nature of social relationality itself and to show the differential (sometimes-incommensurable) modes of relatedness that even allow a concept such as kinship to be thinkable. Strathern is working against an idea of description as synthesis toward one of partial connections, where partiality speaks, in one register, to the constitutive epistemic incompleteness of the very project of ethnographic description itself. It is in this recognition of the impossibility of a complete description that Strathern's politics diverges markedly from a Geertzian normativity.

In a second register, "partial" means *partisan*. The decentering of synthetic paradigms is also a regrounding in order to generate non-phallogocentric descriptions, in order to render something like kinship a feminist concept, not just an anthropological one. This is where Strathern explicitly joins with Donna Haraway on situatedness, revealing the bias in a purported "complete or full description" that claims to be nonpartisan.[9] In the process, Strathern develops a dialogue between feminism and anthropology, using feminism to interrupt anthropology, even as she uses anthropology to interrupt feminism.[10]

Strathern's signature intervention is her placement of incommensurability at the heart of the conceptual problem-space of comparison, even as she shows the power-laden ways in which things are made to relate and be commensurable. In a review of the anthropology of incommensurability, Elizabeth Povinelli begins with a linguistic treatment of the problem, concerning the relationship of incommensurability to linguistic indeterminacy as explored by W. V. Quine (Povinelli 2001; Quine 1960). This relates to the linguistic question of how one commensurates radical alterity. One answer to this is Donald Davidson's, through the assumption of rational linguistic conventions (Davidson [1984] 2001). Povinelli opposes this to a critical theoretical approach (following scholars such as Walter Benjamin, Michel Foucault, Jacques Derrida, and Georges Bataille) that suggests that indeterminacy and incommensurability are the normal condition of communication. A third approach (following Edward Sapir and Roman Jakobson) is the move from considering incommensurability in terms of linguistic *phenomena* to doing so in terms of linguistic *consciousness* (i.e., distortions are not just internal to language itself; there is an anthropological component to linguistic indeterminacy) (Sapir 1949; Jakobson 1962).

Povinelli situates this linguistic trajectory considering the question of incommensurability alongside 1980s debates over concepts of nature, culture, and capital to other societies, of which Strathern's *The Gender of the Gift* (1988), which articulates the incommensurabilities in the very grounds upon which these concepts are framed while talking *of* the Other, is a seminal contribution. Thus on the one hand (as in Povinelli's reading), Strathern's work is located in a nexus of emergent conversations in linguistic anthropology. On the other hand (the reading I am doing here), it is located in the 1980s epistemic milieu of what Marcus and Fischer call "the crisis of representation" in the human sciences, in which the work of Gayatri Spivak makes a seminal contribution, itself drawing on genealogies of post–World War II poststructuralist thought.[11] Thinking an-Other kind of comparison that keeps open a non-phallogocentric multisituated ethnographic disposition involves attending to the questions of incommensurability, commensuration, and translation as they operate within and across the triangulations of linguistic, anthropological, and philosophical treatments of the problem of incommensurability across alterity.

One kind of anthropological move away from a model that privileges rational maximization of agreement as the "solution" to the problem of linguistic indeterminacy that Povinelli discusses at some length are pragmatic interactional approaches (Silverstein and Urban 1996; Irvine and Gal 2000). These approaches, pioneered by linguistic anthropologists such as Michael Silverstein and Susan Gal, focus on the pragmatics of agreement in real-time social interactions and contestations. Agreement, therefore, is not a given as it is in rational models, but it must be forged. How this is done, the processes of pragmatic commensuration (which are a function of linguistic consciousness as much as they are internal linguistic determinants), then becomes an object of ethnographic elucidation. The "how" here is crucially a question of process, and the ethnographic work involves the empirical study of that process (following the ways by which commensuration is pragmatically forged, as it were). It is also a question of situations and background assumptions, of the conditions of possibility for the display of certain kinds of linguistic consciousness over others: what Michael Silverstein refers to as linguistic ideologies (Silverstein 1979). Thus, the linguistic anthropological move is to shift the problem-space of comparison from a "semanto-logical to a social problem" (Povinelli 2001: 325).

One therefore has two contemporaneous and related interpretive moves at the heart of generating an-Other kind of comparison, one indebted to Geertz and the other coming out of linguistic anthropology, which are responding to similar kinds of problems but basing their interpretive moves differently. The latter understands processes of the commensuration of alterity by ethnographically attending to sociolinguistic interactions and their pragmatics, across difference, and grounding them in a concept of ideology that is not false consciousness but rather "sets of beliefs about language articulated by users as a rationalization or justification of perceived language structure and use" (Silverstein 1979: 193). Thus, the basis for interpretation is structural and sociological. The former poses the problem of interpretation as the question of making sense of the "native's point of view," which again cannot simply be discerned from an elucidation of process (what another means when they wink requires a thicker description than just an account of the act of the wink [Geertz 1973]). Geertz's solution, as I have argued, is to read "native's inner lives . . . as a poem": the basis for interpretation lies in *personhood*, which may well be constituted by structural elements but must exceed them. There is a turn, therefore, to the literary and the affective that a Geertzian interpretivism opens up.

This much is methodological. But how to think the *praxis* of an-Other kind of comparison, one that goes beyond generating better description or interpretation to also scripting a non-phallogocentric ethnography? For this, I turn back to Strathern and think about the uses of her method for conceptualizing a contemporaneously relevant critique of colonialism/imperialism/capitalisms/(neo-)liberalism. In other words, how do we think with Strathern's decentering of concepts of nature, culture, capital, personhood, or property through a rescripting of Melanesianist anthropology in order to critically elucidate global political economic structures and systems, which is Marcus and Fischer's call in *Anthropology as Cultural Critique*? Strathern's definition of "partial connections" is not quite the same as Marcus and Fischer's call.[12] She is "looking for taxonomies which are not about overarching principles or central features" (Strathern 1991: xx), a different search than Marcus and Fischer's structural and systemic provocation. Strathern's is a call for a fractal anthropology, one that is "not going to take the form of a map" (xx).

Yet cartography is central to imperialism. Therefore, in turning one's gaze on imperialists, one *does* need genealogies and maps, as acknowledgments and investigations of colonial inheritance. Strathern decenters logocentric comparison. Part of the ethnographic question of attending to global political economic structures, however, precisely involves centering them, *as* an empirical ethnographic object, attending to their modes of constitution and their striations and differentiations. Strathern does so by decentering the conceptual apparatus of Western hegemony as constituted through anthropological knowledge, in ways that potentially open us up to radically other ways of knowing. She does so not as a unidirectional relativizing move that valorizes some holistic Other in opposition to one's own (Western) epistemology (to reiterate, relativization for Strathern is always dual, always turns its gaze back to relativize the West as symmetrically as it relativizes the Other), but as an insistence on the partiality of all knowledge, its constitutively fractal nature. She articulates a politics of knowledge then by paying attention to the modes of relationality between these parts: partial connections, as a necessary and constitutive methodological counterpart to dual relativization in order to develop an-Other kind of comparison.

I juxtapose this next to another modality of decentering the conceptual apparatus of Western hegemonic modes of knowing, one that is less about a circumscription of the scope of commensuration of Western assumptions and more about their *inheritance*. This is a dual-edged, ambivalent, deeply postcolonial deconstructive modality that opens up different methodological and conceptual orientations and provocations. For this, I turn to the work of Gayatri Spivak.

....

I will read two of Spivak's key texts, the "History" chapter in *A Critique of Postcolonial Reason* (1998) and *Death of a Discipline* (2003). As preface to these readings, I suggest that thinking with Spivak toward a decolonizing ethnography requires attending to her stakes in *pedagogy* on the one hand and in *imperialism* (as something that exceeds colonialism and continues to operate in the conjunctural manifestations of contemporary global capitalism) on the other.

While so many of our obsessions about method tend to orient around research, as academics we in fact spend most of our time teaching. To the extent that many of us have any tangible impact in the world as academics, it is through teaching.[13] Pedagogy is conditioned by institutional structures that have affordances and constraints, which are different in different parts of the world. One of the major constraints of American academe is that it operates within a highly capitalized and continually financializing political economic structure, such that the recognition of what is worthwhile and worthy of support has to be rendered legible to capital. This makes it increasingly difficult to do humanistic work that is not seen as fungible.

Questions of disciplinary production have to be asked within the framework of such structural constraints. Spivak argues for a humanistic sensibility—specifically, in *Death of a Discipline*, for a comparative literature supplemented by area studies—at a moment when the very value of these modes of knowing are being put into question by institutions that deem what kinds of inquiry are fungible and valuable and which are not. Today, the value of a discipline itself is a function of whether it can render value to capital.[14] So the question becomes, what does it mean to have a relation to these disciplines, while fully acknowledging their colonial and imperial histories but also recognizing that the world would probably be worse off without them? Spivak's is a critique that is not only about decolonizing the disciplines we inhabit but also about saving them, a refusal to just leave the world to a choice between Galilean paradigms on the one hand and an attack on reason and rationality itself on the other. This is the refusal *of a teacher*, teaching a generation of students coming into a world being constrained out of humanistic modes of knowing.

Spivak's best-known and most-taught essay, certainly within the metropolitan disciplinary anthropological canon, is probably "Can the Subaltern Speak?" (1988), a watershed in clarifying the epistemic violence that is at the heart of even those projects that claim to recuperate the voice of the subaltern. I prefer the second telling of this essay in its reproduction in her chapter "History" in *A Critique of Postcolonial Reason*, because even as it reiterates certain arguments from her initial essay, it supplements them in ways that open up fundamentally new lines of thought. In "History," Spivak juxtaposes "Can the Subaltern Speak?" to the account of the Rani of Sirmur, another essay written initially in the 1980s (Spivak 1985). This concerns a queen of one of the "hill tribes" in the foothills of the Himalayas who became a pawn in the "great game" of the still-consolidating British empire in South Asia in the early nineteenth century. Even this fact only comes to be known because of the odd way in which the Rani—whose proper name is never given, not even deemed necessary—emerges in the colonial archives, briefly, only to then disappear. The emergence is consequent to the deposition of her husband, the king, because of syphilis and the Rani's emergence as a custodian for her son, the young prince. In addition, there was the context of the resulting British worry that the Rani would commit *sati* upon the king's death, thereby threatening the configurations of emergent gamesmanship that the colonists were involved with at the time in relation to the governance of the hill tribes. If "Can the Subaltern Speak?" left us with a diagnosis of epistemic violence as a provocation, "History" goes further.

In "History," through an account of the Rani's place (or rather trace) in the archives, Spivak is providing a deconstructive alternative to the project of recuperating the subaltern voice—a project that is, as she had already argued a decade previously, ultimately doomed to ventriloquizing the intellectual's desire for the subaltern voice. The alternative is to look for traces, what she calls "fragments," of the subaltern in the archive. When does she emerge? When does she disappear? In whose accounts? To what ends? Who *is* the subaltern anyway, given that the Rani is, after all, a queen, but a queen whose agency is so instrumentalized in the great imperial game that is unfolding that even her proper name is immaterial in the recording of her "history"? Spivak is looking for these fragments, however, not in order to recuperate the subaltern but rather to turn her gaze on the imperialists in power. Rather than reading the colonial archive in order to "find" the subaltern (the project, for instance, of the subaltern school of historiography), Spivak looks for traces of the subaltern in that archive in order to "find" imperial power, to make that the object of her ethnographic attention.

The story that then emerges is one of various British imperial figures: the young colonial administrator, Geoffrey Birch; the senior military general, David Ouchterlony; and the board of directors of the English East India Company sitting in London. Spivak shows how each figures the Rani in the image of its own strategic interests and imaginaries, even as they were collectively inscribing the power of colonial rule onto India through both governance and archiving. What Spivak finds through this reading of traces is another game that is at the heart of this historical moment, one that is about configuring and contesting relationships between crown and corporation, between an imperial project of mercantile capitalism and a colonial project of direct rule. Spivak's deconstructive reading of the archive thus resituates and dislocates the objects of ethnographic knowledge and attention.

The Rani is one of two figures of a female native informant in "History." The second, Bhuvaneswari Bhaduri, appears in the second part of the chapter and originally appeared in "Can the Subaltern Speak?" Hers is another story of a middle-class militant nationalist woman who committed suicide (not sati) who again was not strictly "subaltern," but whose death was nonetheless already inscribed in certain phallogocentric ways. She could only script another narrative for herself through the moment of her death—which she ensured happened while she was menstruating, in order to obviate the obvious interpretations of her suicide that would have otherwise ensued. Bhuvaneswari's story performs a vital related function to that of the Rani's, but not an identical one, and it is worth thinking of the function of the juxtaposition of these two incongruent narratives as Spivak's two cases of "the native informant in history."[15]

What I want to flag here are three deconstructive moves that Spivak makes—looking for traces and fragments; turning the objectifying, textualizing gaze away from the subaltern herself toward the imperialists in power; and creating incongruent juxtapositions of native informants—that could each profitably constitute elements of a multisituated ethnographic disposition. I use this as a springboard to considering some broader meta-methodological and praxiological stakes for Spivak by reading *Death of a Discipline*.

Death of a Discipline is an argument for a comparative literature supplemented by area studies, one that is relentlessly concerned with questions of appropriation. Spivak argues for a humanistic, comparativist area studies practice that resists hegemonic appropriation, even as she recognizes its full potential for being appropriated by hegemonic discourses, pedagogies, ideologies, and institutions. In the conjuncture that she is writing, the hegemon is not the colonial state as immediately as it is globalized financial capital (though how can we possibly think globalized financial capital without a theory of imperialism?), which becomes the only register of exchange in which one is allowed to think about exchange within our institutionalized norms and forms. Thinking exchange otherwise, in ways that are not legible to globalized financialized capital, is actively constrained, even discouraged. We must think our disciplinary practices and modes of inquiry in full recognition of this potential for appropriation.[16]

Appropriation is not an abstraction. Spivak locates it within two conjunctures, two examples of progressive sensibilities that have been appropriated by the dominant:

– What is very important for comparative literature is the move toward world literature. I remember when my mother, Rajeswari Sunder Rajan, was a member of Delhi University's curriculum committee for English literature in the 1980s. The English curriculum circa 1987 started with Chaucer and ended with Dickens. Twentieth-century literature or American literature did not count as literature; forget about postcolonialism, feminism, or literature by people of color. This was the canon. Within the next twenty years, this canon came to be radically transformed, such that by the late 2000s Delhi University had become a cosmopolitan center of humanistic thought (before the assault, these past few years, by the Narendra Modi government and Hindutva ideologues on the Indian research university and on Enlightenment thought itself). Especially in the metropolitan university, this cosmopolitan transformation came to be disciplined and appropriated through an idea of world literature, a movement akin to world music: the commodified, packaged, globally disseminable form of the literatures of the Other in ways that are legible to capital and can be made valuable. So the question is how to engage in a project of an insistence on Other literatures, an insistence on Other voices, such that they not be thus commodified? Spivak's answer is that there are no guarantees.[17] Therefore, her investment remains in a comparative literature, but also (as with Strathern's relationship to anthropology) in another kind of comparison. The critical move is not to abandon the comparative project, not to abandon the disciplinary project, but to engage in a praxis that seeks to save something that is appropriable—by the state, by capital, by patriarchy—without any guarantees that it will end up where we want it.

- A second example concerns the figure of the woman. On page 46 of *Death of a Discipline*, Spivak discusses the incorporation of feminism within dominant structures of power, for example, through the establishment of international women's rights upon the human rights paradigm. This must be seen in the context of a trajectory of financialization that provides the setting for such incorporation, whose exemplary instantiation is microcredit: an espousal of an idea and ideal of feminism in which the only idiom through the rural subaltern woman can be figured as a legitimate other is that of globalized financialized exchange.[18] Again, the vital necessity of feminist praxis; again, without guarantees that it will not be appropriated, repackaged, and commodified by hegemonic discursive, ideological, and institutional formations of global heteropatriarchal capital.

In all of this (Other literatures that can be appropriated by global capital, the figure of the woman and feminist praxis that can be appropriated by global capital), the place of indigeneity is absolutely crucial to Spivak. In the final section of the book, Spivak develops the notion of "planetarity": a notion that contains within it an ecological sensibility that globalization does not, and which therefore also has something to do with indigenous modes of engagement with the world. In doing so, she insists that no form of planetary feminist engagement can avoid risking engagement with the indigenous Other. This speaks to the vital place of Mahashweta Devi—an intellectual who is herself not an indigenous person but who spent her life working in rural tribal Bengal—as an interlocutor in Spivak's thinking. Because for Spivak, as for Geertz and Marcus and Fischer, this engagement does not come from transcultural identification, from "becoming subaltern," from knowing what the subaltern "really thinks," and from giving voice to the subaltern. It comes from the work of translation.[19]

There are no guarantees that this engagement with the female subaltern Other will not be appropriated by imperial states and global financialized capital. Spivak's is not an aspiration to a pure, uncontaminated space of engagement. What does it mean to engage in this manner, which keeps one open to the possibility of other and Other forms of knowledge, knowing full well their appropriability? The risk here is not just that this form of engagement gets appropriated; it is that if one is really open to thinking otherwise and Otherwise, our own paradigms of knowing—which, let us not kid ourselves, are as indebted to colonial states and global financialized capital as they are constrained by them—come to be at stake.

So what is to be done? Spivak does not lay out a program, but she does provide pointers to the kinds of empirical and conceptual work that constitute her deconstructive method, involving (1) taking a given construction, deconstructing it, and then constructing it again, Otherwise; and (2) forcing a reading, one that faces, names, and describes imperialism.[20] She also provides pointers from her own biography. She learns languages prolifically. She teaches in rural Bengal every summer, outside of the transactional space of dominant metropolitan institutional legibility. She does something akin to ethnography—not in its disciplined, instrumental sense, but as a stance and disposition of openness, one that necessarily exceeds the transactional sphere of metropolitan academic metrics with their institutional and audit culture rationalities—all the while refusing a claim to have "become Other" in the process.

There are elements to this praxis that are Geertzian, but there is a crucial difference. As I mentioned earlier, while Geertz resists transcultural identification as the mode of knowing, he still remains the author. Spivak is asking us something more radical: what would it mean to be open to a text that is authored by the Other? With Spivak, one is forced to consider the inhabitation and creation of translational spaces where the ethnographer is not the only one performing the authorial work of translation.

While Geertz's position has to have politics read into it, Spivak's call is immediately political. Geertz is asking, how do we know the native point of view when the native is someone other than us? Spivak is also asking, how do we create a politics out of this? One that imagines and articulates modes of worldly collectivity, solidarity, and praxis that resist dominant idioms of globalization?

I want to stay with this question by thinking about the work of comparison that Spivak performs at the heart of *Death of a Discipline*, which makes it as important for the consideration of ethnography as it is for comparative literature. The question of comparison here is not just an epistemic question of knowing the Other. It is also a political question of acting collectively with the Other. What is at stake is not just knowing the other as an object of study, but also *training the imagination*. This speaks to the work of literature in comparative literature, something that I will discuss further in the next chapter. At this point, let me materialize this as Spivak's tangible question at the heart of *Death of a Discipline*: how does one read Other literature? (Alongside, how does one read one's own literature Otherwise?)

The meta-methodological question here concerns training the imagination to the possibility of acting collectively with the other. This is not easy, and it is never innocent. It is in the context of this simultaneously epistemological and political problem that Spivak, at the center of *Death of a Discipline*, reads Joseph Conrad's *Heart of Darkness* (1899), a novel that at once highlights the vicious barbarity of colonialism while being a racist text.[21] Spivak has brought us to a place where the question is not whether one is "for" or "against" *Heart of Darkness*. Rather the question becomes, what does it mean to read Conrad Otherwise?

This is where Spivak's own comparative method comes to the fore. As in the "History" chapter with its incongruent juxtaposition of the Rani and Bhuvaneswari as female native informants, she engages in an act of incongruent juxtaposition by reading Conrad against Virginia Woolf's *A Room of One's Own* ([1929] 2012), Tayeb Salih's *Season of Migration to the North* ([1966] 2009), and Mahashweta Devi's "Pterodactyl" in *Imaginary Maps* (1991). Why these three texts? What kind of incongruent juxtaposition is this, and what epistemic and political work does it do?

For Spivak, acting collectively with the other is not reducible to identity politics (which itself is a certain kind of comparison based on center and periphery). Spivak wants a politics of collectivity that decenters the implicit relationalities of identity politics. So let us go back to the place of the figurations at the heart of the three texts that she has chosen: the figures of the woman (Woolf), the subaltern (Salih), and the indigenous (Devi). These figures are not just Other figures to the phallogocentric colonial rationality of imperial power; they are also Other to what she calls logofratrocentric forms of worldly collectivity imagined out of metropolitan patriarchal centers. (Marxism, of course, is the typical example of such a logofratrocentric collectivity as opposition and alternative to phallogocentric globalization.) In other words, this incongruent juxtaposition is one that resists an imagination of worldly collectivity in the image of brotherhood. Think now of the place of the woman, the subaltern, and the indigenous in a planetary collectivity that is always, even in its progressive variants, structured through logofratrocentric imaginaries. Spivak is not giving voice to the woman, the subaltern, or the indigenous: she is training the imagination to figure the woman, the subaltern, and the indigenous Otherwise. In what ways might one think these figures in complex ways that do not reduce them to the identity categories "woman," "subaltern," and "indigenous" through a reading of these texts? How does that allow for an-Other kind of reading of a metropolitan text such as *Heart of Darkness*?

These figures—the woman (in Woolf), the subaltern (in Salih), and the indigenous (in Devi)—are not Other in the same way. They are different kinds of others. The figure of the woman is something akin to Spivak's suggestion of the universal (as in woman is everywhere and woman is constitutive to species-being). Yet in spite of the universality of woman, collectivity is not imagined in her terms, not by the dominant or by the logofratrocentric progressive alternatives to the dominant.[22] Spivak brings Virginia Woolf, who is not by any means a peripheral writer, who is indeed at the heart of metropolitan literary production in the age of British empire, into the center of her comparative project, because of the question of the figure of the woman. She does so because she is reading Conrad not just to diagnose or absolve his racism, but as a certain kind of text that figures woman as much as it does race. At the end of Marlowe's voyage in *Heart of Darkness*, the heroic figure who is found is not the imperialist hero Kurtz, whom Marlowe goes in search of up the river, but the Black native queen, who is at (or who is?) the heart of darkness. Through this monstrously romantic figure of Otherness and of colonial masculinist desire, Conrad is figuring woman as much as he is figuring race. The racialized female Other is at the heart of his text.

Spivak takes these three texts and asks what it means to read them alongside each other as texts that take the figure of the woman seriously.

Not only are they not all postcolonial texts; they are also not all feminist texts: indeed they are not all even written by women. These are texts that, individually and together, figure woman as species-being through woman as a nonspecial case. Reading them together, Spivak is opening us up to a certain universalizing idea of woman that is not reducible to the heteronormatively binary identity "not man." She is working toward an entirely feminist reading, regardless of who writes the text, forcing a feminist reading out of nonfeminist texts even as she forces a postcolonial reading out of metropolitan texts.

If Woolf is writing a feminist text from the belly of the colonial beast, then Salih is writing a postcolonial text from the heart of the masculinist beast. *Season of Migration to the North* is a text that is located, at once, in Sudan and in London: a narration of a narration that inverts and reverses the routes of colonial voyage narrated by Conrad, and by his protagonist Marlowe, in *Heart of Darkness*. This includes, at its core, the Arab man's elaborate contriving of an Orientalist boudoir in his British residence as a means to seduce a series of white women. All of whom happen to subsequently die.

In many ways, *Season of Migration to the North* is a sexist book, in a manner akin to how *Heart of Darkness* is racist. Yet Salih also, in describing and inverting structures and affects of postcolonial masculinist desire, shows the reader something about colonial and patriarchal violence, just as Conrad does. Think here of the structure of colonial desire that Frantz Fanon describes: decolonization and postcoloniality do not have to be pretty and certainly do not have to be virtuous (Fanon [1952] 1994). No guarantees. The question, however, is one of the refiguration of woman if one thinks it through the relationship between the Black or brown male body and the white female body. How does one think collectivity in this moment, out of this text, in relation to the subjectivity of diasporic Arab masculinity? In these times? What does it mean when Arab masculinity travels in ways that are postcolonial and also sexist and sexualizing?

Then Devi. "Pterodactyl" is a prehistoric figure that indexes indigeneity. What does it mean to take the primitive seriously and not simply as an object of the desire of the metropolitan intellectual to recuperate or salvage the idea of "pure" indigeneity? Yet the protagonist of "Pterodactyl" is not (just) the indigenous: it is the journalist Puran Sahay, who makes his own voyage into a certain "heart of darkness," as he travels from the Palamu region of Bihar where he is from to Pirtha, in Madhya Pradesh. Puran is a journalist who goes to write a story of a strange sighting of a prehistoric bird, the pterodactyl, itself first "revealed" through inscription, the cave paintings of the mute indigenous boy Bikhia. This is a story of the violence and failure of postcolonial nationalist development that never reaches the indigenous peoples of India (designated as scheduled tribes by the government, or just "tribals" for short); indeed, these are people who are constantly expropriated in the cause of this development. The tribals are facing famine, at a time of agricultural abundance in the state of Madhya Pradesh. Theirs is a famine that is entirely a function of property relations, feudal landholding, and dispossession. On the face of it, this is a quintessential story of the violence of liberal modernity as it gets internalized into postcolonial development and visited, most virulently, upon indigenous populations.

Yet there are incongruences to this story. Puran Sahay is himself a flawed character, like Conrad's Marlowe. He is also a metropolitan character, of a sort. What, however, is the metropole? He voyages from Palamu, which is itself a tribal region. The violence inflicted upon indigenous populations in Madhya Pradesh exists just as much in Bihar. This violence has many facets specifically directed against indigenous populations, but it is also part of a more generalized violence against the poor, including the nonindigenous poor. (The specter of the Union Carbide gas disaster in Bhopal, which is the state capital of Madhya Pradesh, hovers over the story.) The story is also haunted by the shadow of Saraswati, Puran's unconsummated love in Palamu, who is dressed as a widow as he leaves her to write his story. Even as the protagonist of the story, unlike many of Devi's others, is male, the figure of the woman is central to it. There is the further dialogic interweaving of Devi herself, the female intellectual who is not indigenous but who has devoted her life to writing about the plight of India's tribal populations, through literature, journalism, and advocacy, and the further layering of Spivak's own dialogue with Devi, as her translator to a metropolitan audience.

These three texts, in their juxtaposition, serve a certain kind of function. Their juxtaposition is deliberate and staged—it is part of Spivak's research design and conceptual labor. It is threaded by the question of the figure of the woman as a universal question for thinking planetary collectivity otherwise, as a figure that is always appropriable, whose function as a basis for thinking planetary collectivity Otherwise is always without guarantees.[23] This juxtaposition also layers different registers of comparison as an exercise in revealing power and difference. Woolf speaks to the quotidian *inequalities* of gender relations in the metropolis. Salih speaks to the *incongruences* and *inversions* (potentially of racial power dynamics, if not sexual ones) of the metropolis becoming postcolonial through immigration, an incongruence that is always laced with inequality, still. Devi speaks to the *incommensurability*, the impossibilities of communication, in the postcolony that builds itself in the image of the metropolis, for the violated bodies and socialities of its indigenous peoples (relationships that show incongruence, and are lacerated with inequalities, all the way down). Each of these texts effects its own work of comparison; Spivak juxtaposes them in a comparative project of her own; and, in reading Conrad through their juxtaposition, she engages in a further rereading and rescripting of *Heart of Darkness*, yet an-Other kind of comparison.

I have read Spivak alongside programmatic texts in the disciplinary history of anthropology, especially Geertz, Strathern, and Marcus and Fischer, in order to show a kinship in the nature of their projects, even if the specific modalities of ethnographic attention and concept work they adopt contain important methodological and praxiological differences. What would it mean to think multisituated ethnography as conceptual— and praxiological—topology through this reading of Spivak, *as* a feminist project? In which "feminism" is not reduced to the identity category "woman," but is a "general critical instrument rather than something to be factored in in special cases" (Spivak 2003: 74)? In which a feminist epistemology is not just about asserting the rights and demands of a marked subject position, "woman," but becomes a mode of forging knowledge and planetary collectivity in non-logofratrocentric ways that require deliberate employments of alternative modes of comparison, attentiveness, and forging relationality? There is particular kinship here with the kinds of questions that Strathern is asking, such that it is essential to read Spivak with Strathern.

Nevertheless, I also want to read Spivak against Strathern, for even as both share impulses toward the development of non-phallogocentric forms of comparison, there is a specific difference between Spivak's approach to comparison and Strathern's. Both Spivak and Strathern turn their critical gaze, through their comparative methods and projects, upon European epistemologies and cosmologies. Spivak does so in order to show mechanisms of appropriation; Strathern, in order to show the always impossible, always incomplete, process of commensuration that attends these appropriative processes. Spivak's is an exemplary demonstration of what Dipesh Chakrabarty has called "History 1," histories that are "posited by capital" (Chakrabarty 2000: 50). Strathern's shows the limits of European epistemologies and cosmologies themselves, demonstrating what Chakrabarty terms "History 2": histories that exist "outside of capital's life processes" (50).

At stake are two distinct decolonizing modalities of critiquing hegemonic comparativist paradigms, based in different objects of the ethnographic gaze and attention. Spivak is a cartographer *of* imperialism: she unpacks it and shows its own internal differentiations and striations. Strathern gazes *beyond* imperialist cartographies, showing their own constitutive epistemic inadequacy. Hers is an insistent, almost obsessive, search for ways of knowing and living outside and beyond the worlds posited by capital; Spivak's is an almost paranoid vigilance toward the ways in which there *is* no pure world outside capital that is not appropriable by imperialist ways of knowing and living. Her insistence, therefore, is that one has to understand these modes of knowing and living on their own terms, not in terms of the radical alterity that one might desire. If Strathern traces the limits of metropolitan knowledge (while attending to the violence that accrues from an epistemic system that constantly refuses to acknowledge those limits), Spivak maps the internal logics and contradictions of those metropolitan systems.

Both Spivak and Strathern script Other forms of comparison by deconstructing the fundamental assumption of colonial modes of comparison, which posits the universality of metropolitan ways of knowing while relativizing the knowledge of the Other. *How* they do so is methodologically different and shows different political orientations. Strathern, by showing the limits of Western commensurability of the Other, thereby shows the inherent partiality of its universalizing claims. Thus, she relativizes the metropole in the same manner that metropolitan knowledge relativizes the Other: another kind of comparison through dual relativization. Spivak, by opening up the black box of Western thought (such as its dependence on the native informant for constructing an authoritative relativist knowledge), engages in a different kind of refusal, keeping open the possibility of a *universalism from elsewhere*. For instance, Bhuvaneswari Bhaduri, her second key female protagonist in "History," is not Other because she is outside Western rationality. Her nationalism, like that of many anticolonial thinkers and actors throughout the twentieth century, is steeped in Enlightenment ideals. These ideals are, however, turned against the colonizer and torqued in the process. Spivak's is thus an insistence on the *multiplicity* of universalisms.[24] For Spivak then, radical alterity is not the horizon of politics (as I will subsequently elaborate), and universalism *itself* is not the epistemological and political adversary. Rather, it is the *possession* of universalism by heteropatriarchal, metropolitan capitalism that has to be fought. This is the fundamental epistemological and political difference between Strathern's method and Spivak's.

To summarize the kinship and difference between the two, consider Homi Bhabha's assertion that "the difference of cultures cannot be something that can be accommodated within a universalist framework" (1990: 209). Both Spivak and Strathern articulate methods that thicken this insistence. Yet in Strathern's method, the "cannot" attaches most vehemently to "universalist" (the difference of cultures cannot be something that can be accommodated within a *universalist* framework), an epistemological and political investment in a necessary attention to the partiality of perspectives, connections, and articulations. Meanwhile, Spivak's method italicizes the "a" (the difference of cultures cannot be something that can be accommodated within *a* universalist framework), an emphasis on the potential for a multiplicity of universalisms, from elsewhere and Otherwise. I thus argue that Strathern comes up with an alternative epistemology and practice *to* the dominant, Eurocentric mode of comparative knowledge production, reconfiguring the comparative project itself, whereas Spivak inverts the gaze *on* to imperial epistemologies and thereby provincializes Europe. The focus on her attention is on the *inheritance of* European histories, rather than *difference from* European ontologies or cosmologies, which is Strathern's. The focus on *incommensurability* (and thus *alterity*) as the horizon of politics in Strathern's case, and on *inheritance* as the condition of politics in Spivak's.

I conclude this chapter by elaborating on this question of inheritance, rather than of incommensurability, as the epistemic and political horizon of Spivak's work. What are the stakes of Spivak's refusal to let her explanations and her praxis rest upon radical alterity and incommensurability?

....

An attentiveness to European inheritance in the constitution of postcolonial modernity is the focus of Dipesh Chakrabarty's *Provincializing Europe* (2000). This is especially important to an understanding of *political modernity in the postcolony*, the object of Chakrabarty's analysis. Strathern's primary ethnographic object, by contrast, is that of British social anthropology, "the society," and specifically the individual/society distinction at work in this epistemology. She does not engage political modernity per se. Thus, even as she provides a decolonizing methodology of comparison, she does not concern herself with a description of the politics of the postcolony from within the situation of the postcolony (which often, in fact, sees a deep internalization of and desire for European inheritance, sometimes with very good reason).[25]

Spivak's comparative method, by contrast, explicitly concerns itself with the politics of the postcolony. An excellent example of how it does this can be found in her essay "Constitutions and Culture Studies," which is an engagement with and critique of Bruce Ackerman's *We the People* (Spivak 1990; Ackerman 1991).[26] In this essay, Spivak deconstructs the originary myths of American constitutionalism, myths that are possible only, she argues, because of silenced histories of settler colonialism. She compares this to the Indian Constitution, which does not have the conditions of possibility for such originary myths. Her project at this point does not move in to a critique of liberal constitutionalism per se. Instead, she sets up these differential trajectories of Euro-American constitutional histories as world making by asking a comparative question to nineteenth-century Ottoman imperial constitutionalism—a constitutional form that was, Spivak insists, *also* universal, indeed as universal as the Western European constitutions of the time. The defeat of the Ottoman empire then was not, in Spivak's reading, the triumph of a "universal" worldview over an "Islamic" one; it was the triumph of one imperial universalism over another, such that in battles over Turkish modernity, the modernists led by Atatürk could *only* be secular in European guise. Any indigenous Islamist alternative was already relegated as peripheral and by definition "religious." Only one universal, because comparison could only be between the (solitary) center and its peripheries. The consequences of this painful Faustian bargain, which had no place for other kinds of comparison that allowed a thinking of difference, are, of course, continuing to be felt in Turkish politics today, in violently authoritarian ways.[27]

In order to further elaborate this method as one that goes beyond a comparative project that establishes radical alterity and incommensurability, I engage in an experimental reading practice of my own, a reading of a reading. I provide here an account of an engagement with "History" in my "Multi-si(gh)ted" graduate seminar, on the part of one of my students, Ji Yea Hong. Hong's intellectual trajectory is doubly diasporic. She is a student from Korea, studying for a PhD in anthropology in the metropolitan American university. Her dissertation project began as a study of the bronze drum, an emblematic cultural object in the history of southwestern China. Thus, her study of China is of "another" society, but she is not a metropolitan ethnographer. She nonetheless comes to a project whose construction is necessarily framed by long intellectual genealogies of metropolitan (and Chinese nationalist) area studies *of* China (and its minority ethnicities). Hong's work, therefore, is by definition performing an-Other kind of comparison, one that cannot simply refuse the inheritance of area studies (including its most imperial variants), but that also cannot afford—for epistemic, political, or autobiographical reasons—to simply re-perform certain kinds of objectification of "the" bronze drum as an emblematic "Chinese cultural" object.

Hong began her reading of "History" at the beginning, from Spivak's first sentence: "If by our old-fashioned reckoning philosophy concatenates and literature figures, feminist historiography often excavates" (Spivak 1998: 198). Thus begins an opening interlude to "History," which is two paragraphs long, in which Spivak tells the reader what the chapter is about, but also makes a declaratory gesture (not fully explicated) about what "feminist historiography" is or might be. This opening, Hong admitted, "still feels very much like a riddle to me. I could kind of understand, but never fully."[28] The "riddle" in question is not so much a query or an obfuscation as much as a hesitation, such that the declaration in the first paragraph that "History" is about the native informant in history is paused in the second:

> In the first paragraph, Spivak declares that this chapter tries to answer the question of "what is the fate of the historians' informant" by giving two stories about the informant in history. She also positions this attempt as an act of excavation, a practice of feminist historiography. In the second paragraph, however, Spivak struggles with her cause that she has just provided in a very straightforward manner. She hesitates. This project has never been a straightforward project for her. She wants me to know that this previous statement is one that must be followed by a "despite," and it is what follows after the "despite" that is more important than her declared act of excavation itself. (Hong)

In diagnosing the dialogue that exists between the first and second paragraphs of "History," Hong is establishing a dialogue between herself and the text, which is also implicitly a dialogue between the reader and the author. Hong notes the importance of Spivak's hesitation, which she marks as a site of vacillation—a vacillation that marks a moment, perhaps, when the writing is unsure of itself, but also a moment when the author is convinced that something important is afoot, precisely, therefore, a moment when certitude is to be most carefully avoided. After saying at the outset that "History" is about the fate of the native informant in history, Spivak qualifies the project with this:

> In the previous chapter, I have tried to argue that a critical intimacy with deconstruction might help metropolitan feminist celebration of the female to acknowledge a responsibility toward the trace of the other, not to mention toward other struggles. This acknowledgment is as much a recovery as it is a loss of the wholly other. The excavation, retrieval and celebration of the historical individual, the effort of bringing her within accessibility, is written within that double bind at which we begin. But a just world must entail normalization; the promise of justice must attend not only to the seduction of power, but also to the anguish that knowledge must suppress difference as well as *différance*, that a fully just world is impossible, forever deferred and different from our projections, the undecideable in the face of which we must risk the decision that we can hear the other. (Spivak 1998: 198–199)

Hong goes on to make an affirmative statement about what Spivak's essay is really about. She does so by attending to the "despite" in Spivak's second paragraph, a "despite" that is actually a "but." "But a just world must entail normalization." Hong, however, forces a reading: she reads it, in her post, as follows: "In her attempt to excavate the fate of the historians' two informants, she is also losing them, and she knows it from the very beginning. '*But*,' she says, 'a just world must entail normalization; the promise of justice must attend not only to the seduction of power, but also to the anguish that knowledge must suppress difference as well as *différance*, that a fully just world is impossible, forever deferred and different from our projections, the undecideable in the face of which we must risk the decision that we can hear the other'" (Hong).

In her reading, Hong places her own emphasis on the "but": "but" becomes "*but*." In doing so, she is recognizing its importance. Hong recognizes that at this moment, (almost) at the outset of her essay, Spivak is not merely proceeding with an establishment of difference *from* a Eurocentric historiographic epistemology as part of her critical method, but is doing so from within the double bind, where there are no guarantees about the outcome of this project.[29] This lack of guarantee is not just because of the uncertainties and contingencies of all (political) actions, but—Spivak's haunting insistence—because the promise of justice *must* entail a suppression of difference. In other words—and this is at the heart of the *différantial* politics of a Derridean deconstruction—*the establishment of difference is not enough for the promise of justice. Différance*—a concept that entails difference and deferral—is one that is at odds with itself.

How, now, at this moment and in this text? Spivak is saying that building an epistemology that insists upon radical alterity and incommensurability—which, as I have described, is at the heart of Strathern's development of an-Other kind of comparison—is a *necessary* and *nonsufficient* condition for justice. What might provide sufficiency is not an intensification of, or a radicalization of, difference, but in fact—a thought that leaves Spivak anguished—its *suppression*. At a general philosophical level, we surely know this to be true: for instance, a valorization of difference is not always concomitant with a politics of equality, and in certain situations it can be antithetical to it.[30] Hong gets specific, by moving to the third paragraph in "History."

This paragraph marks the beginning of a new section, which is in fact a parenthesis. Seemingly, apropos of nothing, Spivak tells us of a conference organized by the sociology of literature group at the University of Essex in 1982, on the topic of "Europe and Its Others." Spivak narrates her attempt to have the conference renamed, instead, "Europe as an Other," and how the conference organizers were not at that time ready for such a nomenclatural (and conceptual) recalibration. This reframing—"Europe and Its Others" to "Europe as an Other"—is central to both Spivak's project and to Strathern's: it is a move of cultural critique, of dual relativization, of provincializing Europe.[31] In critiquing the framing "Europe and Its Others," Spivak is asking what it would mean to empirically attend to a world in which Europe is able to center itself such that it is not-Europe that is the Other. She is also asking what it means that these non-European others can be described as *its* (Europe's) others, a term indicating possession. Making Europe the object of ethnographic attention provides a method to tackle this possessive (indeed, colonial) framing head-on.

There is another thread running, in the "but," and it is a qualification. What does it mean to provincialize Europe in terms of its others, if that makes the non-European Other the bearer of History 2 and Europe the bearer of History 1? On the one hand, provincializing Europe is essential to highlighting and potentially negating Eurocentric epistemology, in ways that highlight alterity and incommensurability. On the other hand, there is the intrusion of the word "justice," which in Spivak's usage is not an instrumental term but is rather (following Derrida) promissory. (Like all promises, it contains within itself the potential for betrayal.) This word "justice" interrupts; it causes Spivak to pause, to quiver, to tremble with the anguish of the knowledge that the establishment of difference may not be the only end at stake and worth fighting for. The story she is about to tell us in "History," which she has informed us (in the first paragraph) is a story of two informants in history, is not a story in which a critique of Eurocentrism causes patriarchy to be vanquished through the rendering of an-Other account. An-Other kind of comparison is not (just) about establishing alterity; an-Other kind of comparison is not just if it only establishes alterity.

"Therefore," says Hong, "in her attempt to excavate the fate of the historians' two informants, she is also losing them, and she knows it from the very beginning." *Also losing them.* Not failing to find them, but losing them—an active, agential act of loss. Loss is not innocent; loss is about grief. Spivak's historiography cannot be the recuperation of the subaltern: it is already, from the beginning, a work of mourning.[32] Spivak forces us to confront questions of intimacy and desire, and the transferential relations of the producer of knowledge to the object being studied, in generating an-Other kind of comparison.

Hong says, "I can't quite grasp the depth of the risk she is taking and her burning urgency to still do it. This is why this text is so difficult to me." This is not the ungraspability of incommensurability and radical alterity, whose demonstration is at the heart of Strathern's Other kind of comparison. This is the ungraspability of the ethnographic relation itself, its singularity, its multiple mediations between ethnographer, informant, and reader, its transferential capacities and limits, its constitutive violences, even when (most definitely when) it serves to establish the value of difference. This is so especially in the context of cosmopolitan encounters in which the diasporic itineraries of ethnographers, informants, and readers of accounts are complexly constituted in ways that simultaneously reify and decenter conventionally colonial metropolitan-periphery relations.

By the end of our seminar, Hong had reframed her dissertation. It was now no longer about "the bronze drum" but about the worlding of the bronze drum in the context of practices of Chinese culture writing, one that simultaneously takes into account the histories of field science in Chinese nation building and the global valuation of "heritage." The *objectification* of the bronze drum, and not the bronze drum itself, became her ethnographic object. This objectification could not be understood without turning an ethnographic gaze on to global political economic structures and systems, including those of area studies paradigms in both the

Chinese and the metropolitan universities. Helped by Spivak's not-quite-graspable riddle, Hong is embarking on an-Other kind of comparison.

....

Spivak calls us to move away from a politics of hostility to a politics of friendship-to-come.[33] She also, following Derrida, establishes a relationship to the future anterior—*l'avenir*, that which is to come rather than that which will be, without which, in Derrida's terms, "there is neither history, nor event, nor promise of justice" (1994: 198). *L'avenir* speaks to a particular register of futurity that is not predictive but promissory: again, no guarantees.[34] It speaks to a mode of relationality that is not clear-cut, virtuous, guaranteed to right wrongs or set accounts straight. Reading Other literature is not going to reverse injustice in that fundamental(ist) way. Rather, it opens us up to the possibility of other modes of relating. Spivak's is a critique of modes of identitarian politics that already frame the Other as a certain kind of essentialized figure (either antagonistically or, in its liberal variants, as pure radical alterity to be valorized and/or salvaged). This has kinship with Marcus's desire to think multisited ethnography without falling prey to the anxiety of "the loss of subaltern voice" (see chapter 1); both Marcus and Spivak share a suspicion of a project of subaltern recuperation.[35]

Strathern's rescripting of relationality, at the end of the day, elides this critical dialogic question. Hers is a concern with generating better *accounts* of relationality, *as an ethnographic object*. It is reflexive in that it critiques the dominant epistemological assumptions that underlie existing phallogocentric accounts. However, it does not implicate the ethnographer within the relational question, except as an observer and epistemologist. One can see this elision in her reading of *Writing Culture* as an entry into *Partial Connections*, as a critique of representation that is focused on exposing the hidden power relations between anthropologist and informant. Surely, it is that. But more: the point I am emphasizing is that in its Geertzian genealogies, the entire project of the "*Writing Culture* moment," which shares affinities with and can profitably be read through Spivak, is concerned with considering the consequences of engaging in an epistemology that requires the native informant as its basis. In some regard, Strathern goes beyond this rescripting of the notion of the fieldworker to demolition of the idea of "the integration of ethnographic experience" itself: partial connections *as opposed to* integration.

Yet it is only by retaining the central concern with the native informant that one can deconstruct the power relations inherent to this epistemology even as one practices it: this is a question of the reformulation of the norms and forms of ethnographic practice itself. At the end of the day, Strathern reads *Writing Culture* (and implicitly, by extension, the moment of the critique of representation of which it is a part) as primarily an aesthetic project, one that decenters a "modernist" aesthetics at the altar of a "postmodernity." My argument, by way of Marcus and Fischer, is that there is rather a radical, promissory methodological call that is at stake, concerning the cosmopolitan praxis of ethnography itself. Strathern herself provides a vital and dynamic method that responds to the phallogo-centric qualms that were being explicitly voiced at this moment. But there are certain directions in which she does not go, having specifically to do with the elaboration of dialogic and autobiographically situated rescriptings of ethnographic praxis—specifically, the question of inheritance, which is not the same as commensuration, but is also not about incommensurability. This question of inheritance is indelibly a part of the subjective and epistemic situation of postcoloniality and hence is at the heart of developing a diasporic anthropology. It is, therefore, central to my further consideration of a multisituated topology in the next two chapters. Even as there are affinities between the problems Marcus, Fischer, and Strathern are writing about, it is Spivak rather than Strathern who helps me articulate some of the subjective dimensions that implicate the cosmopolitan ethnographer within the scene of the ethnographic encounter.

....

In this chapter, I read Gayatri Spivak's argument for a certain kind of literacy, which troubles our expectation to understand those that are radically Other to us through our reading. Her praxis insists that objectivity cannot be reduced to Galilean paradigms; to the extent that they are, Spivak's deconstructive move is to ensure then that the objectifying and textualizing gaze is consistently turned on instruments and institutions of power rather than on the subaltern. This is why, even in the diagnosis of epistemic violence in "Can the Subaltern Speak?," before we even get to the supplementary work that "History" performs, Spivak is not denying the subaltern her ontological capacity to speak. She is even in that moment of the diagnosis of epistemic violence turning her gaze on the Western intellectual, and his re-inscription of her speech as his recuperation of her speech.[36]

Spivak speaks to the relationship between the unintelligibility of radical alterity and the kinds of literacy that are needed across region, discipline, language, and genre to grapple with it, within the scene of metropolitan, phallogocentric, intellectual desire that seeks the intelligibility of that alterity, not just in-itself, but also for metropolitan ideas and ideals of a virtuous politics. It is a desire that is often not explicit but rather institutionalized in our disciplinary and epistemic norms and forms, a desire that a multisituated stance and disposition, as conceptual topology and with a constitutive deconstructive sensibility, can help dislocate and decenter.

The ethnographic challenge that Spivak leaves us with then is how, given this, we might articulate the problem-spaces of political modernity (including and especially as seen from the postcolony) in ways that retain the possibility of a denunciatory critique of the liberal modernist enterprise without being reduced to it.[37] This provokes us, I suggest, to consider ethnographic norms and forms that go beyond the monologic dimensions of sociological analysis and "theory" making. There is a need for a critical objectification of Western epistemologies, articulated to a study of political modernity in and from the postcolony, in ways that grapple with the dialogic, autobiographical, and transferential questions of inheritance that are at the heart of diasporic ethnographic encounters.[38] I consider this in the next chapter, by considering ethnography, alongside and through literature and photography, as an intimate praxis of encounter.

3

Encounter

Gayatri Spivak tells us that the "History" chapter in *A Critique of Postcolonial Reason* (1998) is "two stories about the native informant in history": one story about the Rani of Sirmur, the other about Bhuvaneswari Bhaduri. When there are *two stories*, there is a work of comparison. In chapter 2, I considered the question of how Spivak engages in an-Other kind of comparison. We must, however, consider, further, what we mean by "story." When we are reading history as a story, we are reading it as literary. Indeed, Spivak insists upon this: she is not saying that history equals literature, but she is saying that *she* is not reading the archive the way a historian would; she is reading it as she knows how to, as a literary critic. What is the function of reading history as literary? What kind of relationship is being set up here between history and literature? What are all the kinds of literacies we need to have (and to put on hold) in order to read it thus?

The first story in "History" is about the Rani, except that it is not about the Rani. It is precisely a refusal to tell a story about the Rani. This is the point at which Spivak diagnoses epistemic violence. This refusal-cum-diagnosis is precisely *not* a refusal to make knowledge or to make a claim. The story of the Rani is the story of her appearance in the archives (i.e., the object of the story is the *archive*, not the Rani). Spivak is reading the Rani under erasure. She is not saying I will not tell you what happened, just that I will not tell you about the Rani, only about the place of the Rani in the archives. Spivak is saying, let us get as objective as we can, but let us change the object. There is an assertive and affirmative epistemological stand here, and it is an ethical and political one. The object is decentered and situated, the ethnographic (historiographic) gaze inverted. This leads to a methodological question: *how* do we read the story of the Rani to tell us about the archive? If Spivak is telling us about the archive, what else is she telling us about, alongside?

Spivak is hardly the first person to do a poststructuralist deconstruction of the archive and is certainly not the first to read history as literary. As she proceeds through her argument, she engages two scholars who have foundationally reconceptualized the archive, Hayden White and Dominick LaCapra. White deconstructs the archive by reading it like literature, indeed at virtually the same time that Clifford Geertz is inviting us to read natives' inner lives as poems (Hayden White 1973; Geertz 1974 [see chapter 2]). White suggests that the archive after all is just fiction, a selective construction, the work of those who have the power to author it. Spivak pushes back that it is not enough just to read the archive as fiction. Not because of a positivist concern that refuses the literary function of the archive, but because of the subject/object configuration in White's reading.

Here are these two entities: the Rani and the archive. What the deconstructive reading allows is the displacement of the Rani as object into archive as object. When White is telling us to read archive as literature, there are only two entities at play: the archive and literature. When we are engaged in an act of reading and interpretation, however, Spivak is reminding us of the essential third entity—*the reader*. Spivak's point is that if one is assuming only two entities, the archive and literature, when in fact there is always a third entity involved, the person who is engaging in interpretation, then one is failing to read the powerful role of the intellectual—and his desire—in creating certain interpretations rather than others.

This is where Spivak turns to psychoanalysis, in her move from White to LaCapra (LaCapra 1983).[1] LaCapra's deconstruction of the archive is *transferential*. He engages in a psychoanalytic reading of the reader of the archive, arguing that the reader establishes a transferential relationship to the text.[2] This is the first glimmer in the "History" chapter of the question of intellectual desire: that is, when we read a certain kind of interpretive relationship (archive as literature), there is no way that our own desires as readers do not in some way constitute that reading. This is inescapable—it is at the center of the kinds of knowledge that we produce—even as it is deemed unacceptable, because our knowledge is supposed to be objective. It cannot be "I also want"; it has to be "it was thus." Spivak takes issue not with the fact of intellectual desire itself but with the presentation of phallogocentric intellectual desire as simply "objective."

What allows the legitimate transmutation of "I also want" to "It was thus" across disciplines—anthropology, history, throughout European Enlightenment history? Around what can a claim to objectivity be constructed? It is the native informant, as speaking subject. Without the native informant, there is no ethnography, only opinion. The native informant is constitutive to the very project of ethnographic (and historical, literary, and philosophical) knowledge production—this is Spivak's point throughout *A Critique of Postcolonial Reason*. What I have wrestled with through my reading of Spivak is, how do we displace that native informant in certain kinds of ways to make the relationship less colonial, less patriarchal?

Spivak reads the archive not to find the radically Other speaking subject as an end in itself, but to turn the gaze on power. One of the critical understandings that emerges from "History" is of the imperial moves made by the East India Company. The simultaneous invocation and erasure of the Rani has to be understood in the context of these moves; indeed, Spivak insists, it has to be understood such that these moves now no longer remain mere "context" or backdrop for the elucidation of the Rani's subjectivity, but must become the object of analysis themselves. The question of *corporate* power risks being elided if one misreads the story of the Rani of Sirmur as being one of female subaltern agency.[3]

Yet this is not a novel turn for "History": Spivak had already thus decentered the object of her historiographic gaze onto power in the earlier iteration of the two pieces that constitute the essay, "The Rani of Sirmur" and "Can the Subaltern Speak?" What makes "History" more than just a combination of these two earlier pieces is a crucial, rather peculiar, supplement. At the end of the section on the Rani of Sirmur, Spivak describes a remarkable ethnographic excursion that she undertook to the foothills—going to the Rani's kingdom, conducting oral histories with people living there, even staying in the Rani's palace. It is a most extraordinary passage, because it moves from looking for traces of the Rani in the archives to doing so via an ethnographic expedition. In the process, she finds traces in the scriptures of the Brahmin priests, yet again inscribed by a group of powerful men. But more: almost enigmatically, while describing this particular journey, Spivak confesses, "I pray . . . to be haunted by her slight ghost" (1998: 207).

Thus, Spivak refocuses the object of her empirical attention, turning her ethnographic gaze on the constitution of patriarchy (both religious and imperialist) itself, in all its differentiated specificities. She thereby makes the *hierarchical terrain*, rather than female subaltern agency, the object of ethnographic investigation. Her analysis leads us to question the space that can be created for alternative interpretations, such as those that turn the gaze on to institutions of power. But it is not *just* an objective reframing; Spivak indicates that this space, for her, is *haunted*. It is a subjective, relational space, one that she shares with ghosts: the Rani's ghosts, for sure, but also the ghosts of Spivak's own inheritance, the autobiographical traces of her desire. There is no rescripting of objectivity thus without the transferential resonances that render this work undead within the space of the encounter. This is what one might call, following Michael Fischer, a *third space*.

Fischer defines the third space as "terrains and topologies of analysis, of cultural critique, of ethical plateaus. They are dramaturgical processes, fields of action, and deep plays of reason and emotion, compulsion and desire, meaning making and sensuality, paralogics and deep sense, social action and constraints of overpowering social forces" (2003: 4). Fischer draws on Homi Bhabha's postcolonial sociolinguistic notion of third spaces, which refers to the spaces where processes of hybridity occur in the interstices of cross-cultural encounter, processes that always both operate within and challenge global structures of domination. According to Bhabha, "Hybridity . . . is the 'third space' which allows other positions to emerge" and which thus "gives rise to something different, something new and unrecognizable, a new area of negotiation of meaning and representation" (1990: 211).

Hybridity is the question of diasporic being, and the third space is the question of diasporic space, space that is constituted in and through the encounter. That includes, necessarily, the ethnographic encounter, which as I am suggesting is itself not just dyadic but triadic, encompassing different moments and kinds of encounter, achieved at different places and times, in different institutional situations, such as "field," "classroom," and "university," in a contemporary conjuncture when all three are at stake. This third space "displaces the histories that constitute it, and sets up new structures of authority, new political initiatives, which are inadequately understood through received wisdom" (Bhabha 1990: 211).

The third space is an affective and a psychoanalytic space, a space of identification, transference, and translation. It makes explicit (without necessarily ever resolving) the relationship between ethnography's potential for sociological elucidation at the scene of the encounter and the autobiographical traces that necessarily animate the encounter itself, which bleed into and exceed any "objective" sociological account. Such that a purely Galilean objectivity always requires a certain violence, an excision of the ethos and affect of the encounter in order to establish and preserve the romantic authority of the ethnographer. This is the phallogocentric move at the heart of a Malinowskian ideology of ethnography, one that a multisituated sensibility argues against. How then does one *study* these third spaces, these zones of intercultural and social encounter (Bhabha), through a method (ethnography) that, being a practice of encounters all the way down, itself constitutes third spaces every time it enacts itself? For this, one must read Spivak's lessons for the excess they contain, for their evocative function.

In this chapter, I explore the question of the relationship of evocation and autobiographical trace to training the imagination toward a multisituated disposition, within the scene of writing (with its constitutive violence), but alongside and also in relation to the practice of photography and the scene of seeing (with its constitutive violence). These questions speak to the intimate functions of ethnography as an encounter with an other, with others, with the Other, and its noninnocence. I consider the implicated, noninnocent essence of ethnography to ask how a multisituated sensibility might operate within and through the constitutive violence of this intimate praxis. As with the previous chapter, the argument of this chapter is contained, in part, in its itinerary, one that brings together readings of exemplary ethnographies, theorizations, and critiques of photography, psychoanalytic readings of the literary function of ethnography, and theorizations of the meaning and practice of intimacy itself.

I begin with a consideration of ethnography as a kind of literary knowledge.

....

What would it mean, Spivak asks in "History," to consider history as literary? This is *not* a statement that the archive is (just) a fiction. It is instead a methodological question, asking what it would mean if we were to read the archive like a literary critic would. Analogously, I ask what it would mean to consider ethnography as literary, which again is not an assertion that cultures are texts but is instead a methodological provocation, a question of attending to the objects of ethnography as a literary critic would. It involves considering what *literary knowledge* is (what kind of epistemic thing is the novel?) while also considering the transferential triadic relationships established between author, text, and reader (subsequent, elsewhere, and Otherwise). I emphasize here that I am not discussing new forms of writing within anthropology, including those that blur distinctions between "ethnography" and "fiction." This is undoubtedly an important matter for consideration in its own right, and one of the provocations of *Writing Culture* (Clifford and Marcus 1986) that has remained the object of both inspiration and debate, speaking to multimodal dimensions of ethnographic inquiry and production. The scope of my analysis here, however, concerns the stakes in considering the ethnographic *episteme* as literary rather than sociological, the latter having been the dominant frame through which I have approached the ethnographic function in the first two chapters.

In one kind of pedagogy, the point of reading a text is to settle on its meaning. This is important: I have just after all insisted that reading "History" as recuperation of the female subaltern voice is a misreading. However, if a text also provides the possibility for different responses, then it lends itself to other kinds of interpretive functions. Here the stakes are not about closure, stability, or holding still: the "meaning" of the text cannot be contained within its referential function. In *Imaginary Ethnographies* (2012), a book about the relationship between writing culture and writing psychic life, Gabriele Schwab argues that this evocative function is constitutive to literary knowledge.

The interpretation of literature for Schwab is not about settling on the "correct" meaning of the novel, but rather about the differential evocations of the novel in different readings and different peoples' readings. The potential for interpretation is both differential and singular. Literary knowledge is not just an epiphenomenal addition of evocation to a truth that is already there; it is the very condition of possibility for literature to be a transformative experience. Here we must ask, *for whom*? The question of the evocative function of literature is at once a question of the reader, which itself is an ethnographic question concerning the desire of the reader (a question of subjectivity) and the conditions of possibility for certain desires to be brought to bear within particular contexts of reading (a question of sociology, history, and political economy).[4]

Schwab's definition of literary knowledge comes from a foundational ethical and political concern with cultural contact and otherness, which is what ethnographers are concerned with all the time. If, as ethnographers, we are encountering something unfamiliar or strange as part of our vocation, how can we not evoke? How can we possibly think of the evocative as superstructural to a prior referential function that has to be established first? Schwab says, when I read, I am establishing a relationship with a thing that is itself lively. It is vital, in every sense of the word, to emphasize the place of the reader and the relationship that is established.[5]

One of the central novels that Schwab reads in *Imaginary Ethnographies* is Marianne Wiggins's *John Dollar* (1988). She reads this for its iconic figuration of the cannibal, which is at the heart of colonial imaginaries of cultural contact that simultaneously configure boundaries of the human even as they inscribe the frontiers of conquest. It is a story of a British family expedition to the Andamans, set in 1919; it is also, simultaneously, a reminiscence from sixty years later of an Indian servant-woman, Menaka, as she buries her mistress, Charlotte (both had been on the expedition). The fact and affect of voyage (and voyeurism) as integral to the processes of colonialism is evident, a structure that has kinship with Joseph Conrad's *Heart of Darkness*. Schwab's strategy of reading *John Dollar* mirrors Spivak's concerns with reading *Heart of Darkness* in *Death of a Discipline* (see chapter 2): how does one read this text Otherwise?

John Dollar is already an-Other writing of colonial voyage, by a diasporic female writer writing in the late twentieth century (Wiggins was an American author settled in Britain) rather than a diasporic male writer writing in the late nineteenth (Conrad was an expatriate Polish author settled in Britain).[6] The reminiscence, which is a horrible and disturbing one, comes from Menaka's doubly marked subject position, a contrast to Conrad's protagonist, Marlowe. The expedition ended in a shipwreck, which forced Menaka and Charlotte to survive on a desert island along with Charlotte's lover, the sailor John Dollar. Far from the redeeming, industrious, white masculine capitalism that marks the survivalist colonial imaginary of *Robinson Crusoe* (which depended, of course, on the labor of his man Friday), *John Dollar* ends in an allegory of cannibalism. The colonial stereotype of the cannibalism of the "primitive" Andaman Islander is turned on its head in excruciating detail on to the colonial voyagers, with inversions of relations of gender, sexuality, and servitude further muddying the tale.

When Schwab reads *John Dollar*, she is not just discussing the obviously tragic relationship that is established between Menaka and Charlotte, a relationship that continues for decades after their return together to Cornwall until Charlotte's death. She is articulating her own relationship to the text, as its reader. The lively function of the novel *John Dollar* is not that it is telling you who Menaka and Charlotte really are, what cannibalism really is, or what colonialism really is. Rather, it is establishing a set of evocations that exceed the referentiality of these realities, while also establishing specific references for particular readers: especially, in this case, the evocation of white guilt that is a function of both your own colonial inheritance as a reader and the generations of cannibalism upon others of the world your ancestors have engaged in. What is at stake is not just the epistemic refiguration of "the cannibal" as an ethnographic object, but the simultaneous interrogation of the subjective desires and anxieties of the colonizers' progeny as they establish their relationships to this dystopic tale (a tale that does not offer any of the redemptive possibilities that even *Heart of Darkness* [let alone *Robinson Crusoe*] provide to the descendants of the perpetration of colonial violence).[7]

The question of the autobiographical trace is at the heart of Schwab's reading strategy, which is also an ethnographic method. "Most intellectual choices in our work bear hidden autobiographical traces," she insists (135). Schwab asks us to read those traces in literature; but, more radically, she provokes the question of what it would mean to animate an-Other kind of discipline (whether anthropological or literary) that allows for the differential activation of different kinds of autobiographical traces in the work that we do. If one takes literature seriously in the development of a multisituated disposition, then one is forced to interrogate the kinds of things that evoke, the things that force one to enter into other (and Other) worlds and relationships, and the subjective dimensions of those relationships. This necessarily decenters our own romantic authority, and it leaves us vulnerable—not just vulnerable in the face of the Other but vulnerable in the face of encountering and acknowledging one's *relationship* to the face of the Other. There is a vital anti-phallogocentric ethics and politics to this.

"Autobiographical traces" are not just about confronting or situating one's autobiography; the trace is not reducible to reflexivity. It is, Schwab insists, transferential. An autobiographical trace cannot be reduced to personal investment (which itself is a category of financialization: personal investments require returns on investment, so no rational financialized subject will invest without that expectation of return). The trace is subliminal. In the same way that literary knowledge exceeds referentiality, the trace exceeds the referentiality of something as tangibly financialized as investment. It is something that we cannot escape, something that is always there. Rather than investment, the trace has to do with haunting.

Where is the trace located? Where does the trace come to matter? The trace comes to matter in the *scene of the encounter* (i.e., the trace is not just a description of oneself; it is also a description of the scene of the encounter).[8] What does it mean to be haunted by something strange and inexplicable that is not in the other but that is in the space of the encounter? Methodologically, this opens up the importance of attending to an ethnography of the encounter with the Other (rather than ethnography as a description of the Other herself), alongside the importance of situating oneself, one's own autobiography, one's own inheritances as an ethnographer at the scene of the encounter. It also means, while in the process, articulating and generating an adequate account of this space, the mise-en-scène of the encounter itself.

I briefly mention three ethnographies that are exemplary in doing so: Schwab's *Haunting Legacies* (2010), Lochlann Jain's *Malignant* (2013), and Christine Wally's *Exit Zero* (2013). *Haunting Legacies* is a story of transgenerational trauma, specifically the repression of the Holocaust in Germany in the generation immediately after World War II on the part of the perpetrators. Schwab explores what it means to be of a generation that grew up in the immediate aftermath of these horrors, without any acknowledgment of the apparatus of violence that was her inheritance. *Malignant* is an account of cancer written by an anthropologist who is also a breast-cancer survivor. It is a biomedical and political economic analysis that cannot but be enmeshed in Jain's own story of diagnosis and treatment. *Exit Zero*, which was made as both a book and a film, is a story of changing familial and class relations in Chicago consequent to the city's deindustrialization, focusing on the borderlands of Chicago and Northwest Indiana, where Wally herself grew up.

These are three very different works, in subject matter as well as ethnographic form, but there are threads that unite them in the way they teach us to look Otherwise, through a repositioning of the author *as*, at least in part, the native informant. Being auto-ethnographic, they push the boundaries of intimate accounting/accountability. Yet none of them is solipsistic; all of them look outward, evocatively elucidating global political economic structures through the lens of differentially articulated personhood. The structure that they are all looking at is the experiential structure of the *aftermath*: the aftermath of genocide, the aftermath of a diagnosis, or the aftermath of deindustrialization. None of them is an apocalyptic tale: the very possibility of their writing inscribes the fact of survival, the fact of a future that has continued to exist in spite of and beyond the happening of violence. Yet all of them are works of mourning. This is not a conservative or romantic mourning for a halcyon past; it is a mourning that recognizes that futures that are to come will have to be scripted differently, in ways that live with and bear the burden of specific (and specifically targeted) kinds of loss.

In the process of diagnosing and analyzing this loss, and the pasts of which the accounts are an aftermath, each of these texts makes searing contemporary analysis, one that strips away any possibility of innocence or apology. What does apology for the Holocaust mean, Schwab forces us to ask, if the form of (non)reckoning is repression? How do we account for biomedical interventions into cancer that do lead to miraculous cures and recoveries, Jain forces us to ask, if in the process of medicalization we lose the capacity to ask about the conditions of contemporary living that script etiologies of cancer in the first place? Conditions that have everything to do with late industrialism and corporate unaccountability? How do we generate an adequate (and adequately intimate) sociological analysis of the conditions that have, in the years since the publication of Wally's book, led to the rise of Trump? Wally gives us both description and multimodal ways of seeing our way toward an answer, with an intimacy toward and sensitivity of what class means through generational processes of deindustrialization, without ever resorting to the kinds of zero-sum white supremacist valorizations of the white working class that proliferated ad nauseum in the aftermath of the 2016 US presidential election.[9]

These three works manage something else that is extraordinary: autobiography, for each of them, is not the source of romantic authority. Thus, they are all in their own ways anti-Malinowskian and anti-phallogocentric texts. They achieve this not by insisting on the authenticity of their accounts, but by providing situated perspectives. They are not asking the reader to look *at* them, but rather to look—at the Holocaust, at cancer, at American deindustrialization, at the worlds we live in and have inherited—*with* them. Thus, the author herself becomes a native informant rather than a romantic source of authority. In the process, the author is not telling the reader/viewer what to see or what to feel, but is rather offering her work (and, in some vital way, herself) up for interpretation. She is eliciting labor, even as she is making herself vulnerable.

Ethnography, in these works, is not the act of "becoming other," as it is for Sherry Ortner, or even the dialogic space of understanding "the native point of view," as it is for Clifford Geertz (Geertz 1974; Ortner 1995; see also chapter 2 of this book). There is an anti-phallogocentric politics that involves repositioning the ethnographic relationship to the native informant altogether. This is not simply a reflexive disavowal of, or self-absolution from, racism, sexism, or colonialism *toward* the native informant. Rather, it is a reorientation and deconstruction of subject/object distinctions that are constitutive to phallogocentric modes of ethnographic knowing at the scene of the encounter. There is an intimacy to these works, one that requires an authorial vulnerability and that elicits transferential labor on the part of the reader. This does not necessarily require an auto-ethnographic form, but autobiography in each of these works renders authorial vulnerability and the elicitation of the reader's labor particularly explicit.

....

By "intimacy," I mean, on the one hand, the intimacy of an experience-proximal mode of engagement with others, which is a hallmark of ethnography. What does it mean for such an intimate praxis to be non-phallogocentric and multisituated, that is (as much as possible) not about penetration (reducing the question of ethnographic possibility to one of access), not about taking from the other whom one has accessed (appropriation), and not about a romantic salvaging of the subaltern Other? On the other hand, intimacy is an ethical-political category of praxis: what kinds of solidarities and betrayals are entailed and inscribed in these intimate spaces, and how might creative practices of evocation (such as photography, which I will discuss subsequently) allow for rescripting intimate encounters Otherwise, especially given the vexed representative histories of practices such as ethnography and photography?

I consider this question of intimacy by reading two other exemplary ethnographies, Kathleen Stewart's *Ordinary Affects* (2007) and Timothy Choy's *Ecologies of Comparison* (2011), as intimate works that take questions of encounter, evocation, and the work of poesis in a multisituated disposition seriously. These texts help us think the evocative function of ethnography within a praxis that attends to the intimacies of ethnographic encounter. Before I do so, I elaborate what I mean by a politics of intimacy, for which I turn to the work of Lauren Berlant.

In reading Berlant's short essay "Intimacy," the students in my "Multi-si(gh)ted" seminar came up with a couple of related yet distinct definitions of the word (Berlant 1998).[10] While Jeanne Lieberman read it as "a (perhaps always imagined) relation that will stabilize closeness (but is always haunted by its potential failure to do so)," Nida Paracha noted "the idea of tension or friction that was a part of Berlant's definition of intimacy (zones of familiarity and publicness)."[11] This speaks to a friction between Berlant's idea(l)s of intimacy that exceed the kinds of intimacy that are publicly recognized and valued, and the normative idea(l)s of intimacy that are publicly recognized and valued. These tensions are threaded by the notion of "a life," a *desire for a life*, a phrase that Berlant keeps returning to in their piece. This desire is also, as another student, Ji Yea Hong, read it, "a desire for stable tacitness, a stable *something*."[12] What is this question of "a life" in Berlant's account? What ethnographic, conceptual, and political work does it do?

Berlant is looking for an intimacy "beyond the purview of institutions, the state, and an ideal of publicness" (284), toward "the kinds of connections that impact on people, and on which they depend for living (if not 'a life')" (284). They are thinking through what "a life" is supposed to look like, as opposed to how it might. It is "a life," not "life," in the sacralized sense of *zoe* or *bios* that constitutes the "life" of biopolitics (Agamben 1998). "A life" is always placed on unstable and shifting ground, between the individual trajectories that people script for themselves and the scripts that people are given, institutionally and culturally.[13] This is an idea of a life that goes beyond structuralism, but is not antistructure: it begs the question, precisely and ethnographically, of *relationships* between agency and structure, the individual and the collective, public and private.

These definitions of intimacy—or, more specifically, the ways Berlant straddles them to develop a method of analysis that consistently relates the question of intimacy to the question of how intimacies are worlded— are important for thinking a multisituated ethnography, both for the doing of ethnography and for the consideration of the nature of the ethnographic encounter. How do we inhabit the world in ways that are scripted but also world making? Berlant "seek[s] to understand the pedagogies that encourage people to identify a life with having an intimate life" (282). What is at stake here is something other than changing the subjects and objects of ethnography, the deconstructive move that I have analyzed thus far through Spivak. Rather, Berlant develops a method that moves away from seeking an ethnography of objectified subjects toward an attentiveness to the *atmospheres* of places and times, one in which the conceptual question of intimacy is always interrelated with the ethnographic question of intensities.[14] As exemplary work that renders Berlant's provocations on the simultaneous ordinariness and strangeness of intimacy ethnographically, I turn to Stewart's *Ordinary Affects*.

Ordinary Affects is a carefully constructed, scenic ethnography of everyday life in America. It consists of a series of juxtaposed, sometimes interwoven, vignettes of encounters that Stewart has had that are at once ordinary and strange. Stewart offers and teaches us a mode of engagement with and attentiveness to the stuff of the everyday. My student Melissa Itzkowitz diagnosed this as being "at its core, a book about method, not just telling us where to look but how to look." She elaborated this by thinking of the book as helping her not just with her ethnographic practice, but also with her photographic practice (Itzkowitz is a photographer). A response from another student, Alexandra Kaul, was even more subjective: "I am so emotionally attached to this book that it feels like an insurmountable task to write about it."[15]

Kaul's response was more than just an instinctive affirmative response to a text that happened to move her. She went on to locate this response within her own diasporic trajectory between Germany and the United States, ending her commentary on the book with this: "There's something not quite right, the eerie similarity, the emptiness; this work reminds me of the ways in which I looked at America when I first came here. I wonder what I've lost through training these eyes, moving to major metropolitan cities, receiving American schooling and American citizenship and ways of being. If I can go back to my former eyes, if it's possible to see with two types of places at once. Something's not quite right."[16]

Kaul is saying something very serious about ethnographic practice (and praxis) here, her own emergent one and the one that Stewart is teaching us: our eyes *do* change. We do not look at the after as we did before. This is in part a function of the naturalization that attends all ethnography with progressive immersion in "the field." This is also alongside, as Kaul reminds us, the naturalization that attends immigration, not at all the same thing but also not entirely different, hence bringing particular resonances to the diasporic trajectories that are so central to forging a multisituated disposition. This changing of our eyes is not innocent. As our eyes change, there is loss, including conceptual loss.[17] Kaul sees *Ordinary Affects* as work that refuses a telos, managing to ignite a recognition of a "first encounter" with America in one who came here from elsewhere; that manages both to refuse a comfortable American exceptionalism and a patronizing objectification of the lives, scripted and lived, that constitute the subject matter of the ethnography. This is achieved, I suggest, by a multisituated disposition that has developed a praxis of intimate attention.

One of the things that emerges here is the singularity of the accounts and images Stewart provides us. The vignettes she provides are not simply means to a synthetic end; they stand on their own, not as objects but as relational encounters between the ethnographer and the stuff of her world under question. My student Rachel Howard pointed out that if Stewart had taken someone else along, they would not have written the same ethnography that she did.[18] Howard's observation speaks to the absolute contingency of the ethnographic encounter (which, in crucial ways, is similar, as I will argue subsequently, to the nature and praxis of the photographic encounter). These encounters are powerful and lively precisely because one cannot go back to them in the same way, even if memories, residues, and hauntings of the encounter remain. There is an anti-Galilean, antisynthetic, humanistic praxis here, whose value lies not in the reproducibility of the observation but in its singularity. It lies in the trajectories—autobiographic and transferential—that develop over time, as the encounter gets reencountered in its telling and its various (re)readings. There is a layering that happens between what the encounter was and what it has subsequently become (differentially, for the ethnographer and her readers) that is not mere "writerly construction" but is about the ways in which we (can be trained to) see the world.

The conceptual work that Stewart is doing attends, like Marilyn Strathern's work does, to connections. Stewart and Strathern, however, operationalize the method of thinking and making connections differently. Stewart's is less an epistemological deconstruction of phallogocentric modes of forging and knowing connection, as Strathern's is (see chapter 2). Rather, in bringing together disparate vignettes alongside each together, Stewart's work crackles with potentiality: how do we learn to see the possibility of connections across different moments of encounter? There is an ongoing work of curation here, which itself is at the heart of the theoretical work that Stewart is doing; it requires and embodies a multisituated disposition. Hence, this is not just a random agglomeration of encounters Stewart happened to have. There is a conscious underdetermination of the "meaning," in some objective sense, of each encounter and of the collection of encounters, as an invitation to the reader to inhabit the spaces and times Stewart is telling us about. Knowing fully well that the reader might inhabit it differently. Knowing full well that the potential for making connections Otherwise in the reading of the book necessarily undermines Stewart's own romantic authority, opening up the space for the reader to establish her own transferential relations to the text.[19]

Thus *Ordinary Affects*, as an ethnography, provides "literary knowledge" in precisely the manner that Schwab describes and advocates for the works of literature she reads. This is a non-phallogocentric alternative to certain conventional (colonial and masculinist) ways of staging and reflecting upon the encounter with the native informant.[20] This is done by capturing the ordinary in a rigorously constructed manner. If Stewart's connections between vignettes are conscious works of juxtaposition and curation, then each vignette in itself functions as a kind of still life. The work of the still is not just the representation of the object, but also and vitally the capturing of an atmosphere. Stewart provokes us to think a praxis of ethnographic connections, similarly and differently to Strathern, even as she presents the possibility of developing ethnography as providing descriptions of what Berlant calls "a life," of the conditions of "a life," of desires for "a life," as a means to thinking the politics of the contemporary. The question to be asked—and the pedagogical and institutional responsibility this beckons—is how one might operationalize and encourage such a mode of intimate ethnographic attention, attunement, and attachment at the dissertation stage, given the normativity of phallogocentric modes of knowing within institutional spaces that valorize disciplinary reproduction and epistemic modes that privilege the sociological functions of ethnography, often valorizing them as "Theory" at the expense of its more literary functions.[21]

....

A second exemplary and multisituated "still life" that engages in a praxis of intimate attachment that attends to atmospheres is Choy's *Ecologies of Comparison*. This book is about the politics of global environmentalism as it touches down and inscribes itself in Hong Kong. It is also about encounters—of East with West, colonial with postcolonial, Hong Kong with China, global with local, air with breathers, cosmopolitan with traditional, ethnographer with field of study, environmentalists with planners,

planners with villagers, dolphins with airports, media with dolphins, bota-nists with orchids, orchids with classifications, classifications with air . . . encounters all the way down.

What Choy does particularly well as an ethnographer is constantly look elsewhere. His is not the style that sees the object, the field, the an-thropological problem and attempts to capture it, study it, solve it in any direct manner. Instead, he goes for a swim. Climbs a mountain. Drinks orange juice with a fruit seller at a polluted street corner. These are not just stylistic narrative interludes—they provide the sites and substances of Choy's engagement with his worlds of study and concern, thus providing texture, to use one of his phrases, to the "warp and woof of the network" he is weaving (Choy 2011: 147). Choy is deeply invested in complexity, both as an object of analysis and in his own ethnographic and conceptual method. It is a vigilant, attentive investment. It is worth paying attention to the modalities of Choy's vigilance, of his attentiveness, of his excess, of his deferrals, of his refusals.

On page 137, Choy goes for a hike, through the remains of an old school, in August 1998, with, "a fake country girl" who was going to Hong Kong University. He tells her about his project, and "with the same wide smile she said, to be honest it sounds like a very Western research project." Choy continues: "I sat with that a while, sometimes I still do, bemused in a ru-ined British fortress, wondering what to say." This is the encounter of the metropolitan-located anthropologist with a theory from the South: a call-ing out of the very modalities, frames, and ambitions underlying the work that Choy was undertaking. Yet it is not a critique "from the outside," not staged in the context of disciplinary conversations about theory and method in anthropology within the metropolitan university itself. Rather, the critique happens within an intimate context, the context of friend-ship and dialogue in formation. As Choy ponders a response, bemused, his solution is not—cannot be—a simple embrace of radical alterity, a simple reframing of the project Otherwise or "from Hong Kong." Part of the eth-ics of responding to a provocation such as this is precisely one that pauses, that defers, that establishes a relationship of listening and engagement, that refuses to substitute one set of phallogocentric framings for another set of desires that wishes to "become Other."

There is an ethics of deconstruction to this deferral. Yet Choy's mode of deconstruction is not quite Derridean. For Derrida, the deferrals of deconstructive practice are a function of the constitutive inability for closure within the text, within writing itself. Choy's pauses, on the other hand, are more conscious, willful, an active part of his method of figuring things out. Indeed, he says as much. He is, after all, researching a highly politicized and overdetermined field of action, environmentalism, one in which the subtleties of the ethics of the encounter harden quickly into the right-and-wrong dualisms of moral positions. Choy is in deep solidarity with global environmental politics, but he insists upon a slowness for himself, thus distancing himself from his activist comrades. He does not want to commit himself to a response within the time-scales in which response is often demanded in these fields. This is not an apolitical gesture but, rather, I would suggest, a supremely political and an intensely difficult one. He wants to keep asking what kinds of thought and writing would emerge if we just slowed down and paused for a while?

This slowing down, this pause, and its connection to fieldwork, writing, and reading, entails a refusal of a certain kind of declarative analytic style. This is not, as with Stewart, simply an "aesthetic" choice. Rather, Choy is questioning the adequate representational modality by which to ethnographically investigate complex structures and questions. He is invested in poesis, both in his own ethnographic praxis and in the stuff of the world that he encounters.

This poesis, akin to Stewart's but differently manifested, is praxiological, for Choy is constantly in dialogue with environmentalism as a field of collective political action. The collectivities he feels accountable to are not merely constituted by those who have the vocation of environmentalism. There are two moments when the collective comes to be theorized. The first occurs in the chapter "Articulated Knowledges," which, for Choy, can be understood only in light of what he calls "unarticulated knowledges." Choy articulates articulation, following Stuart Hall, as a process of utterance and of bringing together (Grossberg 1996). Environmental knowledges are articulated knowledges, but not everyone gets to articulate. Choy is interested in those who do not, in spite of clearly having a certain local knowledge that would be relevant to the problem at hand. Choy is not giving voice to the subaltern who cannot speak; rather, he is considering the place of people with the capacity for enunciation, yet not for connection, within the articulatory terrain of global environmentalism.[22] This lack of connection has to do with certain individual discomforts and refusals—on the part of the village head of Ha Pak Nai, or an elderly woman from Lung Kwu Tan, both fishing villages on the outskirts of Hong Kong that Choy writes about. They also have to do with the recognition of the structural, political terrains on the parts of actors, who know the value of expertise, how it gets constituted, and how their knowledges get excluded from those constitutions.

Choy considers a different kind of collective subject in his final chapter, "Air's Substantiations," in which he introduces the figure of the breather as a political subject of contemporary ecopolitics. What kinds of political articulations and conceptualizations are possible when we think together the terrains of environmental articulation that constitutively unarticulate certain kinds of knowledge from the connectivities (and collectivities) that it forges, with the figure of the breather, given that, as Choy reminds us, we are all breathers? Choy confesses to being troubled by the universal address of the breather but it is also an address that, not unlike Marx's call in the *Communist Manifesto* to the workers of the world to unite, contains within it a calling-into-being of a collective that does not exist, but that perhaps could, in politically consequential ways. Choy here is asking the question that Spivak asks, of multiple (and, in this case, differentially articulated) universalisms (see chapter 2). Following Derrida's invocation of the specters of Marx, it could be said that the breather is a promissory figure, a promise that might never be actualized but that nonetheless provides a horizon of ethics and of politics.

In subsequent work, Choy develops the notion of the breather by thinking of her/it as an experimental subject, by drawing into relations different figures that are made to breathe experimentally—smell-chemistry sniffers who grade matsutake mushrooms through olfaction along with neonatal asthmatic rats used as experimental models for air-quality research (Choy 2018). Thinking such apparently disparate and yet obvious interrelated things together is a task in unsettling what is figure and what is ground and also how one makes explanatory articulations that are themselves functions of our own analytic moves toward universalization and specification and hence never innocent.[23]

I use *Ordinary Affects* and *Ecologies of Comparison* as exemplary texts here in a slightly different register to how I used *Van Gogh on Demand*, *Speculative Markets*, and *Advocacy after Bhopal* in chapter 1. There is a different quality to their multisituatedness. For Winnie Wong, Kristin Peterson, and Kim Fortun, the multisituated aspiration is most specifically a multiscalar one: how to knit the contingency of the experience-proximal encounter into an observational analysis of structure itself. Stewart's and Choy's multisituatedness is of a more evocative kind, attending to moments of encounter, their affective resonances and intensities, that inhere within moments that perturb and excite. This is not to say that there is no structural analysis here: both are essentially books about value, *Ecologies of Comparison* considering value in relation to knowledge and *Ordinary Affects* doing so in relation to (classed and gendered) American culture. However, the stakes here are not so much about the specific transit *from* the contingency of the ethnographic encounter to something structural and abstract, but rather about staying within the trouble of the encounter itself. Hence, it is not so much about a transition from "micro" to "macro," but a concern with what Roland Barthes, in his discussion of photography in *Camera Lucida*, refers to as "infra-knowledge" (Barthes 1980). I turn to Barthes next, as I bring photography into play in this discussion of the politics of intimacy, the scene of the encounter, and the evocative function of ethnography.

....

According to Barthes, the photograph speaks of desire and of mourning. The desire that Barthes captures is not reducible to the telos of romantic love. The mourning that he speaks of is not programmable into stages of grief. Desire and mourning, in the way he thinks about photography, are not separable as opposites of one another (the one speaking to animation and life, the other speaking to sadness and death, for instance). Rather, they are intimate counterparts of one another.

Barthes's *Camera Lucida* is an extraordinary, poignant work. He spends much of the first part of the book as an observer of photographs, pulling out and discussing various photos by famous photographers that have been important to him and that he most loves. Here, he is not doing the work of the critic; he is not interested in establishing in any objective sense the value of a body of work. Indeed, he says that he very rarely appreciates a photographer's work across an entire oeuvre: certain photos in particular speak to him. This is the animation that the photograph achieves, and it is purely relational—a subjective relationship between the observer and the photo, one that is shot through and through with "contingency, singularity, risk."

Barthes's interest is not in the *studium* of the photograph, its "very wide field of unconcerned desire, of various interest, of inconsequential taste," which is of the "order of *liking*, not of *loving*" (27). Rather, it is in the *punctum*, that which pierces, which pricks—an often inconsequential detail that animates the photograph, that animates the viewer, that animates the relationship between the viewer and the photograph, that is purely subjective (a function of the relationship) and absolutely contingent. It is a detail that, however, once noticed, cannot be ignored or forgotten and that takes over the relationship to the photograph, that takes over the photograph itself. It is at this point that Barthes makes his only mention of "the ethnographical" in his essay, as he mentions how the photograph provides him access to an "infra-knowledge."

Once seen, that cannot be forgotten—this is all about attentiveness, one that is purely contingent but that cannot be reduced to mere empirical detail, that has to deal with the ways in which that absolute contingency borne of a singular relationship between viewer and photograph comes to matter, to inhabit that relationship in irrevocable ways and over time. The core of the ethnographical and the photographical lies in a certain moment—and it is quite literally a moment, one that is im-mediate and that can never be recaptured or reiterated in the same way—of intimacy. The sensibility, and indeed the mode of conceptualizing the world, is of a quite different order to a "big picture," macro-structure, the representative or the illustrative function. Barthes highlights a register of analysis—one that operates in ethnographies such as *Ordinary Affects* and *Ecologies of Comparison*—that is precisely not illustrative of the ethnographic endeavor in any formal or proper sense, but that exists in a different relationship to it (indeed, I would suggest, in a *différant* relationship to it). For what we are dealing with here is nothing other than the trace that Derrida writes about (Derrida [1967] 1976). It is a trace that manifests in a particular and specific manner through the techne of photography, which is different from other technes, such as of writing, which is the subject of Derrida's concern (and Schwab's, when she considers the autobiographical trace as constitutive of literary knowledge). The trace is haunting; it is implicated in the work of mourning.

Even if the punctum of the photograph is contingent, there is a constitutive work of mourning in the subjective relationship that is established with it. The photograph captures something outside of oneself at a particular moment of encounter. A moment that, even by the time the photograph is made, is already gone but is transmitted to a future-that-is-to-come. Yet what is transmitted is no longer the present moment, no longer the presence of that moment, but its absence. What is transmitted is something that no longer is; what is transmitted is not an other, but her trace. What is revealed is not the thing outside, but a fragment of ourselves: our fears, our desires, our loss. This is why photography, the desire for a life that it expresses, is for Barthes (and for me, in my own photographic practice) always a work of mourning.

The specificity that exists in the techne of the photograph, according to Barthes, is a function of the fact that the photograph tells us that *this was there*, in a manner that is inescapable: "Photography's Referent is not the same as the referent of other systems of representation. I call photographic referent not the *optionally* real thing to which an image or a sign refers but the *necessarily* real thing which has been placed before the lens, without which there would be no photograph. Painting can feign reality without having seen it. Discourse combines signs which have referents, of course, but these referents can be and most often are 'chimeras.' Contrary to these imitations, in Photography I can never deny that *the thing has been there*" (Barthes 1980: 88–89, emphasis in original).

Arguably, this realist idea of photography is dated with the digitalization of photography and the increased potential for its manipulability with technologies such as Photoshop. Nonetheless, I see something philosophically irreducible in Barthes's account here, which cannot be reduced to realism. After all, photography was always a fabrication, from well before its digital turn, and surely Barthes knew that. The "this" that was there, therefore, is less a statement of fact and more one of affect. Barthes is not telling us about photography as a representational technology as much as he is about the transience of time that it captures. Barthes's account of photography, one that is idiosyncratic and parochial even as it has become a canonical reference point in the theorization of the medium, contains within it a noninnocent and vital ethos that is at the heart of my elaboration of the intimate praxis of the ethnographic encounter, one that resonates not just with my stakes in multisituated ethnography but also with my photographic practice and my own aspirations as a photographer.[24]

Barthes goes on to develop the second part of the book by discussing a photograph of his mother, who had died just months before he wrote the book. It is the one photograph that he discusses in the book that he does not show—quite simply, he says, because its punctum exists for him and would not do so in the same way for anyone else. Showing it would simply be irrelevant. The photograph establishes for him the authenticity of her that was, of her that was even before he was born, before he knew her; it establishes the authenticity of a presence before his time, one that matters only in his relation to her and to her photograph. This is the haunting that the photograph achieves. This is the work of mourning. With the photograph, it is something other than, alongside, beyond memory. Barthes asks that "instead of constantly relocating the advent of Photography in its social and economic context, we should also inquire as to the anthropological place of Death"; he goes on to say that, in the photograph of his mother, his own death is inscribed.

The haunting by the photograph of his mother (signifying love and death in the most intimate of relationships) shares skin with Spivak's desire to be haunted by the ghost of a Rani whose name she cannot even know, the scene of the encounter in "History." This concerns a particular structure to the event/subject and its relation to memory, inscription, and the work of mourning—which, as Derrida pointed out, is also the work of learning how "to live finally" (Derrida 1994: xvii). In both cases, the ghost that has to be lived with in the present is not that of the dead woman herself; it is of the particular relationship between her existence and the trace that it leaves behind, one that has specific relationships (structural and contingent, necessary and singular) to ethics and to politics. It concerns the gap that exists between that which was there, that which could not have been known at the time, and that which we cannot not know now, at the moment of reinscription, of reiteration, of establishing the singular relationship of mourning through acts of writing or viewing or reading or variously attending. (Barthes's mother could not have known about Barthes's future existence at the time that her photograph was taken. Much less could the Rani have known that a postcolonial scholar would go looking for her in the archives and in her palace nearly two centuries after she lived.) Both Barthes and Spivak exist in *l'avenir*, the future-that-is-to-come for that which was there.

The capacious, polymorphic, and careful ways of attending to the world that ethnography allows are animated and refunctioned in particular ways through encounters with literature and photography, which themselves develop singular, fragile, intimate relationships to that which was and to that which was-to-come. These singular, fragile, and intimate relationships are not relationships to history—they are relationships to being itself, to "a life," to living in the company of ghosts, with one's inheritances. This is what Derrida calls hauntology, and it is at the heart of both ethnographic and photographic attention and praxis. It is not innocent, and it is not without its violence.

....

If Derrida writes of the violence of writing, then John Berger writes contemporaneously about the violence of seeing, specifically of certain masculinist ways of seeing that have developed in the history of art, which reach their apotheosis in the kinds of photographic images that are mediated and appropriated to serve the interests of capital (Berger 1972). As I approach ethnography through Barthes and photography, the multisituated question at stake is what it might mean to see Otherwise. Deconstructive and transferential questions lie at the heart of thinking through what it means to read Otherwise, given the constitutive violence of writing.[25] Albeit posed, framed, and operationalized differently, so too are they at the heart of thinking what it means to see Otherwise, given the constitutive violence of the visual image.[26] Just as Derrida considers the violence of writing within the scene of writing (hence rendering this violence an ethnographic question as much as an epistemic one that is internal to writing itself), it becomes important to consider the question of seeing, the violence of seeing, and seeing Otherwise within the ethics of encounter at the scene of seeing.

Berger is concerned with how the act of seeing art becomes an act of appropriation. The rawest form of this appropriation is the male gaze; the most capitalized form of this gaze is the objectification of women as objects of male desire in advertising. The representational practices entailed in this objectification, Berger shows, have, however, a long history in Western art, all the way back to the figuration of the female nude in the Renaissance.[27] The question of seeing Otherwise then becomes a question of how to reject this appropriative modality of representation, while remembering that in fact there are two visual encounters at stake, spatially and temporally disjointed from one another. The first is the encounter of the maker of the image with its (potentially objectified) subject; there is then the subsequent encounter of the viewer with the image itself, with all the transferential relationships entailed therein.

My student Melissa Itzkowitz asked the question thus: "How do we look at our interlocutors with intimacy rather than desire?"[28] This question is qualified by Itzkowitz knowing full well, following Berlant, that intimacy itself is vexed and not innocent and that desire is not merely objectifying, being itself a complex and often mutually (if differentially) articulated subjective relationship. The critical part of this question, however, is its methodological component: *how do we look?*[29] The question of how to see Otherwise is a question of learning how to look; it is a question of attention and attunement and also of sensorial, bodily presence that includes yet also exceeds and decenters sight. How might a photographic practice help work through this question, given photography's own history of objectification and appropriation of its subjects?

To answer this, I elaborate Itzkowitz's own reflections on her photographic practice after she read *Camera Lucida* in my "Multi-si(gh)ted" seminar (her second reading, having earlier read it shortly after graduating from college):

> This is . . . the challenge (or at least my challenge) with ethnography. Fieldwork is easy—you talk to people, you go places, you do and see things—but doing ethnography that adds something to the world is nearly impossible. It takes work and it requires persistent attention to the *punctum*: "the detail . . . says only that the photographer [or ethnographer] was there, or else, still more simply, that [s]he could not *not* photograph the partial object at the same time as the total object" (Barthes 1980: 47). . . . [T]his moment—this being there—is (for me) the first encounter. The first encounter is the encounter with the camera (or the field) and with myself as a pensive photographer (or ethnographer). This is more a feeling—a bodily presence—of the way I approach my work. Then the second encounter is my encounter with the thing/person I am photographing (or researching): why this out of anything else in the world I could be looking at, even if "anything else" is just a few degrees away from where I'm looking now ("of all the objects in the world: why choose [why photograph] this object, this moment, rather than some other?" [6]). The third encounter is when I look at my work later, as I go through contact sheets and pin my prints around the room (or my field notes, my scribbles, my drafts), and see what I've done. Then it's thinking about that work, feeling it, remembering it (see 53), and coming back to it over and over. The fourth encounter—showing someone else my work—is only possible if I've been wounded by my own photographs (or research) in the third encounter.
>
> Now that I've written all of this, it feels sort of strange and vulnerable.[30]

In this reflection, Itzkowitz both thickens and decenters sight. She articulates seeing Otherwise as a mode of bodily presence, something that exceeds merely seeing to incorporate both the unseen and the felt. Itzkowitz sums up the shared im-mediacy of ethnography and photography that relates to the development of intimate attunements in terms of *the quality of the encounter*. Further, there is its simultaneous singularity and multiplicity. Every single photograph that is made, successfully, involves encounter*s*, plural and sequential. It cannot just remain the encounter between the photographer and her subject, the ethnographer and her native informant; as long as it does, it cannot but be appropriative, however "ethical" we may procedurally be. It must also be an encounter with oneself, pensive, wounding, vulnerable making (autobiographical traces), a relationship to one's own desire and mourning. It is also an encounter with a third entity (viewer, reader) in a third space: one that is necessarily in *l'avenir*, the future-to-come, as yet unstable and undecideable.[31]

Itzkowitz's grandfather was also a photographer, as she recollected:

> I'm reminded of two photographs that my grandfather took of my grandmother: the first in approximately 1952 when my grandmother was around 17 and about a year away from marriage and the second in 1977 after she had had two sons and was a year away from having a third. In the first photograph, my grandmother looks timid, scared even. She looks down away from the camera, her shoulders hunched up and back, and a mysterious hand (perhaps of a doll?) lurks behind her as if ready to grab her right shoulder. She is vulnerable and we are watching. In the second photograph, however, my grandmother appears in control and glamorous. They appear to be in a car and she appears to be driving (the window is just to the left of her and the side mirror appears hazy beside her). The light catches her face in such a way that her eyes are in shadow, but you can see her eyelashes, long and curled, and her lipsticked lips are pulled back in a smirk. She is glowing, literally, in a way that makes her appear both angelic and fiercely feminine, dazzling and strong all at the same time. The first time I saw this photograph, when my grandfather was living in a rehab center after a bad fall that left him with a broken neck, I turned to my grandmother and said "he really loves you." This photograph, for me, is the epitome of love, of nakedness, and of intimacy. There is no one else in the world who could have taken this photograph of my grandmother because no one else in the world has ever looked at her in the way that my grandfather did. This is turning the ordinary, the everyday, into the mundane particularly that defines intimacy.[32]

Itzkowitz is calling here for a certain kind of praxis that is not reducible to procedural instrumentality. The ethics of the encounter here is not about some formal notion of "consent." Itzkowitz's reflections suggest that looking Otherwise, in nonobjectifying ways, is not just about the self-policing of objectifying behavior. It demands asking how we intervene in the very structure of the objectifying encounter: a reformulation of the norms and forms of ethnographic practice itself. In thinking about her own ethnographic praxis through her photographic practice of sequential encounters, and then illustrating it with an example of her grandfather's intimate gaze, one that cannot but leave autobiographical traces on his granddaughter who learns from him, Itzkowitz offers us one kind of method to see Otherwise. This is not one of the authorial conferring of subjectivity upon the object of the photographic gaze, a move that would be akin to "giving voice to the subaltern," nor is it about necessitating a certain level or particular kind of intimacy between ethnographer and interlocutors in the field. It is rather about developing a mutual, relational subjectivity over time, an ethics of indebtedness and inheritance and, necessarily, of mourning. Itzkowitz shifts the problem of looking Otherwise beyond just the problems of *our* eyes (our racism, our sexism, our heteronormativity as authors and producers of image or text), which can be "dealt with" through our moral self-improvement, to render it a problem concerning the form of the (ethnographic/photographic) encounter. In seeing Otherwise, how can we put the *form* of ethnography itself at stake?[33]

Itzkowitz, following Berger, is calling for *the establishment of the reciprocity of sight*. Looking Otherwise is not about "how do I see?" but rather about, as Ji Yea Hong put it, "how were my eyes reciprocated?"[34] In other words, the subjectivity of the object of ethnography/photography is maintained not by becoming Other (an act of authorial appropriation) or by giving voice to the Other (an act of authorial condescension) or simply by obtaining consent in some reductively formal or procedural sense (an act of authorial instrumentalization). All of these moves preserve the romantic integrity of the author and hence cannot escape objectification and appropriation in the very form of the encounter. The ethnographer (photographer) still owns the encounter on his terms (think again of the encounter between Lévi-Strauss and the Nambikwara chief, and the absolute nonreciprocity of vision entailed therein). Reforming ethnography, in a multisituated disposition, has to be dialogic, even (eventually, unpredictably) trialogic, with subsequent viewers and readers of the work who come to it with their own eyes, their own investments, their own transferential resonances.

....

Camera Lucida straddles analysis and affect. It does so in two ways, through the figuration of the personal at the heart of the text. First, it provides an extremely subjective response to a group of photographs whose own selection is purely a reflection of Barthes's liking. Second, Barthes inscribes the death of his mother, and an account of the photo of his mother, into the heart of his analysis. In this analysis, Barthes locates himself in a third space, in relation to the subjects and objects he writes about. If the first space (of the authorial producer of knowledge) is an objective space, marked with the phallogocentric histories of objectivity, and a second is a more interpretive space where this objectivity is always in tension with the subjectivity of the Other from whom objective knowledge is derived in ethnography (see chapter 2), then the third space is an *affective* space, one of transferential relationality, as Schwab shows through her reading of literary knowledge. This is especially so, as Barthes emphasizes, in relation to love and death. The various dimensions of the notion of the punctum, as the expressive element of the "ethnographical" in Barthes's sense of infra-knowledge, have a role to play in articulating this space.

There are at least two dimensions to the punctum:

- The punctum is, in Barthes's terms, "the accident which pricks me" (1980: 27). This speaks to the contingency and im-mediacy—the eventness—of the punctum. It therefore also makes the question of the punctum a question of time. As Rachel Howard diagnosed, "It is not just the fact of the arresting details in a photograph, but the 'disappearance' (94) of the moment it has produced."[35] This "disappearance" is precisely that which lends photography its creative as opposed to simply documentary aspect. (Howard went on to emphasize "produced *not* REproduced, this is crucial.")
- The punctum is the detail that prompts "giving myself [the viewer] up" (45). Thus, the punctum here is not the affective manifestation of a contingent encounter as much as it is of the deliberate focus of attention. What it evokes is not accidental but inevitable, the inevitable outcome of the photographer's mode of attunement, which imprints itself irrevocably upon the photograph that is made. Further, this is a detail that "expands to capture the whole attention of the viewer."[36] Hence, it is not just a detail, but a lively, animate, expansive detail.

What makes a detail expand? On the one hand, the answer to this question is entirely personal and contingent, having to do with the transferential attention of the viewer. On the other hand, this has to do with the scene of the photographic encounter, at the time of making the image and at the time of its subsequent viewing, which has to do with what Berlant calls an atmosphere. Thus, the punctum has something to do both with time and with atmosphere—hence both with inheritance and promise (Derrida's concerns) and with intimacy and affect (Berlant's). What is at stake here, thinking multisituatedness through the punctum, is *singularity*, the absolute singularity of the im-mediate image and each of its viewings, having to do with, as Derrida has maintained throughout his work, the absolute singularity of responsibility toward the Other. In Barthes's terms, this singularity has to do with "love, extreme love" (13).[37]

"What would it mean," Alexandra Kaul asked, "to approach one's interlocutors with extreme love while not producing a romanticized notion, but to truly see people, with all their flaws?"[38] This love, Kaul points out, is not just what we *feel* (which would be its romanticized version) but concerns what we *do*. How do we see? How do we approach? These are questions of bodily praxis, not of sentiment or morality. Kaul went on:

> I once read somewhere that you can dehumanize people in two ways; by objectifying them and by idolizing them. I suppose both are objectification, but how do we create intimacy in Berlant's sense without (re)producing the tropes of love found in popular discourse of talk shows and romance novels in our work? . . . How do you write something that is not dead, that doesn't kill? How do you photograph someone, with a camera or with words, that at least grasps at the totality of self? I want to think more about how to craft works that produce labor (as opposed to just momentary affective response) within the viewer/reader.[39]

This responsibility is immediately layered upon and in tension with the authorial work of photography and ethnography. This is the searing authorial desire of *wanting* to craft a work in a way that elicits a certain response (again, not reducible to a question of audience and with no guarantees that this response will be elicited in any given viewer/reader). What is at stake is not mere distancing from authorship, not mere refusal or disavowal, but a reclaiming and rescripting of authorship Otherwise, with responsibility toward and a nonromanticized, noninnocent love for the Other. That type of love contains within it a certain equanimity and is not restricted to that or those we have prior admiration or desire for, or identification with.[40]

The irrevocable, irredeemable, necessary, and necessarily dangerous contradiction at the heart of the praxis of vulnerability that Itzkowitz describes is that "there has to be a level of self-indulgence and pretentiousness involved because if you ever arrive at the fourth encounter, you assume that what you've done is worth looking at."[41] There is a constitutive relationship between vulnerability and wanting to show one's labor. This is the noninnocence of the praxis of intimacy.

It is also its politics. Itzkowitz *wants* to make photos that people look at; she *wants* authorship, even as the four encounters that constitute her photographic praxis make her vulnerable. There is a radically deconstructive move here, because the craft that is at stake has to *produce labor* within the viewer/reader, as Kaul puts it. It is not just the labor of the author that matters: it is the elicitation of labor on the part of an Other who is as yet unknown. This, Kaul goes on to say, is "a collective adventure and a social project." This is at the heart of the notion of collectivity that Spivak is pushing toward when she argues for a comparative literature supplemented with area studies, tied into a promissory ideal of planetarity, in *Death of a Discipline* (see chapter 2). This is the labor that Stewart elicits in her readers, such that she refuses to let us just be voyeurs of small-town Texas, refuses to allow us to simply consume her accounts of the ordinary in contemporary America. There is a displacement away from making the *subject* vulnerable (which is the phallogocentric act of representational appropriation, the violence of writing and of the image), toward making the reader/viewer vulnerable, making her labor too. The reader, as consumer, desires the vulnerable (objectified) subject. Not offering that, in making the reader/viewer work for something else, is at the heart of a multisituated disposition. Itzkowitz, Kaul, Spivak, and Stewart are not refusing authorship per se: rather than feeding the diet of consumerist desire on the part of the reader/viewer, they are forcing them to work.

....

Thus far in this chapter, I have read exemplary multisituated ethnographies that foreground the intimate encounter as constitutive to a method of attention and attunement (Stewart and Choy) through Berlant's conception of intimacy and Barthes's of photography. I have suggested that there is kinship (not identity) between the work done by the ethnographic and the photographic. This kinship operates at the level of the evocative work that both perform, in their own different ways, alongside the labor that they produce on the part of the reader/viewer. I elaborate this next by juxtaposing Stewart and Choy to the work of a narrative photographer, Teju Cole, and his recent book of images and text, *Blind Spot* (2017).

Blind Spot is a text that self-consciously operates through fragmentary ways of seeing the world. It is a deliberate juxtaposition of text and image, both made during the course of Cole's travels around the world. It is in one sense a travelogue, with images of different locales (hence multisited in a quite literal sense). Yet it avoids the romanticized, phallogocentric sensibility that fills genres of travel writing and imagery, with their constitutive colonial genealogies (for which, see Pratt 1994). How does it do so? How does it manage instead to be a work of mourning, rather than one of objectification and appropriation? There is a quality of the *flâneur* rather than that of the cartographer here, a quality that one finds in Choy's ethnographic style as well.[42]

Answering this question involves attending to the process of the book. It is a book filled with images: well over 150 of them. It is also a book filled with text: each image has corresponding text that relates to it, though not all the textual pieces correspond to their respective images in a direct, representational manner (i.e., the text is never just the description of what the image *is*, nor is the image ever just the illustration of what the text *says*; rather, each supplements the other). Thus, even as the images and the text work in their own right, there is a work of authorship, as well, in the combination of the two. Even if this combination does not adopt a directly representational relationship, it is carefully authored, like Stewart's vignettes. Each image/text interlude is an ethnography of an encounter, but there is a further encounter that is staged in the creation of the book, *between* image and text. At the same time, and in apparent contradiction to what I have just said, each section of text is titled with the name of the place where the image is taken ("Queens," "Tivoli," "Treasure Beach"). Thus, the apparently nonrepresentative, evocative work that the nonliteral juxtaposition of image and text performs is overwritten (undercut?) by the proper noun at the top, telling the viewer where each image is made. Cole simultaneously highlights and effaces the literalism of the multisited nature of the work, within each text/image vignette, repeatedly.

I wish to hone in on four images in the book, because they were ones that my students responded to in ways that shed light on a multisituated sensibility, in relation to place and to personhood and to intimacy and mourning. The first, on page 157, is apparently a photo of a curtain, drawn up, with dark, blurred images of leaves outside (fig. 3.1). The crispness of the curtain's texture contrasts with the haziness of the night outside. There are no landmarks, no indication of a sense of place. The photo is one of a number in the book titled "Milan." The text speaks of the summer of 1943, when Milan was reduced to rubble by bombing.

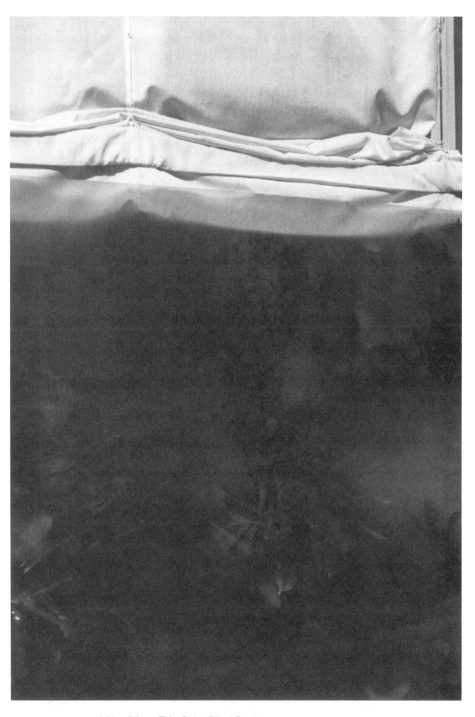

FIGURE 3.1 "Milan," from Teju Cole, *Blind Spot*.

Itzkowitz diagnoses the process behind this image as "the idea of showing something else, [in order to elicit] the *feeling* of something . . . that makes you think of something else."[43] Itzkowitz here is speaking of the "something" that is at the heart of Stewart's attunement to and engagement with the ordinary—what could be more ordinary than a curtain? Yet not every picture of an ordinary curtain pierces, makes the viewer think of something else or feel.[44] There is something about *this* curtain, even in the absence of knowing that this is a curtain in Milan, that somehow this image of this curtain in Milan is a memorial to a city reduced to rubble six decades previously. This is not because of any direct representative correspondence, but because of an authorial association that is purely transferential, and perhaps engendering of other transferential associations, elsewhere and among others.[45] Yet Itzkowitz is pointing not just to "something"; she is also pointing to the "else"—a word that speaks of otherness, of that which is not in the frame, of peripheral vision, of blind spots.

When Itzkowitz speaks of "showing something else, finding the *feeling* of photography," she is not speaking in abstractions. This for her (and for me) is a literal description of photography. If you want to show war, both she and Cole are saying, show a curtain, not rubble. This "showing something else"—and, in the process, avoiding the appropriation that would otherwise be constitutive to a pornography of violence—speaks, in a nutshell, to Derrida's project of deconstruction. For he is always looking elsewhere, deliberately, whenever he writes "of" something. This can never avoid the violence of writing entirely, but it can decenter and displace it. This process of looking elsewhere is central to Cole's own itinerary, as it emerges over the course of *Blind Spot*.

Yet it is not any curtain. It is in Milan. The viewer could not have known this had Cole not told her so. The proper name, of a real place, matters to Cole. Cole's images take us to the heart of the complex dialectic between the (at times necessarily) specific and literal multilocality that constitutes an operationalizable multisituated trajectory, and multisituatedness as conceptual topology (see chapter 1). In doing so as a traveler, a quintessentially colonial figure, but also as an African-born, American-located traveler considering (in this case) the incalculable violence that Europe inflicted upon itself not that long ago, Cole further pushes us to think the situated embodiments of colonial ways of seeing and knowing and their complex inheritances, with their potential for rescripting and inversion.

The place that is at stake in *Blind Spot* is not just the physical location that is photographed. It is also the relation established with it, for the viewer, for different viewers, differentially and transferentially. Consider two other photos, both of Seoul (each titled "Seoul"), on pages 119 and 195. Neither is an exceptionally dramatic photo, not even abstract or evocative in the way "Milan" on page 157 is. One is taken from the interior of a high-rise, a lounge area of an apartment building perhaps, or a reception area of an office, showing some tables and sofas and looking out on to the top of other high-rises in the cityscape (fig. 3.2). The second shows a street corner under construction, taped off in a slightly haphazard manner (fig. 3.3).

Ji Yea Hong responded thus to these images, after suggesting that she had found it difficult to respond deeply to many of the others in the book:

> There were few rare moments when I felt like I almost get it, that I was either in his dream or dreaming with him. Seoul (119, 195) are the ones that took least time to feel that way. Well, to be honest, it's also the only place in the book that I feel like I know (Chicago is still a little foreign to me). I know he doesn't want me to *know* that place, but still, this happened to be this way. Both photos see horror and wound that is also mine. One appears to be tidy, calm, toned down, and well-organized, another chaotic, obsessive, and hysterical. Well, maybe both are obsessive: obsessively calm and obsessively chaotic. I hear both photos scream. They are the same wound, same horror that is extraordinarily ordinary, so much so that it hurts. Inside me, I scream with them.[46]

The question of location is the place from which I started my consideration of multisituatedness in this book: a question, literally, of sites, of going to multiple sites in order to do a multisited project as conventionally understood. Yet Hong's searing response immediately shows how location is not just an objective rendering on a map (a cartographic, phallogocentric idea of location) but is immediately subjective. It is haunted not just by autobiographical traces but by diasporic trajectories (consider Hong's vital parenthesis, about the foreignness of Chicago). "Seoul," the images, through Cole's images and Hong's reading, becomes a site of cultural contact, between the Nigerian traveler-photographer living in America (whose racially marked and diasporic subjectivity is equally important to the ways he scripts his images) and the diasporic anthropologist who views his images. Even within two images about place, two images with no people in them, multisitedness becomes multisituatedness: situated, embodied, relational, and in the moment of encounter through the image, dia- and trialogic. Possibilities for imagining both collectivity *and* difference (where

FIGURE 3.2 "Seoul," from Teju Cole, *Blind Spot*.

FIGURE 3.3 "Seoul," from Teju Cole, *Blind Spot.*

the latter does not necessarily translate into the former: for which, read Hong's reading of Spivak in chapter 2) emerge.

Thinking through the juxtaposition of these three images, two of "Seoul" and one of "Milan," and these two responses, one Hong's and the other Itzkowitz's, highlights another aspect of Cole's process: its self-consciously fragmentary presentation. This is a reflection of what Marilyn Strathern (1991) has called a "fractal" ethnography; but in considering its transferential resonances, one can see something more at issue than generating comparisons through partial connections, which are Strathern's stakes in such a nonsynthetic, nonholistic process (see chapter 2). This is precisely because they elicit, as Jeanne Lieberman put it, "memory associations that take one elsewhere."[47] Not just "something else," a decentered and displaced object, but one taken "elsewhere," a transferenced viewing subject, scripted into a relation with image and text. In other words, they are partial connections that *depend on the reader/viewer* to be fulfilled, differentially.[48]

A final response to read concerns an image of a person, not a place (even though the title of the image, "Zurich," is emplaced like all the others).

This is an image on page 283, and the response I read is again Itzkowitz's. The image is of a woman on a bus (fig. 3.4). Cole takes the picture from behind her, apparently without her cognizance. One can see the reflection of the back of her head in the bus window. Most of the picture is dark, negative space, though one can see out the grimy front window of the bus, streaked with stains from its windshield wiper. What is lit up, dramatically, is the outline of the woman's head, such that one can see the strands of her hair, unkempt and luminous.

The text that juxtaposes to it is incongruous, precisely because, unlike most other textual vignettes in the book, it directly explains the image: it is representational, not evocative. Cole tells us that as the woman's hair was pulled up, he could see her neck tattoo clearly. It had a woman's name and a date. (In the image, her neck is dark, and the viewer cannot even tell that she has a tattoo.) He goes on to say, "Later, when I looked up the name, I found an old newspaper article: a woman of that name had died in a small town in Phoenix, Arizona, in 2007, and it had happened on the date in the tattoo. In the car that night, the article said, had been two other people, both of whom survived the crash, and both of whom, at that time, like the woman who died, were in their early twenties, a man, the article said, and another woman" (Cole 2017: 282).

The representational here interrupts the evocative and the transferential. Itzkowitz responded to this image by wishing she had not read the text. When she first saw the image, before reading the text, she saw how the light from the window of the bus illuminated the outline of the woman's head: "I feel like she's a *real* person . . . whom I want to know about without actually knowing."[49] Yet once she learns of the objective fact of the tattoo on the woman's neck, once she "really knew," something was lost. In this response, Itzkowitz is locating intimacy in (as) the desire to know, not least because of the transferential residues and relational affects activated in the moment of that desire (Itzkowitz went on, almost as a parenthesis: "her hair reminds me of mine").[50] On the one hand, this desire to know is not an appropriative desire: it is in the objective knowledge obtained after the internet search that appropriation resides. (Though the risk of appropriation, the risk of violence, cannot be avoided in that desire to know. It is after all Cole's desire to know the stranger who captivated him that led him to his internet search, to her naming and placing, to, ultimately, an intrusion into a stranger's intimacy and her past.) Rather, it contains within itself a Levinasian ethics of relating to an other, to the possibility of knowing the Other, a suspended animation of a future that is to come—

FIGURE 3.4 "Zurich," from Teju Cole, *Blind Spot.*

l'avenir—that is ruptured by the internet search. On the other hand, the condition of possibility of such an ethics is transferential identification ("her hair reminds me of mine"), which is interrupted when the other's actual, distant social relations are determined. This potential identification through transferential identification is by no means innocent: it is the deeply risky condition of intimacy, but it also opens the possibility of solidarity, of collectivity, of the possibility of mourning, even (especially) for a stranger.[51]

Like any artwork, *Blind Spot* seeks to produce affect, and it succeeds (or fails) in producing a range of affects. My reading of the work is predicated not just on the book itself but also on some of the response it engendered, in a specific, overdetermined pedagogical space. For the most part, the genre of Cole's work is apparently that of street photography: he takes a camera, walks through space, and makes photographs of what he sees, invariably while on his travels. Yet throughout the book, there is a differential, inconsistent decentering of the representational work of street photography. The work is not an attempt to move away from representation altogether—on the contrary, the insistence on the proper naming of the places where photos are made, or the work of finding out who the woman he saw on a bus in Zurich "really" is, is explicitly representational, even objectifying. Rather, it keeps open the active tension between the representational and evocative work of photography: a tension that is at the heart of ethnographic practice as well.

This tension requires a transferential identification with that which is being photographed (such as Hong's "Seoul" with Cole's "Seoul"); but it is also deconstructive, because it is the moment when the photographer loses control of her image because a viewer adopts a different (and potentially *différant*) relationship to it in ways that interrupt, or at least defer, possession.[52] It is in this difference, this deferral, this *différance*, that opens to the promise of something, some horizon, that we might imagine as and call justice.

....

Encounter is necessarily a question of ourselves and our relation to others, to an Other. This is why it is a question at the heart of ethnographic and photographic praxis. This relational question, further, *has* to be the question of the relationship between stranger and kin, as scholars from Levinas and Derrida to Strathern and Haraway keep reminding us. This is why the encounter in either ethnography or photography, with all its potential and actual intimacy, can never be innocent. A deconstructive praxis that decenters and displaces the violence of seeing does not—cannot—do away with that violence entirely. A politics of sight at the heart of a multisituated sensibility cannot pretend to be an innocent one, much less a moral one.

Therefore, my attempts here to wrestle with the evocative potentials of photography, dependent on transferential identifications on the part of viewers, subsequent and elsewhere to the making of the image, are resolutely not an argument that somehow "evocation" is more virtuous than "representation" or "transference" less phallogocentric than "objectification." It is precisely such binaries that I wish to suggest cannot be drawn, on one side of which would lie moral innocence. Indeed, Barthes's *Camera Lucida*, the quintessential text that gets at photography as an evocative medium that exceeds mere objectification, is hardly an innocent text. Not only is the punctum, the concept at the heart of Barthes's analysis, ultimately a phallic and penetrative imaginary, but Barthes's reading itself could be attributed to that of a solipsistic French white male intellectual who is especially inattentive to questions of race.

The opening chapter to Shawn Michelle Smith's *At the Edge of Sight* (2013), "Race and Reproduction in *Camera Lucida*," diagnoses the punctum as an inexplicable response that often has nothing to do with the photograph.[53] In other words, its purely transferential character, even as it serves to decenter the objectification of the image, replaces that objectification with the absolute, authorial subjectivity of the viewer of the image. This might, of course, open up the possibility of imagining forms of identification, even solidarity and collectivity, with the stranger, as I have just suggested. It might also equally serve to authorize and validate the gaze of the viewer, in this case the metropolitan philosopher viewing images that are in many cases racially loaded, in ways that doubly erase the subject of the image.

The difficulty—the constitutive risk of the encounter—is that these very different outcomes cannot be parsed out in advance through a technical formula that reduces the encounter to a purely contractual one, tabulating risks and benefits (even as, in certain times as places, certain such formulae are a necessary minimum to prevent gross violation). This is where a praxis of vigilance, to go alongside one of authorial vulnerability, is essential. Also necessary is the creation of dialogic forums, authored and curated, within which mutual teaching and learning (not just from "faculty" to "student") can occur. These are vital institutional questions concerning the building of reflexive pedagogical spaces of listening, of queering, and of a certain forgiveness.

Smith's reading provides a critical method that incorporates this praxis of simultaneous vigilance, queering, and forgiveness. An image that Smith reads into the heart of her critique of Barthes is James van der Zee's 1926 "Family Portrait."[54] Smith shows how Barthes, in his insistence on reading the punctum of this group photograph of a Black family, dismisses the studium of the photograph in a manner that is "notably condescending":

> He states that the photograph "utters respectability, family life, conformism, Sunday best, an effort of social advancement in order to assume the White Man's attributes (an effort touching by reason of its naivete)" (43). Barthes's explanation of the studium is laden by a paternal racism that readers are asked to ignore in pursuit of that which really interests *him*, the punctum. He calls upon the studium as if it is apparent, transparent, as if this lovely formal portrait could not be read in any other way, as if all readers should share his bemused reaction to the image and its subjects. (Smith 2013: 24, emphasis added)

Smith is not just troubled by Barthes's naturalization of the cultural codification of the studium. Rather, the actual detail of the punctum that Barthes identifies, a necklace that one of the women in the image is wearing described as "a slender ribbon of braided gold," is in fact misseen and misremembered by him, for the necklace in the image is in fact a pearl necklace. The stakes of this mistake, for Smith, is the way in which Barthes allows "personal connotation" to "efface representational denotation" (26). It is one thing to displace objectification. It is quite another to just get the details wrong and pretend that it does not matter because one's personal reaction and relation to the image trump what the image actually contains. Think here of the fine line between a transferential reading and a racist misreading. That line cannot be drawn formulaically, but it has everything to do with the modalities of the reader's own intellectual desires and the ways in which they interpose upon the text.

The necklace in van der Zee's "Family Portrait" that Barthes mis-sees serves as his punctum because it reminds him of his own aunt, who never married, and her necklace, which was "shut up in a family box" and forgotten, unmourned. Smith reads the connections, transferential yet oddly coincidental, between Barthes's aunt and the woman in the image who triggers Barthes's punctum, Estelle Osterhout, who also as it happened never married. At the heart of his work of mourning for his mother, who produced him, Smith shows the transferential and haunting presence of a nonreproductive figure in Barthes's meditations. When Barthes reads the winter garden photograph of his mother (without showing it to us) in the latter half of the book and tells us that in her death his own death is inscribed, there is something left unsaid. For, of course, he is there to mourn her; but who will mourn him upon his own death? What is at stake is not merely the solipsistic (and in this case racist) misreading of an image by a French white male intellectual, but also the queer lament of the nonreproductive self who is looking toward a death without progeny to mourn it. *Camera Lucida* is of and for his mother, but Smith points out that he himself occupies, as viewer, the place of the aunt.

Smith's reading of Barthes is ultimately a brutally honest and sympathetic one. She does not allow us to sit comfortably with the seductiveness of Barthes's analysis, to wallow in its evocative power. She also does not dismiss a transferential reading as unnecessary or simply self-indulgent. There is a gesture of solidarity and openness in this reading, through a refusal to read Barthes's phallogocentrism as *just* that, which ends in a most remarkable transferential reading of her own, of a photograph of Barthes:

Barthes's personal exploration of photograph demands, in part, a personal response—one I now undertake with some trepidation. I find I can meet Barthes part way, by choosing a path of "sympathy." . . . Using the punctum as a pathway to the that-has-been, I will try to meet Barthes as living effigy. As one aunt, I will consider another, and agree to imagine, at least, that I agree to see Barthes in one of the images he has left behind. I am drawn to a photograph of the adult Barthes preparing himself to tackle the blank slate of his writing tablet. It is an unusual photograph, perhaps taken on vacation. The typically dark-clad Barthes, pictured in enclosed, wooden offices, here sits perched on a plush white rug, in a bright, airy room, dressed entirely in summer whites. . . . I gaze at him from behind and to the side, and wonder which close admirer might have taken this photograph. I marvel at my access to this intimate scene. Entering into the image of Barthes, embracing what is dead, this is the photograph that I promise to keep. This is the one I will rescue from the advance of a Life Force that forgets and obscures those who do not biologically reproduce. (Smith 2013: 38)

Smith's sympathy to the question of queerness is, of course, a function of Barthes's own homosexuality, but it is not reducible to it, just as her antipathy to his racism cannot be reduced to his white masculinity. Something other than or beyond just identity is at stake here. Similar to Spivak's reading of Joseph Conrad's *Heart of Darkness* through Virginia Woolf, Tayib Salih, and Mahashweta Devi (see chapter 2), the question of how one might see Otherwise is riven and undercut through multiple axes of identification that do not sit easily with one another. Certainly, there are no guarantees that one marked body will see another, differentially marked one in non-phallogocentric ways. Thus, Smith contends with her sympathy toward Barthes's nonreproductive body alongside the violence of Barthes's transferential reading of van der Zee's image that erases the subjectivity of its Black female subject. She poses a praxiological question of the relationship between (non)reproduction and kinship: how to think self and other, kin and stranger, through an empathy for the nonreproductive yet white, patriarchal, colonial viewer/reader? How to think the politics of site, sight, and situation when the protagonists do not align simply along moral lines of perpetrator (unmarked, objective) and victim (marked, subjected, effaced, and erased)?

Smith's methodological answer to this question is to focus on reproduction again: on the reproduction and circulation of images. The politics of photography does not just lie within the triangulated relationship between photographer, subject, and (subsequent) viewer (elsewhere). It also lies in the manner of the image's own multisited and multisituated itinerary, one that crucially depends on its own modalities of valuation in commodified and globalized (and deeply mediated) markets that enable and constrain particular ways of seeing rather than others. Smith's analysis of Barthes is not an end in itself: it is an opening to a series of essays throughout *At the Edge of Sight* that considers this question of reproduction and circulation in relation to the racialization of photography.

Smith's concluding chapter to the book, "Afterimages: Abu Ghraib," is a reading of the circulation of photographs from Abu Ghraib that symbolized the depth of violence of the American occupation of Iraq. Smith discusses the work of these images, showing the abjection of naked, male Iraqi prisoners being humiliated by American occupation forces. What was particularly shocking was that the images were taken by Lynndie England, a female army reserve soldier: thus, the sexual humiliation, which became emblematic of American imperialism and racism, had a complex gender politics layered onto it, with the emasculation of the male Arab a significant part. Here, it inverts the sexual dynamics of *Season of Migration to the North*, for instance, one that again shows the complexity of intersectionalities that are not necessarily reinforcing toward a pure or virtuous politics. England came to become the culpable and individualized actor held accountable for the prisoner abuse, the "bad apple" who could be sentenced and dishonorably discharged, as the Bush regime's "honorable" war waged on. Even as England's acts themselves were unconscionable, how does one locate them within a broader global politics?

Specifically, Smith asks, how does one locate them within a global *reproductive* politics? For, central to the trajectory of the story, to the question of which accountabilities were scripted and in what ways, is reproduction. Not just of the images, but also of the (American) nation-state, whose place in its own exceptionalist worldly imaginary as custodian of democracy, freedom, and human rights (an imaginary shared by many Americans who were opponents of the US war in Iraq) was at stake. How does one think of a postcolonial/decolonizing, multisituated ethnographic praxis in relation to these images? Which at once gave lie to noble American myths, while also allowing them to be prosecuted in ways that left those myths intact? Which at once held the perpetrator of an outrageous act accountable, while decontextualizing and individualizing it in ways that kept American military masculinity (and not just virtue) intact?

Gayatri Spivak, in "History" (and previously in "Can the Subaltern Speak?"), famously alluded to the structure of the "white man saving the brown woman from the brown man" as constitutive to the structure of imperialism (as reproduced and reinforced by metropolitan intellectual desires to give voice to the subaltern subject). This structure is inverted in the Abu Ghraib images. Here it is the white woman humiliating the brown man in front of the white man; what is more, the woman doing the humiliating is quite literally the female subaltern. (Remember that the original meaning of "subaltern" is a lower-level military officer.) At the same time, the structure of imperialism is paradoxically reinforced, for what Abu Ghraib, the images, and the "afterimages" make explicit, as Nida Paracha pointed out, are all the women the white man may not want to save but want to crush.

One of those women was Lynndie England, but Paracha's point is larger than this. In responding to Smith's essay, Paracha referenced her own meeting with two young Pakistani women:

> I was reminded of the intertwined stories of Malala and Nabila, the girl who fought for education and the girl whose family was bombed by a US drone strike respectively. I remember meeting them both when they were invited to the United States for the first time, while Malala was to meet Obama, Nabila was to work with representatives of the Southern Poverty Law Center. Today, while Malala is known as the girl who changed Pakistan, studies at Oxford, and wants to join Pakistani politics, Nabila lives in poverty, with no guardian, depends on Malala to share her wealth and is largely forgotten. Maybe I am writing this story down because I don't want to be complicit in the always absent Other and while Smith talks about the effacement of colored women in the US military as well as the women who the white man (and bad women) want to save, I want to make sure that we also mark all the women the white man (and bad women) don't want to save (and conversely might want to crush—the bad colored woman?)—a different kind of effacement, or perhaps a telling absence or a willful blindness?[55]

The "Malala" whom Paracha references is none other than the young Nobel Laureate Malala Yousafzai, undoubtedly a remarkable woman but also a poster child for a virtuous American humanitarian interventionism, a justification both for the military interventions in Afghanistan after 9/11 and also for their continuation and intensification through drone strikes in Pakistan under the Obama administration. Malala is the brown woman doubly saved by the white man: first through his military intervention, and then through subsequent education at a premier metropolitan university whose entanglements in the colonial project are as old as the history of the project itself. How many Nabilas have been crushed for each Malala who is "saved" to assuage the imperialist humanitarian consciousness, Paracha forces us to ask?

Malala is the native informant at the heart of a project of salvage whose historical tentacles, of course, reach deep into the disciplinary history of anthropology and into its still continuing norms and forms. Paracha is one of many diasporic anthropologists who reckon with the tensions between these enduring disciplinary histories (and their concomitant consequences for professionalization into both canon and method) in the contemporary metropolitan university. She is also one of the anthropologists who come with accountabilities to other communities of practice: Paracha's own background before joining an anthropology PhD program at the University of Chicago was as a human rights lawyer in Pakistan.

The politics of ethnography does not just lie within the triangulated relationship between ethnographer, native informant, and subsequent reader, elsewhere, but also depends on its reproductions and circulations: hence the question of accountability to multiple communities of practice. We are back to where I started this book: with the question of disciplinary reproduction and its vexed relationship to a truly multisituated ethnographic praxis that embodies diasporic empirical and political commitments. Another student I have advised from Pakistan, for instance, found it impossible to publish a critique in disciplinary anthropological venues she had written of American drone strikes in her country and their representation in American public discourse: her reviews repeatedly dismissed her piece as "too personal an account." Malala the native informant who sticks to the reproductive script (of American exceptionalism) is venerated, but there is no place for the Pakistani cultural critic who queers that script by turning her gaze on American imperialist violence itself.

A multisituated ethnography will not simply give voice to the "subaltern" elsewhere. It will create institutional space and disciplinary affordance for diasporic political commitments, including those that will queer the project of disciplinary reproduction itself, with its established norms and forms. The transferential scenes of the multiple encounters that constitute ethnography (as they do, nonidentically, photography) and the evocations engendered therein speak to a literary function of ethnography that cannot be reduced to a representational, sociological function and that exceed even the most careful, calibrated, and sophisticated methods for scaling and comparison Otherwise. The institutional space of anthropological pedagogy, I argue, must enable such expressivity. Yet as with deconstruction, transferential evocation is not absolution. It could simply be a justification for phallogocentric misreading. Transferential evocations must be vigilantly queered, and there is no simple technical formula for how that might be done virtuously and without risk. There are, however, potential strategies for how one might refunction the norms and forms of ethnographic practice in order to create new kinds of conversational spaces for its enactment, which is what I explore in the next (concluding) chapter.

What is clear, however, is that a pedagogy that concerns itself with only disciplinary reproduction, and does not therefore keep itself open to the stakes and potentialities of multiple kinds of diasporic investments, is doomed to reproducing phallogocentric ethnographic practice, however moral its intentions might otherwise be.

4

Dialogue

In the prologue to *Emergent Forms of Life and the Anthropological Voice* (2003), Michael Fischer asks how we might understand something like the panic around the Y2K bug ethnographically, in terms of both the hype that surrounded it and the infrastructural pragmatics required to address a complex technosocial problem that had not in fact yet materialized.[1] What is at stake is not just Y2K as a thing (a bug, a software problem) but the *scenario* within which Y2K unfolded as a technological, and for the ethnographer an anthropological, problem.[2]

Fischer provides the example of Y2K as a complex scenario that both defined the global present within which he was writing at the time and demanded ethnographic elucidation not just in itself but for an understanding of contemporary technopolitics. The question that arises is, from *where*? From where does one write about such unfolding scenarios when one is embedded in and directly impacted by the worlds one sets out to study? This cannot pretend to be the study of the radically incommensurable Other, elsewhere. The location from which Fischer argues is an institutional milieu of interdisciplinarity in a program such as the Science, Technology and Society (STS) program at the Massachusetts Institute of Technology (MIT), itself a corporate and globalizing university. Any theorization of method therefrom is intimately connected to the question of the contemporary metropolitan university, in this case one at the vanguard of technoscience that prides itself on its self-professed culture of innovation, deeply tied to the commercial and entrepreneurial milieu of its environs and emerging out of MIT's Cold War imbrications in the military-industrial complex.[3] Part of the task of ethnographic elucidation is to generate a thick account of the scenario under study and also of the ethnographer's position within these unfolding socialities of action.

The question of situation is at once cultural, societal, and locational. It has two additional dimensions that are crucial to a multisituated disposition. One is temporal: the question of where one is writing from while ethnographically elucidating complex terrains and scenarios contains a conceptual dimension that concerns the *emergent*, the uncertain, the anticipatory, and the speculative, *l'avenir*, the undecided and undecidable future that is to come. The second is (auto)biographical: specifically, the question of the relationship between individually situated (auto)biographies and "moral systems of larger societies or segments of society" (Fischer 2003: 11). This reflects Fischer's unwillingness to give up a focus on individual ethical agency and struggle.[4] This refusal to elide or subsume accounts of individual agency with the framework of a larger sociological analysis (which is never, for Fischer, a simple rebuttal of the latter, as this is not a zero-sum game) is, I would suggest, crucially constituted by his own diasporic inheritance. I am interested in how Fischer situates the ethnographer not just as a traveler but as an *immigrant*. It is impossible *not* to think of individual agency when one's own autobiographical and ethical trajectory as an ethnographer is bound within it. This speaks to a certain praxis of cosmopolitanism that scholars such as Fischer inhabit, as a function of their own autobiographies and inheritance.

"Deep Play and Social Responsibility in Vienna" is Fischer's opening essay in *Emergent Forms of Life*. I was privileged to be in the audience at the presidential plenary of the annual meeting of the Society for Social Studies of Science (4S), held at the University of Vienna in 2000, when Fischer first delivered this essay as a keynote address to the conference.

He spoke of the resonances both of speaking in that place, a university where both of his parents had studied in a city that they had considered their home, before they were forced to migrate to America to escape the Nazis, and of speaking at that time, when the neo-Nazi Freedom Party led by Jörg Haider had recently become part of Austria's ruling coalition. Two decades later, Haider's fascism has been overtaken by even more virulent right-wing politics in Austria, Europe, and the world. How can one *not* think individual ethical agency and struggle as constitutive to the problem-space of a multisituated praxis today?[5] This is not reflexivity as choice or self-indulgence, but a thick, situated reflexivity, where one's own itineraries as an ethnographer are part of the constitution of the mise-en-scène of the complex, interrelated, and hybrid worlds one seeks to elucidate—not just connections, but long histories of intimate and often violent entanglements. For Fischer, what follows methodologically is a concern with infinite commentary and questioning rather than ontology.[6] There is a Judaeo-theological ethics at stake here, one that, following Emmanuel Levinas, entails a nonfinite interaction with the Other, and where the praxis of ethnography is not about the sociologically grounded outcome of these interactions but rather about the ethos and praxis of the interactions themselves.[7]

Fischer had exemplified this praxis over a decade previously in *Debating Muslims* (Fischer and Abedi 1990). That ethnography focused on Iranian culture, Shi'ite Islam, and Iranians in the United States. It describes and performs this dialogical call at three registers. First, it elucidates infinite commentary and questioning as that which *describes* an Islamic ethics (the dialogue and debate as *object* of study).[8] Second, it articulates infinite commentary and questioning as method of analysis: Fischer and Mehdi Abedi do not declaim about Islam as an object of study as much as they dialogue with Islam's own traditions of dialogism. Third, there is a performance of debate and dialogue between the coauthors, Fischer and Abedi, themselves. What the dialogue does, in both its declamatory and objectifying refusals and in a form that illustrates a certain cosmopolitics of idea(tiona)l exchange, is refuse radical alterity as the point where explanation runs out.[9] It contains within itself the trace of the Other, which is always necessarily also an autobiographical trace.

How to think the autobiographical resonances of diasporic ethnographic itineraries as a question of a multisituated method that reformulates the norms and forms of ethnographic practice toward non-phallogocentric modalities of encounter? This is the problem that I explore in this chapter, as I consider multisituatedness as an explicitly *dialogic* practice, one that necessarily goes beyond the sociological monograph. The question of dialogue is one of whom one is conversing with, but also of where one is conversing from. This is not just an identitarian question (what race/class/gender/sexuality/nationality am I?) but also a situated one (what is the experiential milieu out of which my ethnographic attentiveness has been sculpted?).

Fischer is arguing for an ethnographic methodology that goes beyond following the object to trace connections. It cannot, however, just stop with tracing connections and must continue to follow "*differentials* of connectedness and their fragility" (Fischer 2003: 2, emphasis added). The nature of complex interactions must itself be the ethnographic object of study. This involves documenting hierarchies. Thus, Fischer's programmatic call is, like that of Marilyn Strathern, to attend to difference as an organizing principle of ethnographic attention. While Strathern's attention to difference was structured by an investment in incommensurability and an idea that no description or account is ever full but always partial, Fischer's, in a manner closer to Gayatri Spivak's, is structured by a concern with making interests, access, desire, and power visible (see chapter 2). Identifying the mise-en-scène, the form to be studied, including forms of life, especially at moments when "life is outrunning the pedagogies in which we were trained" (Fischer 2003: 9), is at the heart of such an endeavor.[10] For Fischer, ethnography must involve and exist alongside a host of investigative, interpretive, and creative modalities that complement, supplement, and interrupt the knowledge it produces. It must also aspire and conspire to articulate new and reflexive institutions for an evolving society.

In this concluding chapter, I explore this promissory call through an exploration of what Douglas Holmes and George Marcus call para-ethnography (Holmes and Marcus 2005), via the example of an institutionally engaged research project of my own that followed the establishment of India's first biomedical translational research institute, the Translational Health Science and Technology Institute of India (THSTI). In the process, I elucidate one potential modality for rescripting the norms and forms of ethnographic practice toward more dialogic ends, suggesting both the kinds of engagements and insights that are possible, and the constraints, limits, and challenges (both epistemological and ethical) such endeavors might face. This is an attempt to end this book by articulating one potential promissory agenda for the development of a multisituated ethnographic praxis, while insisting that this does not in any sense represent a *solution* to the problems, paradoxes, and politics with which I began this book. Rather, it is a working through of the conceptual and meta-methodological problem-space of contemporary ethnographic research through emergent and experimental modalities of dialogic engagement, one that generates its own set of problems that demands both pedagogical exploration and institutional recalibration, necessarily in ways that think beyond disciplinary reproduction as the endgame of ethnographic research agendas and projects.

....

The subtitle of David Westbrook's *Navigators of the Contemporary* (2008) is *Why Ethnography Matters*. Westbrook, who teaches law but has been in conversations with George Marcus and others about refunctioning ethnography, has a simple answer: *conversation*. The real value of ethnography, Westbrook suggests, lies in its ability to create shared spaces of conversation, including and especially across diverse epistemic and political commitments. How does one do so, including and especially with expert interlocutors who are in positions of power? The inspiration for such a question derives from Marcus's suggestion that the ethnographer's position, especially in projects of "studying up," is *alongside* one's interlocutors (Marcus 2011)—not the view from nowhere that objectifies the subjects of ethnographic attention, but equally not the reflexive turn that accounts for such objectification by professing self-knowledge of it. The praxis that is at stake is one of critical interlocution: if many of our conceptual aspirations today revolve around understanding instruments and institutions of global power, how do we actually engage those institutions ethnographically? This is not a question of "access"—which again reduces the problem to one of penetrating the constructed object of ethnographic attention—but rather of the possibilities for generative interlocution.

Most of all, it insists on an ethnographic ethos that decenters the position of the ethnographer vis-à-vis the native informant. What would it mean if the native informant was instead considered interlocutor and collaborator, such that what is at stake is not merely a reconfiguration of the norms, forms, and epistemologies of object-subject relationships, but a more radical reconsideration of the native informant, under erasure, as a way of rescripting their place in the ethnographic encounter? This is the praxis of what Holmes and Marcus call para-ethnography in their seminal essay "Cultures of Expertise and the Management of Globalization: Toward the Re-functioning of Ethnography" (2005). The idea and ideal of para-ethnography attends to the constitutive conversational modality of ethnography, not just as an instrumental means to an objectifying end of generating sociological elicitation but as a more situational elicitation of a dialogic praxis that articulates an ethos of commentary that cannot but be implicated, in part, by the ethnographer's own autobiography and inheritance.

In discussing Holmes and Marcus's notion of para-ethnography, I am articulating the operationalization of the design and performance of ethnographies of a certain kind. Elaborating this kind of operation requires the groundwork that came before—of conceptualization and refusal—in the absence of which para-ethnography might simply seem like a mechanistically technical element in a program for a literalist multisited ethnography. Rather, para-ethnography is a meta-methodological problem-space, one that contains within itself a call to praxis.

Para-ethnography raises the question of how to work collaboratively with informants, rendering informants as interlocutors and creating the possibility for dialogic forms of ethnography. This requires the enablement of conversations that are not just about the ethnographer "getting" knowledge from the native informants, but must also be productive for one's interlocutors in ways that necessarily decenter or rescript ethnographic authorship and authority. However, once we acknowledge these working definitions and seek to operationalize them, we very quickly confront the normative intervention Holmes and Marcus are making into a certain prevalent ideology of the participant-observation function of ethnography, which is the implicit imperative not to interfere in what we are studying. Holmes and Marcus are not just making a claim that ethnography does intervene in the system under study; they are saying that it *ought to* and can self-consciously do so. There is really no way to reconcile a method that privileges participation in the system that one is studying and a presumption that as an ethnographer, I am going to be a fly on the wall who is just taking notes. There is no way to take Holmes and Marcus seriously and then just presume and assume the role of a passive observer. This is directly related to the dialogic call of *Anthropology as Cultural Critique* (which I also read into Spivak, and which is at the heart of any kind of research project that is also a pedagogical one)—it is not possible to be dialogic and just observe. That is just a bodily impossibility. There has to be some kind of active and relational intervention into the scene of the ethnographic encounter in order to render it dialogic. This is not about "activism." It is simply an acknowledgment that as a function of the ethnographer having been there, as part of a conversation (including perhaps conversations that she has staged and authored), her trace exists in the ways those conversations develop.

What does Alan Greenspan, Holmes and Marcus's textbook example of the para-ethnographic in "Cultures of Expertise," have to do with this? Why do Holmes and Marcus pick Greenspan, who is not someone they have had conversations with, not someone who has been their direct interlocutor, not someone they are directly establishing dialogic relationships with, as an exemplary figure in their elucidation of the para-ethnographic?

Holmes and Marcus are interested in how expertise is constituted within particular social milieus that are themselves located within (and in the cases of the US Federal Reserve, which is the focus of their analysis, significantly script) global political economic systems. What calculative rationalities are established, and how are they made to count? The Greenspan example is important not because it is a heroic account of a historical figure: it is not. Rather, it tells us about the ways in which Greenspan produces knowledge, which is reliant on his intuition, judgment, and biographical experience. It then tells us how such subjective, experiential knowledge is legitimized, valorized, or discounted within the Fed, which, Holmes and Marcus relate, requires Janet Yellen's translation of such often anecdotal knowledge into legible and actionable "facts" through quantification, a passaging through Galilean paradigmatic rationality in order to render it justifiably "expert." In this trajectory, the hegemonic system becomes the ethnographic object. It is the figure of Greenspan, not Greenspan the man, that is ethnographically important for Holmes and Marcus. Figures have functions. Figuring out how figures operate has something important to do with understanding how systems operate.[11]

I elaborate this with an example of what to me is a classic para-ethnographic reflection, Nahal Naficy's essay "The Dracula Ballet" (2009). This is a brief reflection on fieldwork, published in James Faubion and George Marcus's edited volume *Fieldwork Is Not What It Used to Be* (2009), in which Naficy articulates the double binds of being a diasporic Iranian anthropologist studying American geopolitical interventions into Iran in Washington, DC, in the mid-2000s. She describes how any position she would take would be caught within a discursive environment structured by a fundamentalist, authoritarian Iranian regime on the one hand and a neoconservative American one on the other. Any critique of the former would immediately be appropriated by the latter, even as any refusal of such a critique would be seen as a betrayal by friends and comrades struggling to oppose the regime.

There was no way for Naficy to be an ethnographer in DC in the mid-2000s and just be an observer, because there was no way that people were not attending to what she was writing and saying with a view to appropriating it to their own ends. One of the things that this points to is that institutions of power tend to be constituted by very small groups of people who structure the discursive terrain within which ethnographic knowledge can circulate and out of which it can disseminate. We are often immersed in fields in which people construe us in certain kinds of ways that we do not have full agency to shape. There is no way that any feminist or postcolonial para-ethnographic praxis can avoid this risk of conscription and the attendant actual and possible betrayals that might ensue.

In "The Dracula Ballet," Naficy renders the absolute political importance of the figure of the violated Iranian expatriate in DC in the mid-2000s. She recounts her argument with her friend Shirin, who was running an NGO involved in resisting the authoritarian regime in Teheran. For this resistance to work, discursive circuits had to run uninterrupted, but they also required the native informant—in this case, Naficy herself as someone who grew up under authoritarianism in Iran. The thing with native informants though is that they have to simultaneously be figured as the speaking subject while being spoken for. Naficy's problem was that she insisted on speaking herself and did not stick to the script: in a dinner-time conversation that involved Shirin and a journalist, she refused the subjectivity of victimhood to the Iranian regime that Shirin expected of her, much to the latter's anger. The speaking subject was the subject of intellectual desire; the subject who actually speaks, on her own terms, was a betrayer of that desire, a betrayer of friendship itself.

Why did Naficy have to function as a certain kind of violated figure? Why was the only subject position she was allowed one of victimhood? Would she have had to function as the same kind of figure had she been a diasporic Iranian in London?

In a profound sense, Naficy's brief vignette is an ethnography of *Washington*. Washington is the scene of the ethnographic encounter, and it is overdetermined. One could not be a diasporic Iranian in Washington circa mid-2000s without being conscripted—and her account is telling us about that system of conscription. It is articulating a principle of method that, as Kim Fortun puts it, ethnographically attends to discursive gaps and discursive risks (K. Fortun 2012). It is telling us about a place that offers no discursive possibilities for being a diasporic Iranian otherwise. It is telling us about a time that does not allow a diasporic Iranian to simultaneously be opposed to the Iranian administration *and* be opposed to American neoconservatives.

The work of ethnography has to be about subverting hegemonic frameworks. At the same time, asking the question of Greenspan as exemplary figure tells us something about the nature of globalized markets, speaking to the question of whose subjectivities get to count as expert knowledge. Think that alongside Naficy's haunting question—what does it mean if they only get to count at the moment of appropriation? When Naficy's subjectivity and her conjectural knowledge only mattered when it could travel in three steps to a senator to whom Shirin wanted to make a case against the Iranian regime, a cause in which Naficy's testimony to the journalist (who had access to the senator) was to be conscripted? This circuit of articulation required Naficy to stick to her script, a script of victimhood.

An autobiographical trace haunts this essay, for Naficy's parents were at different times arrested by the Revolutionary Guard, and family members were killed. The reader is told of these facts but is not allowed to linger upon them. Naficy's refusal of an autobiography of victimhood in spite of this history is also her insistence, at once political and personal, on an autobiography of a normal childhood. This is important to Naficy not just as an individual who has to live with the consequences of tragic events, but also as an ethnographer who insists on producing a certain kind of knowledge that refuses a co-optation into dominant expectations of how she ought to live and to know. This trace is not allowed. American neoconservatives do not allow it. The Iranian regime does not allow it. Her own friend, the interlocutor in the NGO who is supposed to be on her side, does not allow it. This tells us something about institutions of power in Washington and in Teheran that constrain peoples' biographies and capacities for living in certain ways. Something that could not be told outside the space of the encounter as subjective, tinged and singed with inheritance, haunted by the collisions between the constraints of geopolitical machinations of power and the singularities of lives lived, died, built, and re(-)presented.[12]

....

Holmes and Marcus's methodological argument is that thinking the ethnographic function of such encounters (and thinking the production of ethnography out of such encounters) is not just contingent happenstance (Naficy happening to have a friend who happened to know a journalist who happened to have access to a senator whom the friend wanted to influence). The scripting of the para-ethnographic encounter requires openness but cannot be fully arbitrary. This leads to questions of design and staging as one mode of operationalizing the para-ethnographic. For this, I want to discuss the para-site as an ethnographic third space.[13]

The para-site is perhaps the most scripted version of the para-ethnographic encounter. It is a conversation involving key informants or interlocutors that attempts to stage certain debates in a manner that is unfamiliar and hopefully generative, both to the ethnographer, who is hoping to gain certain insights into the way actors are thinking about a problem, and to the actors themselves, who ideally confront new modalities of problematizing familiar debates through this staging. A lot of authorship goes into designing a para-site. The ethnographer does not determine the trajectory of the conversations but must determine their mise-en-scène. I give the example of a para-site organized by Philip Grant, a former PhD student at the University of California at Irvine who was studying secular Iranian activism. In a remarkable dissertation, Grant wrote about this topic while consistently refusing to write about the activists in any manner that would objectify them, writing instead about how gender materialized as a key matter of concern within activist praxis (Grant 2011).

In the course of his research, Grant organized a para-site around the question of the figure of the secular Iranian intellectual. On one side of the room were members of the Million Signatures Campaign (who were all Iranian, mostly female, many graduate students—maybe forty or fifty of them). On the other side was Rameen Jehanbegloo, a prominent Toronto-based secular intellectual, a charismatic figure on the secular intellectual scene who had been arrested by the regime. George Marcus, Étienne Balibar, and I were the faculty who were invited. Balibar was on Grant's committee but had also been Jehanbegloo's teacher in Paris.

The para-site started with Jehanbegloo's reflection on the nature of being an Iranian intellectual. Balibar responded, after which members of the campaign asked questions. What was most interesting was not what Jehanbegloo said: he reiterated well-known public positions he had taken previously, being after all as much of a public figure as Greenspan is. The telling moment was when one of the women in the campaign asked him a question; he got up, turned around, and made himself a cup of coffee while giving a half-answer. What was so striking was the gendered performance of the intellectual. What happened here was, to quote one of my students Jill J. Tan, the "staging of performing the labor of difference."[14] Thus, the para-site performed the conceptual and political work of illustrating the question of gender in Iranian activism and the generational differences in how such questions came to be articulated (or disregarded). Not a question of the (in Jehanbegloo's case, heroic) activist himself, but one of the mise-en-scène of Iranian secular activism as a gendered field of action that is itself contested and evolving over time.

There is an institutional politics at stake here, to put it mildly. One that moves away from the recuperation of the subaltern voice elsewhere, toward more proximal interventions that dialogue with institutions of power, including necessarily with the metropolitan university and its role. In the process, the para-site also reflexively turned the ethnographic gaze onto the metropolitan research university itself, as a space that is normed in ways that render this gendered performance of the intellectual commonplace. After all, actions like Jehanbegloo's happen all the time in the spaces that we inhabit as academics. The para-site, precisely because it is a staged encounter of a certain kind, renders explicit what might otherwise have been a taken-for-granted act of masculine entitlement through its rendering within an ethnographically authored and observed performative space. The question here is not a reductively activist one of whether we can change these institutions: Holmes and Marcus are not going to change the Fed by writing about the figure of Greenspan, and the para-site with Jehanbegloo is not going to change the gendered performance of the Iranian intellectual within the space of the metropolitan university. Rather, what is at stake is a pedagogical project in which, as ethnographers, we could potentially teach our interlocutors to be attentive to some of the things we have learned to pay attention to, even as we develop and maintain an epistemic and ethical openness to learning from our interlocutors as well.[15] Integral to this, as I will elaborate next with an account of a para-ethnographic excursion of my own, are the biographies of the people who people these institutions of expertise. This opens up the question of the relationship between structure and peopling, and the place of the biographical and life-historical in elucidating political economic structures (Fischer 2005).

....

Between 2008 and 2012, I ethnographically followed the establishment of India's first translational research institute, THSTI. This was being established by the Government of India's Department of Biotechnology (DBT), partly in collaboration with the Division of Health, Science and Technology (HST) at the Massachusetts Institute of Technology (MIT). HST is an unusual program that attempts to bridge the engineering and science capabilities at MIT with the clinical capacities at Harvard.

Translational research had by this time become a ubiquitous category in Western biomedicine, certainly in its audit cultures. Under the rubric of the "bench-to-bedside" formulation, there are a couple of comfortably assumed definitions of what constitutes translational research. One working definition is that translational research is basic research that can lead to therapeutic applications. This definition often operates in basic research and university settings—an implicit idea that basic research quite often focuses too much on esoteric aspects of a biological mechanism and ends up becoming too divorced from actually advancing human health. Generally, this idea of translational research has its origin story in cancer research, where mechanistic understandings of how cells proliferate, aggregate, or die have had direct implications for the development of new anticancer therapeutics. A second working definition of translational research begins not with the moving downstream (or outward) of basic research, but rather with the incorporation of a research sensibility and ethos into clinical practice. Both of these working definitions are institutionally enshrined in funding programs for translational research, such as, in the United States, through the National Institutes of Health.

Linear imaginaries of processes, such as the "bench-to-bedside" formulation, are invariably more useful in understanding the ideologies behind those processes rather than the processes themselves. In practice, translational research, far from being a singular idea or process, is polyvalent and, far from being a unidirectional flow from x to y, is relational in all sorts of ways. It is, to paraphrase Andrew Pickering (1995), a mangle of practices but also discourses, ideologies, beliefs, investments, and ideas about biomedicine, about cells, about organisms, and about the world.[16]

Methodologically, one can find complexity by looking at the *practice* of translational research. I wished, however, to focus not on the practice of translational research alone, but on its multiple *conjunctures*, the specific conditions of particular instantiations of translational research in certain places, times, and institutional milieus.[17] An empirical unpacking of the microsociological intricacy of translational research is undeniably valuable, but it does not necessarily allow us to understand the larger structures and contexts within which various research enterprises unfold under the sign of translational research. For this, I wanted to look at how translational research was an unsettled category. What translational research actually means for different actors varies greatly depending on who one talks to. These variations occur on professional lines (basic researchers versus clinicians, for instance) and on disciplinary and institutional lines. (For instance, at a historically entrepreneurial university like MIT, ideas of translational research couple to an ethos of commercialization, which may not be the case, to the same extent, elsewhere.) Additional variability is introduced when a concept such as this is ported to different national contexts, with different institutional histories and social realities. Yet what makes translational research such an interesting ethnographic concept is not just that its meaning is variable, but also that most translational researchers tend to act *as if* its meaning is constant.[18] Hence, there were layers of assumptions, naturalizations, and variations in the meaning and practice of translational research as it was instantiated institutionally in an initiative such as THSTI.

For me, the empirical and conceptual interest in the project lay less in settling what translational research "really" is and more in exploring its polymorphism as itself something ethnographically interesting. This is especially because translational research does not refer just to epistemology but refers also, immediately, to institutions. Questions of institutional structure, culture, and articulation are central to any kind of translational research, however defined. What this means is that translational researchers necessarily have a sociological imaginary. The polymorphism in ideas (and ideals) of translational research is itself reflective of different sociological imaginaries that are at play. Hence, I was less interested in tracing the microsociologies of translational research per se and more in tracing the macrosociological imaginaries within which the polymorphic instantiations of translational research were materializing in an emergent, collaborative, transnational institutional endeavor.

One of the axes around which different conceptualizations of translational research by various key actors in the THSTI initiative operated was around the opposition between imaginations of the "bench-to-bedside" formulation of translational research in terms of either "bench-to-market" or "bench-to-community" solutions. The former was articulated quite consistently out of MIT, where scientists find it difficult to imagine translation without commercialization. (One scientist there told me, in so many words, "But, of course, you can't have translation without a boardroom.")

It found resonance among many scientists in India who have embraced an imagination of hypercapitalist, neoliberal technoscience as the means to become a player in global knowledge economies. But it also encountered deep opposition among others who came to the table with stronger clinical/public health/postcolonial sensibilities and who questioned how a market-based imagination of translation could possibly be useful in a country such as India where 30 percent of the population is destitute and falls out of the market altogether.

I set up a para-site to stage and elaborate the debate between bench-to-market and bench-to-community ideas of translation, by porting the various debates occurring around THSTI into a more general conversation around capacity building for translational research. This was held at MIT in November 2009, and it brought together various people who could contribute to the debate around translational research from both the United States and India (some, but not all, of whom were involved in THSTI). This included basic scientists; people in industry; a number of people from, or affiliated in some way with, the HST program as examples of researchers who worked at the basic research/industry interface; people working in public health and community health; and social scientists who had expertise in organizational issues in the life sciences.[19] Polymorphic ideas and ideals of translational research were articulated (and disarticulated) in this simulated setting, and these opened up certain conversations having to do with THSTI. This para-ethnographic encounter for the anthropologist served, in turn, as a para-theoretical encounter for my interlocutors, allowing the conceptualization of certain critical issues in a manner that, for practical reasons, is impossible to do within the context of formal institutional planning meetings.

For me, the stakes were twofold. At its simplest, the para-site was purely a staged field site: it was an attempt to bring key interlocutors into the room to engage in a dialogue, including those who might not normally encounter each other in the course of their normal everyday practice. For example, a senior executive at Johnson & Johnson, and a physician and community health activist from Dharwad, Karnataka, are not two people who ever usually meet. Yet both, in different ways, were engaged in projects of translational research that potentially had resonance, even if antagonistically, within THSTI, and in this para-site they had the opportunity to converse with each other. The fact that they utterly failed to do so is itself a telling and useful insight into the ways in which structuring sociological imaginaries operate (or fail to do so) in relation to one another, even as it is a revelation of the hierarchies of expertise that were operational among this group.

The para-site was also an attempt to bring certain otherwise marginal positions into the room in a conversation on capacity building, which both at MIT and in India tended to be dominated by market-driven and technocratic imaginaries. This required careful curation. The oppositional positions to such market-driven technocracy in the Indian context were strongly articulated, but they still represented a minor thread in conversations around translational research and institution building for biomedicine. The challenge was to bring these otherwise minor voices into the conversation, in this venue, in ways that were not merely symbolic and that were not violent. Part of what the staging of the para-site allowed was a simulation of epistemic equivalence among the different invited actors, where a community health activist from northern Karnataka could air his views about what translational research might mean during the same time and space that an executive from a big pharmaceutical company received. (The community health activist was still largely ignored, and that in itself, as I mentioned, is telling.)[20]

These were my stakes. From the perspective of some of my key interlocutors, however, the stakes of the para-site were different. The actors at THSTI were involved not just in building an organization but in conceptualizing notions such as translational research. The para-site became a para-ethnographic field site for me, but I was not the only one who was engaged in generating concepts or theory out of that site. So too were my interlocutors. "Conceptualization" for them was not a theoretical abstraction, but it concerned the actual ways and means by which institutional cultures could materialize. As an example of this, I quote Martha Gray, who headed the HST side of the THSTI collaboration, as she explained (to a potential funder of the para-site) its importance to the conceptualization of THSTI:

> To a large extent, any effort to build a translational research effort must involve a change in (or building of) culture. Some may argue this point, but one can easily see that if the present academic culture were sufficient, then there would be much more translation (however defined). Now many more people call their work translational, but one could argue that some of this is a re-branding, and not a change. Put simply, changing culture is hard! (And, I say this backed by my 13+ year experience trying to sustain and grow culture change within

well-established institutions.) Having begun to work with Kaushik, I have immediately come to appreciate the enormous value of bringing an anthropological perspective to these discussions. With the framework and perspective he and his profession provide, I believe that we have a much higher likelihood of developing and executing on strategies to build institutions and programs in India (THSTI) and around the world. This won't all happen in this workshop, but the workshop is a critical first step.[21]

Gray saw the para-site as providing the potential for cultural reflexivity. These were not the same stakes, necessarily, that others in the room (or others involved in THSTI who were not at the para-site) had. For a number of the Indians involved in the collaboration with HST, the biggest challenge was not a difference of *culture* as much as it was a difference of *power* that existed between a global corporate university such as MIT and a "developing" nation trying to establish institutional capacity. This speaks to the praxiological tensions opened up through the para-site, both as they existed in the actual development of the THSTI initiative and the ways in which it allowed an explicit articulation of my investments to some of my interlocutors and, indeed, to myself as I attempted to think through my own stakes in this project.

....

I wrote up some of my THSTI material for the first time shortly after the para-site, for a conference I organized on the theme of knowledge/value (K. Sunder Rajan 2011). I shared it with some of my key interlocutors at THSTI. One of them, Satyajit Rath, who was at the time a scientist at the National Institute of Immunology in Delhi, asked me, "Isn't this paper both relativist and dishonest?"

This was not a hostile question. Rath was attuned to some of the complexities of social scientific research, and he was himself one of the most sociologically reflexive of all the actors involved with THSTI. He was also well acquainted with the larger trajectory of my work, having read a number of things I had written by then on clinical trials and access to medicines, and both of us had been involved in activist interlocution on some of the issues that had arisen in those arenas.

What Rath was pointing to in his critique was a different ethnographic modality that he saw in my writing on THSTI compared to that on clinical trials and access to medicines, where the political emerges quite clearly as interventionist. This latter register of the political, as reflected in *Phar-mocracy*, is not an attempt to "change the world," tell activists what to do, or rescue the voice of the victim (K. Sunder Rajan 2017). Rather, it oper-ates a modality of critique that explicitly points to crisis, contradiction, exploitation, and alienation, and that tries to make sense of that through structural and historical analysis. The THSTI paper, however, showed a stronger residue of another ethnographic ethos and sensibility. This fo-cused on unpacking the intentional or motivational side of social action and on understanding the operation and trajectories of sociological imagi-naries in translational research, as a function of both individual and in-stitutional biographies. These two ethnographic modalities sometimes sit uneasily together.

Some of the unease comes from the politics of representation that are involved. In the *Pharmocracy* project, it was clear where my affinities lay: toward a politics that resists the appropriation of health by capital and even insists on the necessity of imagining what a socialization of health might look like. In the THSTI project, the binaries were not so easy. Crudely speaking, there were at least three kinds of political sensibilities that were reflected in the THSTI initiative. There were hypercapitalist, neoliberal sensibilities operating out of many quarters in India, in explicit tension with leftist, postcolonial, and public- and community health–driven sensibili-ties that provide the possibility for alternative imaginaries of translational research to the dominant ones. The liberal entrepreneurial positions that came from HST were of a third kind, occupying neither position but occasionally forming affinities with one or the other.

This led, for me, to the tension of writing something faithfully descrip-tive of all the positions that were on the table, while pushing and writ-ing *for* some of the minor, alternative, or nonhegemonic imaginaries that might actually think of translational research in nontechnocratic terms. The tension that is contained here consists, at its heart, of the two mean-ings of representation, as portraiture and as proxy. In terms of providing an empirically thick, analytically rich description of the terrain that I was studying, drawing as thick a portrait of that terrain, constituted as it was by multiple biographies, stakes, and sociological imaginaries, was essen-tial. In terms of taking a critical stand, pointing out how some of these imaginaries were in fact more sociologically rigorous than others was es-sential. Thick portraiture does involve a certain distancing from taking a stance, it does require informants' voices and perspectives to speak for themselves, and it involves a privileging of the actors' point of view—it entails a language of complexity that makes decisive analysis and critique difficult or impossible. Meanwhile, taking a stance does involve privileging certain voices over others, certain positions over others—and that contains within it the seed of betrayal. Hence, Rath's point about relativism and dishonesty is not denunciation: it points to the double binds within which projects of cultural critique, especially when multisituated, comparative, and relational, are located.

This betrayal felt particularly tricky in relation to my interlocutors at HST. While I needed to be rigorously descriptive of the hypercapitalist positions coming out of India, it was easy for me to also adopt a critical attitude to those positions, because my antagonism to those positions was evident (and not particularly threatening) to those interlocutors who adopted such positions. It was also easy for me to be critical of the left and activist positions at play in India, because I had developed enough comradeship with those actors that they knew my critiques came largely from a place of solidarity.

HST provided a more difficult problem. On the one hand, the scientists from HST who were involved in the THSTI collaboration formed a group of imaginative, innovative institution builders, committed to fostering multidisciplinary research, open to social science interlocution, and imagining a global biomedicine that involved building capacity in other parts of the world. This was not a group that went to India telling Indians how to do translational research: Martha Gray, for instance, always emphasized that the institutional milieu being fostered would have to be relevant to Indian contexts and grow organically out of and in response to those contexts. These scientists spent an enormous amount of time and energy on the institution, such as in coordinating a faculty search for the founding faculty of THSTI (which was a yearlong process that involved reading four hundred applications and coordinating with search committee members in India). The level of commitment that went into this initiative from HST was nontrivial, and I developed a deep respect for my interlocutors there over the course of my research.

On the other hand, this was the story of an American corporate university engaged in a partnership with a developing country to "build capacity" in a context that the concerned American actors actually knew very little about going in. They often did not understand the historical, sociological, institutional, or cultural nuance that rendered the collaboration full of friction. Meanwhile, both the power differentials and the capital differentials in the collaboration were stark. The collaboration used Indian public money, as the Indian government paid MIT five million dollars toward their involvement in the endeavor. From the perspective of Indian bureaucrats justifying this expenditure to Parliament, there was pressure to show accountability, to show tangible results of particular sorts. From the perspective of MIT, the collaboration from a financial point of view was relatively insignificant, peanuts compared to the half-a-billion-dollar collaboration that was ongoing with the Singaporean government.

From an HST perspective, what was at stake was the ethical imperative to build global scientific capacity. The relationship of this perspective to an "MIT perspective" is itself a vexed, complicated one that changes depending on one's situation, as I will elaborate. From an Indian perspective, the stark differentials in global power relationships were more apparent. Foregrounding the former seemed like relativism to someone like Rath, who was well aware of my own stance, in other intellectual contexts, which would insist upon highlighting the latter. Foregrounding the latter meanwhile would potentially betray the relationships I had developed with my interlocutors at HST. A number of them were well aware of my leftist, postcolonial sensibilities, but they built affinity with me based on other shared sensibilities, around things like the importance of multidisciplinarity in discipline-dominated university structures. They did not necessarily understand the postcolonial subject positions that were at stake, often assuming that the world of technoscience is flat, even while operating on a deeply striated terrain. After all, one could not imagine a world in which American taxpayers would be paying millions of dollars to an Indian university to tell MIT how to build capacity.

Even the question of power differentials was vexed. There was the radical inequity between a corporate university with the brand value of MIT and a yet-to-exist Indian scientific institution. But many actors in India, especially of the hypercapitalist ilk, were more than willing to trade in the fungibility of that brand value, not because they shared the HST ethos but because it could be leveraged to their own ends. While a more post-colonial, nontechnocratic imaginary of translational research in India did exist as a minor strand in the debates on capacity building, in relation to what was perceived as the hegemonic, market-driven imaginary of HST, actors at HST saw their imaginary of biomedical science as the minor discourse, operating at the margins of the discipline-driven institutional structure of MIT. The spatial structure of this terrain was constituted in such a way that HST was hegemonic in relation to India, yet marginal in relation to MIT: hence, the activation of antihegemonic sentiments on the part of Indians was seen as a further marginalization of well-intentioned sensibilities on the part of actors at HST. The temporal structure of this terrain was constituted in such a way that the emergent forms of life that were at stake were always underwritten by questions of what stays still—in this case, the endurance of relational structures that are colonial in effect, if not necessarily in intent.

I am arguing here that a multisituated disposition foregrounds the ways in which different kinds of stakes can be made to implicate each other. The question is, how might such stakes be staged? There are uncomfortable tensions and double binds that reside within such implications for analysts who seek to combine faithful portraiture with faithful interlocution and intervention. Postcolonial contexts highlight this in particularly sharp and resonant ways: this is the very ground of postcolonial dis-ease.

The conceptual challenge of the THSTI project was a scalar one, concerning the relationship between structural elements of a political economy, constituted by global aspirations on all sides and marked by power hierarchies and different sociological imaginaries of translational research, and the ways in which these aspirations, hierarchies, and imaginaries actually materialized on the ground in institutional form. The latter was always a function of both individual investments and preexisting structural constraints, an intercalation of both the structures of political economy and the ways in which those structures were peopled.[22] On the Indian side, this included bureaucratic constraints imposed by the Department of Biotechnology, a public funding body answerable to the Indian Parliament and therefore eager to show tangible and measurable success in the building of THSTI. On the American side, there were constraints imposed by the interests of MIT as a global corporate university investing its brand in capacity building for life sciences around the world. The very specific investments of, and affective relations between, those who peopled THSTI created, enabled, and constrained these structural relations and institutional forms. At stake here is a conceptualization of how relationships between global macrostructures—that involve states, corporate universities, and capital flows—intercalate with the micro-intimacies of individuals and their aspirations and commitments. The meso-scale of analysis here is the institutional.

This project threw up questions relating to structure and agency, structure and contingency, and scales of analysis (macro, meso, and micro). These are not new questions but a reiteration of some of the oldest dilemmas in the human and social sciences. My ethnography of THSTI was of a very small, elite, highly networked group of people who became institutional founders and leaders. Yet stories such as this—having to do with the globalization and recalibration of contemporary biomedicine—must aspire to illustrate something beyond the particular investments and idiosyncrasies of such specific individuals and networks. How can we reconcile this fundamental contradiction, of the absolute particularity of the aspirations and commitments of certain individuals and their relationships (the kind of particularity whose elucidation is indeed the function and value of ethnography) with the more general historical, structural, and conceptual currents in relation to which they must be located, which constitutes the potential for theory?

There were several structural contexts at stake in this project, layered onto various agential ones. The structural contexts—having to do with the laboratory-clinic interface, on the one hand, and the idea of innovation, speaking to questions of commercialization and the academic-industrial interface, on the other—speak to two common registers within which the problematic of translational research is commonly posed. There was also the context of globalization and the particular ways in which the American corporate university encountered Indian efforts at institution building through particular imaginations of a "global" biomedicine, imaginations that were often incongruent, and sometimes incommensurable, across various elements of the collaboration. The agential contexts speak to the stories, trajectories, and investments of the various people involved with THSTI. These operate at the level of psychobiography (ambitions, desires, ideological, and political commitments), of sociobiography (the social contexts out of which actors come but also their explicit and implicit sociological imaginaries), and of relationality (questions of trust, collegiality, and friendship but also, in various ways and at various stages, of pedagogy, mentoring, patronage, mistrust, and betrayal).

Structure and agency, structure and contingency, macro and micro: none of these is a simple binary. They are layered, striated. The work of theory here is not to arbitrate the binary or to find some adequate point (such as the institutional) at which explanations can rest but, rather, to work the striations, to elucidate the topologies that constitute something like THSTI. This is, in part, a mapping project. The nature of the ethnographic entanglement that emerges in the process of such mapping is consequential. The relationship between conceptualization and contextualization, I suggest, is a problem of conjunctural attentiveness, but also a problem that concerns postcolonial diasporic cosmopolitanism in the context of corporate, imperial hierarchies, a problem of the relationship between structures and peopling, between political economy and personhood, between chapters 3 and 4 of *Anthropology as Cultural Critique* (Marcus and Fischer 1986; see chapter 1 of this book).

My own entry into following THSTI was a function of the fact that Shiladitya Sengupta, at the time a faculty member at HST and involved with the establishment of THSTI, was an undergraduate with me at the All India Institute of Medical Sciences (AIIMS), New Delhi. When I attended my first THSTI planning meeting in Delhi in July 2008, at Sengupta's invitation, I walked into a room that contained ten people, including myself. Of these ten, five of us had links, current or past, to AIIMS. Indeed, four of us had been in college at the same time. One of us (myself) was now an anthropologist taking notes at the meeting (with an STS PhD from MIT, a postdoc at Harvard, and a master's in biochemistry from Oxford). A second (Sengupta) was a biomedical scientist with dual appointments at Harvard and MIT researching nanotechnology-based drug-delivery systems (with a postdoc from MIT and PhD from Cambridge). A third (Uma Chandra Mouli Natchu) was one of my best friends from college, who at the time was finishing his PhD in public health at Harvard. Five people also had current or past links to Harvard and/or MIT. While this networking speaks to only one trajectory of the origin of THSTI, the one that I had most immediate access to, it was a consequential trajectory. There were other trajectories and networks within the founding group of THSTI. Their investments sat uneasily with those of this group in ways that would ultimately contribute to the unraveling of the THSTI-HST collaboration.

Individual investments and biographical trajectories were deeply significant to the story of THSTI. At the same time, it would be too simple (and simply wrong) to suggest that the emergence of THSTI was just a function of these very particular investments and trajectories. The question that arises then is, had this particular configuration of people not happened to get together at a particular moment in time, would others have taken their place? The answer has to be yes and no. For example, the very imagination of a translational research institute as a nodal institution in developing biomedical capacity depended in significant measure on M. K. Bhan, the then-secretary of India's Department of Biotechnology, who happened to be the first clinician occupying such a position and who happened to have deep investments in bridging clinical practice with research. His own research trajectories crossed those boundaries, which in the Indian context remain for the most part rigidly enforced even today, more than a decade later. At the same time, one can fully appreciate the investments of figures such as Bhan only when situated within the arc of broader historical trajectories in India over the past two decades, such as an investment in the knowledge economy and an embrace of American institutional models as imitable in order to become a "global player."

Similarly, there is no questioning the uniqueness of HST as a model to base an imagination of a translational research institution on, and it is likely that, had it not been for the contingent networks that brought Bhan into contact with HST, different imaginations of this institution might have emerged. Yet the basic elements of the THSTI-HST relationship—as involving an elite US university, primarily in hiring and training fellows or faculty who will initiate projects in India—were not unique. For instance, a parallel initiative with Stanford University, called the Stanford-India Biodesign Centre, was underway at exactly the same time. The pattern of MIT's relationship with the Indian government in building life science institutions in other parts of the world is also not unique: HST itself subsequently became involved in a similar collaboration, M+Vision, with the regional government of Madrid. MIT as a global corporate university has over the past decade been involved in multimillion-dollar collaborations for scientific partnership and institutional capacity building with the governments of Singapore and Russia. These reflect emergent and *longue durée* structures of global capital, imperialist relations of production, and the neoliberal corporatization and globalization of the metropolitan research university.

At stake then are enduring histories of global, capitalist, and imperialist relations of production that animate the structuring of an institution such as THSTI; also at stake are the sensibilities, motivations, desires, and aspirations of the individuals who people it. How, for instance, does one understand Gray's motivations for getting involved with a country that she had no prior context for, animated by fierce commitments to and ideals about how research should be institutionalized—commitments that reflected her own pedagogical formations, legacy desires, and also what can only be called an ethics and politics? The fact that Rath, intellectually and politically opposed to a simple incorporation of an "HST ethos" across THSTI, cochaired a search process designed by HST, an enormous commitment of time and energy? The intellectual and indeed emotional labor of the search-committee members from HST, none of whom were formally involved in THSTI, not all of whom had connections to India, all of whom undertook the process of sifting through four hundred applications for faculty positions? Or the hubris of Sengupta, younger than most of the other key actors yet believing that he could remake Indian science in an image of his own making? These were the animating factors behind THSTI, and they were deeply striated both at the level of global structures and of individual aspiration and affect.

Fischer's attempts to think through the relationships between structure and peopling in contemporary life sciences at a moment of its globalization, which is a development and realization of the promissory call of *Anthropology as Cultural Critique* to ethnographically conceptualize global political economies *and* personhood, through a conceptualization and inhabitation of third spaces, is apropos here. It insists on attentiveness to structure in ways that render difference visible, without resorting to relativist essentialism. Structure is not determinate; it is what elucidates relationships, across place (concerns with location, geography, and globalization) and time (concerns with history). Perhaps the most fundamental structuring factors were the differentials in hierarchy and the different perceptions of what those differentials were, as already elucidated. Thus hierarchy and power were not simply objective facts (even as there were fundamentally objective elements to it, having to do with the directions in which money and expertise respectively flowed, and to how different perspectives were heard, not heard or coded) but deeply situated, expressed through the individual and often idiosyncratic perspectives of India- and HST-based actors, who were themselves not homogeneous but striated and internally differentiated.

The most substantive difference, however, was this: *whereas the Indians had to act diasporic, those at MIT did not.* By this, I mean that for conversations to occur across the collaborating entities, the Indians had to recognize constantly where HST actors, literally and figuratively, were coming from. They had to understand a normative structure of "global" science that was being instituted as if it were placeless but that was, in fact, deeply inscribed not just by American value systems but also by MIT and HST value systems (commercialization; multidisciplinarity; problem-focused research; collaborative, nonhierarchical work environments; and betting on potential). Actors at HST, most notably Gray, constantly attempted to understand and negotiate Indian sensibilities on their own terms, but they often coded such sensibilities as "cultural difference." This had practical consequences. One was the construction of a faculty-search process that involved nine faculty members from HST, of whom only Gray and Sengupta ever visited India as part of the search. Although some of the others did have an acquaintance with India, and a couple were diasporic Indians themselves, it was believed that one could search for faculty members of "the right phenotype" simply by having the context of HST and without ever encountering THSTI on the ground in India.

A related consequence was the ability on the part of HST actors to assume *terra nullius*—the Indian institutional landscape as a blank slate that could be mapped, inhabited, and normed in the image of HST. That Indians might express different value systems and ideals of institutional development, scientific investments, or translational research consequent to cultural difference was accepted. Gray even came to understand that different sociological contexts might render different meanings of translational research desirable or operable (e.g., a more limited value to purely market-based approaches than at MIT). Yet there was never appreciation in my conversations with HST faculty or in any of the meetings I attended that included them, that Indian life sciences already had a deeply striated institutional landscape that had developed over half a century of postcolonial history, and that the positions of Indian actors reflected this. Terra nullius, of course, is the most foundational of colonial imaginaries. As individuals, actors at HST exhibited a progressive liberal sentiment about building global scientific capacity and interacted with Indian actors with a great degree of personal humility and respect. Nonetheless the fundamental structural, and structuring, aspect of the collaboration was one in which it was always possible—even easy—for HST actors to imagine India as a clean slate that could be written on. Such an imagination constructs the world as flat, constructs collaborations as simply the articulation of networks, and evacuates from itself the need for the recognition of structure, history, or conjuncture.

Such an imagination afforded the Indians, structurally, with more or less three choices: a willingness to be reinscribed through an intensely located imaginary of "the global" that comes out of a very particular institutional environment but has the power to act as if placeless; reluctant, resistant collegiality; or, simply, opposition and disengagement. All three affects and behaviors were on view from different Indian actors, in ways that pulled in different directions, enabled, engaged, or obstructed in different ways and to different degrees, and eventually proved too much of a burden for the collaboration to bear.

In this example of a para-ethnographic instantiation of third spaces, I have discussed the sociotechnical imaginaries at play in the biomedical notion of translational research and suggested that, layered onto that, is the constant importance of cross-national translation in collaborations such as that of THSTI with HST.[23] If the former represents an institutional and epistemic mobilization of the notion of translation, then the latter represents its sociological mobilization in (depending on one's location) either cultural or postcolonial terms. Additionally, there is the "translation" that is at stake in individual biographies. The story of contemporary institution building in the Indian life sciences involves that of people who have themselves lived diasporic trajectories, whose biographies have invariably entailed significant spells of study or research outside the country, usually in the United States or the United Kingdom (or, in one case, Australia). In this regard, virtually every Indian scientist who was involved in the THSTI initiative is, to use Salman Rushdie's autobiographical phrase, a "translated man" (or woman) (Rushdie [1983] 2008). Whereas virtually every Indian involved with THSTI had experienced "global" science in Anglo-American institutional environments as part of their own formation as scientists, most HST faculty rarely, if ever, experienced Indian institutional environments even as part of their active involvement in the faculty search for THSTI. They just did not have to translate themselves in the same ways as the Indians did.

Rushdie provides a counterpart to Fischer for thinking about the striated relationship between the structural and its agential/contingent/biographical others.[24] In *Midnight's Children* (1980), Rushdie asks a foundational question that links, as the entire premise of the book, the biographical to the structural: what might it mean to think of an individual's destiny as entwined with that of a nation? The story of the protagonist Saleem Sinai, and his doppelgänger Shiva, both born at exactly the stroke of midnight on August 15, 1947, as India acquired freedom from British rule, highlights this question through a magical realist mode of extreme caricature. It is a question that has to do with the role of the Indian elite as custodians of a nation in formation; the ways in which individuals shape nations and nations shape individuals (the cracks appearing in Saleem's life mirroring the cracks appearing in the foundational dreams of the Indian nation at Independence); the contingencies of fate that create differences in the biographical trajectories of those who inhabit the nation (the switching at birth of Saleem and Shiva by the nurse Mary, allowing Saleem to grow up as the son of the rich Sinai household and condemning Shiva to a life of poverty); the ironies of those trajectories as, possibly, always materializing in contingent and unexpected ways (Shiva emerging as the hero of the 1971 Indo-Pakistan war while Saleem's life has been torn apart); the constant questions of paternity and inheritance (who is Saleem's father?, a question that, even when answered, has no easy answer, and speaks not just to questions of familial kinship but also to cultural and diasporic inheritance, the postcolonial elite Indian as always, inescapably, in some measure a British creation); the dream of the nation—and the individual—as, ultimately, inscribed in a dream of a radical democratic cosmopolitanism (the image of Bombay as, constantly, the image of the ideal nation of midnight's varied children, in stark contrast to conservative authoritarian Pakistan); and, perhaps most importantly, the story of the imbrication of biography and nation as being a particularly generational story.

There is something that Rushdie is portraying that is important to understand in relation to the contemporary moment of institution building in Indian science and that speaks to a foundational conceptual striation in the understanding of the relationship between individuals and institutions as perceived by the Indian actors and those at HST in the building of THSTI. The HST actors could imagine a "global" biomedicine that did not have to transit through an explicitly nationalist sentiment (a function, in part, of the way in which an institutional context such as at MIT can self-render itself as if placeless, in spite of its absolute particularity). Yet there was necessarily always some kind of nationalist animation at the heart of the actions and hopes of the Indian actors (a function, in turn, of occupying an emergent and aspirational but nonetheless undoubtedly minor location in the institutional, financial, and reputational hierarchies of global biomedicine). Such nationalism would manifest in many forms, ranging from the desire to be a global player to a desire to shun the global and focus on national self-reliance. In varying degrees and different ways, it was a diasporic, cosmopolitan, and postcolonial nationalism, seeking to engage the (especially Anglo-American) "global" world, although often in terms different from those that had been set for it.[25]

Yet something more than nationalism is at stake here: it is the possibility of individual biography shaping a national destiny. However significant Martha Gray might have thought the "HST ethos" was, there was just no way in which she could imagine her role as a codirector of the program for thirteen years as shaping American national destiny (even just at a scientific, institutional level) in the same way. Gray's stakes were high, and she was certainly invested in HST as a model for a better way to teach, do, and institutionalize the life sciences. However, these stakes were not articulated to the nation in any explicit way. When she saw THSTI as a nodal organization that would reshape the landscape of science and its institutionalization in India, what she hoped for was a reshaping of *biomedical research* through the norms and forms that HST would provide. When Indian actors saw such a role for THSTI, what they hoped for, alongside, was a reshaping, in one way or another, of the *nation*. This differential, based as it is in the imagination of something like the HST ethos as potentially universal *because* it is not emplaced (even as it is thoroughly, specifically located, in relation to MIT, to Cambridge, Massachusetts, to the history of twentieth-century American science and technology), provides the conditions of possibility for imperialism, in structure if not in intent. Imperialism is, after all, always structural, and its power comes from the capacity to legitimately disavow intentional violence. The ways in which this would manifest at moments of cross-national, cross-cultural encounter across differentials of power were always telling.

Here, for instance, is an example that speaks especially to the different ways in which place and nation were implicitly embedded in differentially situated technoscientific imaginaries of institutional collaboration. THSTI planning meetings would occasionally involve scientists from MIT (sometimes at HST, sometimes not) presenting various "models" of institutional innovation operational there, for THSTI to take inspiration from. At one such meeting in Delhi, David Baltimore, who was on the Board of Scientific Counselors at the Broad Institute of MIT and Harvard, spoke about the institute as one such model to emulate. As was quite common in such presentations, he did so in terms of MIT's aspirations to globalize good science through the dissemination of institutional models that would facilitate its conduct, alluding to the various transnational collaborations and partnerships MIT had as an example of such salutary globalization. At this point, an Indian scientist in the collaboration asked, "If MIT is so invested in the spread of such institutional models, could you tell me why they are only being spread in other parts of the world, and not in Kansas or Alabama?" Baltimore had no response but at least had the good grace to look sheepish.[26]

There is, in addition, a generational story at stake here. The generation of scientific institutional leaders in India involved in THSTI—many of whom were at the time in their fifties—came of age as scientists and citizens between the mid-1980s and 1990s. They were in the main trained in the United States or the United Kingdom and were for the most part invested in a less hierarchical and gerontocratic institutional mindset than was prevalent in the generations that preceded them. Their coming of age also happened in a politically tumultuous time, marked by the rise of radical right-wing Hindu fundamentalist and nationalist politics, the mobilization of caste politics of both progressive and reactionary varieties, the emergence of a feminist politics that would influence legislation and social activism, the growth of a certain kind of grassroots civil society advocacy marked by events such as the Bhopal gas disaster, and India's transition, very rapidly, to a neoliberal economy from a state socialist one. The consequences of these changes were not discernible in any simple pattern across the various Indian scientists involved in this institutional initiative (and others) in the life sciences. There was nonetheless a discernible generational ethos, marked not just by different conceptions of institutional hierarchy from the past but also by an absence of a sense of neoliberal entitlement that one sees in many younger Indian diasporic biologists.

I once asked Satyajit Rath about this in regards to his own investments in THSTI. I asked him why, given his criticisms of the dominant rationales under which translational research and institutional development were being conceived, given his disagreements with the "HST ethos," given his general or openly articulated sense of despair regarding the establishment and direction of THSTI, he gives so much of his time and energy to the institution. His response: "I am an upper-class, upper-caste male in a casteist, patriarchal society. Guilt, of course."[27]

. . . .

The example of my para-ethnography with THSTI serves a number of functions. At its simplest, it demonstrates one trajectory of operationalization of Holmes and Marcus's call to refunction ethnography, through the activation and inhabitation of ethnographic third spaces. At the same time, it helps elucidate global political economies, in this case as biomedical research and the research university come to be globalized in both corporatizing and postcolonial ways. Importantly, it intercalates these structural and systemic trajectories to the ways in which they are peopled, thus rendering globalization and the postcolonial condition in terms of metropolitan desire and postcolonial diaspora. One of the things most at stake in my ethnography of THSTI concerned the elucidation of the nature of emergent global relationships in institution building for biomedical research: not just for a metropolitan academic audience, but crucially for the involved actors, at least those of them invested in cultivating reflexivity and dialogue in institutional development.

I had initially imagined this chapter as an academic book project, with some para-ethnographic and para-sitic interludes alongside. However, I decided against publishing this account as a description of THSTI's establishment for the metropolitan academe. This is largely because I could not see any way of doing so that would be simultaneously accountable to Rath's legitimate accusation of producing a relativizing account that elides the fundamental issues of power at stake in such an initiative, and I did not want it to feel like an exposé or denunciation of people I had developed relations of trust with at MIT. I should emphasize that I had the luxury of doing an ethnographic project for four years without publishing it—thus maintaining my accountabilities to the biomedical communities of practice I had worked with, but also rendering this work entirely invisible on my academic CV—because of the career stage that I was at. I already had tenure when I started this project, and I was doing fieldwork for *Pharmocracy* alongside. The professional risks entailed in such a deeply para-ethnographic endeavor would be of a different order if this were a dissertation project. Thus, even as I insist that multisituated research is feasible at the dissertation stage (see the introduction), there are strategic dimensions to conceptualizing the extent, scale, and timing of para-ethnographic and para-sitic elements of early projects, given the constraints imposed by the nature of professionalization in anthropology departments in the contemporary metropolitan university.[28]

Nonetheless, in many ways this project was a failure—not because it did not result in a monograph, but even in its para-ethnographic dimensions. Or, at least, it was a limited success. I believe that the para-site I have described, for instance, could serve as a template for operationalization of one kind of dialogic interlocution that rescripts the nature of the ethnographic encounter while potentially undertaking a comparative analysis that elucidates global political economies. Nonetheless, the limits to what it could achieve—or, more precisely, how far I could go with it—signal current institutional constraints on such experimental ethnographic modalities that go beyond projects of romantic authorship and disciplinary reproduction.

The question that I want to specifically end with is, how to think of the next steps beyond a para-site? A para-site is never intended to be the totality of an ethnographic project. It is one mode of situated dialogic engagement, which becomes strategically viable at a certain stage of a project, within certain kinds of interactional milieus. Once it is done, once it has highlighted certain things for the ethnographer and (hopefully) certain other things of value for the participating interlocutors, then what? One of the most telling elements of the para-site that I authored (which mirrored that of the para-site that Philip Grant authored with Rameen

Jehanbegloo and members of the Million Signatures Campaign) concerned the diagnosis of moments of failed conversation, almost always an incommunicability borne of speech that was not heard across differentials and hierarchies of power, institutionally consolidated and enshrined. What I was not able to do, indeed did not even have the tools to think about, was to consider how to moderate or facilitate subsequent conversations as the next step beyond incommunicability. This would have required a lot of upstream work and a clearer idea than I had of what the objectives of the facilitation could be.[29]

One imagined outcome for such work, beyond the diagnosis of incommunicability and institutional hierarchy, is the potential for building institutional reflexivity, a key ambition for Michael Fischer's imagination of the work of a refunctioned ethnography (Fischer 2003, 2009, 2018). The para-site itself potentially does so, up to a point. What rubric of outputs, however, would be generative after its completion? After the THSTI para-site, I wrote up a white paper with key insights that I learned and submitted it to the Indian Department of Biotechnology. That was more or less that and was the last I heard of it. There was also no institutional incentive for me to follow up on it further or to expend the time or energy required to turn it into an epistemic thing and follow its itinerary, since it was unlikely for any of this work to register in my own disciplinary audit cultures unless it was made legible as a work of romantic authorship, perhaps as some kind of monograph. In other words, even with shared desires to generate institutional reflexivity on the part of both the ethnographer and their interlocutors, there is a mutual absence of institutional incentive to generate the forms of longer-term para-ethnographic engagement, beyond the event, that could consolidate reflexive dialogic forms within institutional practice.

The larger question at stake here is, what is the horizon for conceptualizing ethnographic praxis beyond creating occasional spaces and forums for dialogic and collaborative reflection with one's interlocutors? I do not have an answer to this question, but it is the provocation that I want to end with—not least because pondering possible answers to this is essential to generating a feminist, decolonial ethnographic praxis that does not merely end up appropriating the native informant to our authorial ends. This, I insist, is one of the important promissory horizons for thinking a multisituated praxis; it cannot be reduced to a contractual ethics calculated purely in risk-benefit metrics; and it cannot ever adequately materialize if the endgame of ethnographic work within the space of the metropolitan university remains confined to disciplinary reproduction. The institutional ends of ethnography, and its enshrinement in anthropological pedagogy, have to be broader, more ambitious, more variegated, more open to a multiplicity of diasporic stakes and investments, such that alternative norms and forms of ethnographic practice and praxis do not remain risks that can be taken only at a certain career stage or at the margins and borderlands of the discipline. The promissory horizons of multisituated ethnography, unfulfilled in my experiments with studying THSTI, have been explored in myriad ways in the decade since my own small parasite, but there is much to be further imagined and conceptualized, not just epistemologically and methodologically, but also by creating institutional affordances and pedagogical sanction for further experimentation with both the forms and the ends of ethnography.

Conclusion

Toward a Diasporic Anthropology

I attended an *iftaar* one evening in BoKaap, Cape Town. It was a public event, held in solidarity with the Palestinian struggle. A lot of people were there; some very moving talks were given; some of the ongoing residential battles against gentrification in the area were touched upon; questions of the relationship between apartheid in Palestine and the legacy of the apartheid struggle in South Africa were articulated. We broke fast with dates; people unfurled their rugs on the ground and gave *namaaz*. The sun was setting over Signal Hill, shining translucent on the pastel-colored houses of the area. An autumnal sunset, mingling with the maulvi's voice as it carried in the air. Long sheets were spread across two perpendicular streets, food was served, and the air was filled with the gritty scent of freshly cooked *kebabs*.

The maulvi said a prayer: for all the Palestinians living under oppression, he said, and for all the Jewish people in the world who were standing up for justice. There was a certain universality to his gesture, and a world was brought into being. One that spoke of and against the violence and injury and injustice perpetrated upon certain bodies, because of their identity, but who refused, in doing so, to reciprocate that violence. A cry for justice, a promise of justice, that recognized an injustice done in the name of race, religion, and ethnicity and whose response, whose responsibility, was to name that injustice and to imagine a reciprocal horizon that exceeded its identitarianism. A certain universality, but not one scripted by the oppressor.

....

Jacques Derrida dedicated his book *Specters of Marx* (1994) to Chris Hani. Hani was assassinated shortly before the publication of the book. The book stemmed from a lecture given at the University of California at Riverside, at a conference titled "Whither Marxism?" The conference was held in the aftermath of the fall of the Soviet Union, a moment when Francis Fukuyama had declared "the end of history" (Fukuyama [1991] 2006). It asked the question of where "Marxism" was at this time and also of whether this marked the withering of Marxism, a certain end of a political program or sensibility. It asked this in America, in Southern California, hardly a place where "Marxism" had any kind of historical or political hold, and many of the protagonists in the conference were Americans or Western Europeans. Derrida reminds us, through his dedication, that there were transformative moments in world history happening elsewhere at that time, not just in the image of the West; that histories were beginning, not just ending, even as one of the most important labor leaders in South Africa's anti-apartheid struggle had just been killed, a murder that was one marker of a death of Marxist possibilities that was about more than just the tragic ending of an individual's life. What would it mean, Derrida was whispering to the reader in this dedication, if we asked the question "whither Marxism" from South Africa, at that world-historical moment of transition?

In that whisper, Derrida reveals, indeed betrays, his own diasporic sensibility. As a white male European intellectual, of course, but also as a Jewish French-Algerian, whose intellectual and political pedagogy was forged across Algeria and France. Just like Frantz Fanon's was. At the same time, entirely unlike how Frantz Fanon's was.

The early 1990s, when Fukuyama's history was ending, when a post-apartheid South African present was emerging, was a time of historical transition in India as well, where I was completing college. A time, simultaneously, of the assertion of the power of so-called backward castes in representative electoral politics; of the emergence of hard-line, right-wing Hindu fundamentalism; and the embarkation of the Indian government upon a program of neoliberal economic reform. A time when I left India, after a college education entirely funded by Indian taxpayer money, for further study in the United Kingdom and then America: the beginning of an itinerary that has led to my becoming a diasporic academic. And somewhat accidentally, without ever having been formally trained in the discipline, an anthropologist.

....

I visited South Africa for the first time in 2015, and something happened that I had not expected: I fell in love with the country, in ways that I still do not fully comprehend. This made me anxious, especially as I contemplated doing ethnography there. I worried about romanticizing, misunderstanding, and miscoding a deeply complex place at an extremely fragile moment in its history in terms of my own biographical history that had learned, in very thin but consequential ways, to think of the anti-apartheid struggle as the defining world-historical political struggle of my time while growing up. Nonetheless, over time and gingerly, I have developed a set of ethnographic curiosities and interests, and I am in the process of beginning a new research project there. This book was written in the midst of this emergent engagement with South Africa, one that, of course, aspires to intellectual rigor and sociological insight yet cannot but be marked by my association with this place, at this moment in history, at this time in my own intellectual formation, an association that is affective, transferential, an inheritance of sorts. Another, and another kind, of diasporic itinerary.

....

My first diasporic itinerary, to America, ended in citizenship. It took a while to get there, twenty years in fact, and it took Donald Trump's election to get me to take the plunge. India does not allow dual citizenship, and I was not ready to give up mine. Until I was forced to: not just because being a noncitizen in America no longer felt safe, but because being a nonvoter no longer felt responsible. It helped (although it was a perverse kind of help) that the India I grew up in, that the generations of my parents and grandparents helped to build, was—is—being shredded to pieces. By a nationalism that does not allow one to love one's own country in different ways to those it mandates. That does not allow one to express a shared humanity—a certain universality—if it includes those that a self-anointed majority proclaims to be Other. Some of my leftist academic friends tell me that this residual nationalism I feel is idealism at best, something much darker at worst; I am told that the ideal of nation is itself a corrupt and exclusionary one, that there is no way one can feel affinity for nation and not be aligned with something fundamentally violent. There are enough examples to bear this out and to back their claims. And yet the India that I grew up in always had a certain universality, a certain humanity, a certain *insaniyat*; but it is torn apart now, replaced instead by insanity.

It was with this dual ambivalence—toward the idea of nation itself, and my own attachments to the Indian one that once existed—that I took my oath of American citizenship in early 2018. It was on a Tuesday, three days after Trump had described African nations as "shithole" countries. Before we took the Pledge of Allegiance, the presiding judge, John Tharp, said that he wanted to say a few words. He started by telling us that there were one hundred and ten of us in the courtroom that day, from thirty-eight countries. He named all thirty-eight, in alphabetical order, starting with Australia and ending with Zimbabwe. He told us that it was very important for us to understand, especially in these times, that we were all getting citizenship not because of our wealth or education or social status or special skills, but because of a commitment to an ideal; that even though he had been an American citizen since birth and everyone in the room was becoming one later in their lives, his citizenship meant nothing more than anyone else's in that room; that every one of our citizenships had exactly the same meaning and value. He hoped that people would bring their memories and cultures and traditions with them as they became Americans citizens. Judge Tharp had been nominated to the court by George W. Bush.

....

FIELD NOTES, AUGUST 15, 2019

Yesterday was one of those incredible days of fieldwork, where so much happens in so many different directions, in what feels like a culmination of some sort (full moon!). I had two extraordinary interviews with lawyers on either end of the day—the one in the morning worked on the huge silicosis and TB class action settlement, which was just certified two weeks ago. And in the evening, with another couple of lawyers from the ****, a legal advocacy group—a 4 hr conversation that spanned all sorts of issues, but especially a really fascinating case they have been involved in representing drug-resistant prisoners with TB.

Each of these conversations is substantively important in and of itself, but I'm trying to weave in a component of life history into each of my conversations with lawyers, because there is such a strong generational component to this project. And the generation of these three lawyers is particularly interesting, because they were old enough to have lived through apartheid and are therefore aware of the impor-

tance of the constitutional project, are not opposed to it the way the "born free" generation is . . . but they are also white, and so the intersections of race and generation in articulating a relationship to, and a career trajectory toward, the law is so fascinating and complex. I'm still learning how to weave this into interviewing, but (inspired by the work of David Scott) I think I'm getting a little better at it.

In between that, I went to the Wits Art Museum with Stacy to view a scroll by Dumile Feni. Feni is arguably the most famous Black anti-apartheid artist, who was exiled to London in 1968 and died in exile. He painted this scroll, which is 53 meters long, over 7 years, from 68–75. It has only ever been publicly displayed once, a very short section under glass, so hardly anyone has ever seen it. Stacy was commissioned to write a fiction on the scroll just after we met, and she's been interested in Feni because, among other things, he had TB (and she is very interested in the link between TB and creativity). So she got me to come along, into the bowels of the museum. We weren't allowed to handle it or photograph it, as it could only be touched by the Keeper of the Scroll (quite literally), and it was just a most extraordinary, moving, incredible work. Hard to know how to describe it, or how I will even write about it, but it is a kind of animation. An animation both because of the form of the scroll, which reveals things as it unfurls, but also because his work is so much about animism and shape-shifting, people turning into animals, living beings turning into nonliving beings . . . as the scroll unfurls, for instance, you see a picture of a snake becoming a trumpet. The recurring motifs, throughout, are of mother with child. And there are scribbles alongside, all in English, all in fragments, which I noted down, and which is its own form of poetry.

Then at night I got home, and read the news that the Modi government, on the eve of our Independence Day, has now approved an amendment to its anti-terror law, to give powers to the central government to designate an individual as a terrorist and seize his or her properties. Meanwhile, the hot and urgent topic of conversation of those in my class position in India is who the next coach of the Indian cricket team will be. So as I continue to be moved by the immense complexities of this country that I am learning about, I am mourning the loss of my own. It is poignant, difficult, and beautiful to be among these constitutionalists, many of whom fought the brutality of apartheid to build this fragile place such as it is, as I see fascism take root and triumph with astonishing swiftness in the place where I grew up. As I think about the questions of generations, this is the transferential ethnographic relationship that haunts me.[1]

. . . .

We, who write for a living, always do so at certain times, from certain places, out of certain situations. We also do so, today, in uncertain times, from uncertain places, out of uncertain situations. This book, a call for a "multisituated" ethnographic praxis, is no different. As I stated in the introduction, I write at a certain (and uncertain) disciplinary conjuncture, when the norms and forms of ethnographic practice are potentially at an inflection point. When they are certainly at stake. When experiments in both the practice and teaching of ethnography are proliferating, but also when the university is under attack from both authoritarianism and financialization. When the academic job market is precarious. When the ideological inheritances of canonical norms and forms remain strong, even as they sit uneasily with the decolonizing aspirations of many ethnographic practitioners. A praxis, in such a situation, cannot be "method," reducible to a mechanical formula. It is a mode of attunement, of being and relating to the world and its others, of embodying curiosity and openness, of attending to difference without romanticizing it. Its ethos is deconstructive at its core.

In starting this book, I had situated the concept of a "multisituated" ethnography in a certain intellectual, institutional, and political conjuncture. In ending it, I wish to situate my own writing of it. Both in relation to a certain autobiographical conjuncture in my research trajectory and immigrant itinerary, but also in relation to the shape, aspirations, and dilemmas of my own politics, as an ethnographer, as a teacher, and as a citizen. For there is something to say here, about my own vexed relationship to certain pressing political questions today concerning the liberal metropolitan academy (and decolonizing critiques of it from within) and how it manifests in a constitutive antinomy, and a certain hesitation, in the anti-phallogocentric and postcolonial politics that I articulate.

Even as universities are caricatured and attacked from the right as being too "liberal," one form of contemporary violence enacted and justified on American campuses today is the liberal acquiescence of right-wing politics, whose resonances and stakes became heightened in the age of Trump. In the week after the 2016 US presidential election, I was approached by students at the University of Chicago's Pritzker School of Medicine to help them conceptualize emergent institutional conversations at the school, already underway, on "inequality and inclusion." Students were keen to ensure that such conversations could seriously explore what it means to think about race in the Trump regime, as doctors-in-training at a university hospital on the South Side of Chicago, with already vexed histories between the university and the surrounding community that has manifested most recently in protests against the closure of the university hospital's trauma center, the only one serving the entire South Side. Yet when I accompanied some of the students to discuss this with an administrator at the school, we were informed that the most pressing question concerning identity and inclusion was the marginalization of the voices of white conservative students. This conversation took place on a Friday, ten days after the election. Four days previously, the campus had been plastered with swastikas. The ways in which institutions mediate the tensions between racism and fascist xenophobia on the one hand, and student demands for decolonization and antiracism on the other, including and especially through recourse to liberal ideas and ideals of free speech, are neither abstract nor innocent. This is just one kind of violence liberalism enacts on marked bodies in pedagogical environments, one of many instances when a decolonizing critique seems to require a critique of liberalism as much as it does a critique of liberalism's intolerant and xenophobic antagonists. For liberalism too rarely refuses, let alone exits, phallogocentrism.

That a decolonization of ethnography should fight against colonial legacies and epistemologies is obvious. A more vexed question in these times, one that I want to conclude this book with, is, what should the relationship of a decolonial project be to liberalism? Ethnography today is perhaps uniquely suited to offer a certain epistemic requiem for liberalism, a function of ethnography's grounding in a relentless attentiveness toward and methods for an articulation, conceptualization, and understanding of difference, as itself grounded in structures and histories of power, hierarchy, and inequality.[2] Even as ethnography comes with its own baggage, inheriting epistemic modalities of objectification and appropriation that are deeply phallogocentric. The ongoing decolonizing critiques among its practitioners, in which this book participates, are an attempt to confront the ghosts of these epistemic histories and to forge a future promissory agenda for its practice. This requires more than simply "playing nice" with one's informants, and it must go beyond the proceduralism of informed consent, which is itself grounded in a liberal rationality that too often justifies objectification and appropriation as long as it is done with permission, presuming free expression of the liberal individuality of the contracting parties to the ethnographic encounter. One must decenter and dislocate the ethnographic object itself, deconstruct the conceptualization and role of the native informant, recalibrate and proliferate the norms and forms of ethnographic practice. I have suggested some ways of doing so, through a reading of exemplary ethnographies and non-phallogocentric reflections on the conceptualization of method. This is hardly an exhaustive book in this regard, and what emerges is not some kind of comprehensive formula or synthetic program—just a consideration of certain modalities of fieldwork and concept work that inhabit and rescript the difficulties of ethnographic practice, of ethnography as praxis.

Yet there is a hesitation here, an uncertainty, a quivering of my own. For even as this book is a relentless argument against phallogocentric modes of ethnographic knowing, it is also, more implicitly and from a place of greater solidarity, a relentless argument against certain trajectories of decolonizing thought that valorize radical alterity at the expense of a certain universalist aspiration. One sees these trajectories at multiple levels and scales in both the metropolitan and global Southern academe—from a student's refusal in my university to take a class because it would involve reading Clifford Geertz (whom presumably one does not need to read because he is a white man), to the Afro-pessimist repudiation of pan-Africanism in certain manifestations of the decolonization debate in South Africa (and its potential and unintended articulations to the emergence of a xenophobic politics in the South African public sphere), to certain increasingly glib and fashionable critiques of liberalism in the metropolitan academe (critiques that often contain important conceptual and political lessons while being inattentive to the multiplicity of liberal inheritances), or to the radical ways in which liberalisms are being rescripted in the global South (for instance, through strategies and pragmatics involving the law and constitutionalism). In other words, even as I share skin with the ethnographic requiem to liberalism, this book is simultaneously a visceral, insistent refusal of that requiem. Not because I disagree with the sentiment behind the requiem, but because too many critiques of liberalism assume a homogeneity to it that, in my mind, too easily accept its most hegemonic and oppressive framings to be its essential, fundamental, defining ones.

The critique of phallogocentrism at the heart of the book is an insistence on attending to difference and otherness: something that ethnography as a method is uniquely suited to doing. But there is an equally insistent critique alongside, a refusal to let radical alterity be the point at which explanation runs out, at which an alternative politics rests . . . especially if that articulation of radical alterity takes recourse to some notion of identitarian virtue grounded in the historical experience of oppression. This is why, at the end of the day, it is Spivak rather than Strathern that I rest my own arguments with. For her deep mourning of the recognition that the establishment of alterity as a necessary *and insufficient* condition for justice; for her obsessive concern with her own inheritance; for her relentless recognition of the fact that diasporic inheritance is not pure or virtuous, but implicated in all manner of historical and ongoing injustice. Somewhere within all of this lies the contradiction that the call for an infinite partiality of connections as the mode of thinking relationality is not enough, that the promise of justice entails the thinking of a certain universality as well, albeit Otherwise to dominant or hegemonic modalities of constructing and appropriating the universal.[3]

....

Let me consider this with an example of my emergent research interests in constitutionalism. Both in my new research in South Africa and in my tentative forays into civic participation in the American democratic process as a citizen, I find myself involved in experiencing and articulating a certain ethos of constitutionalism, fully aware of its fragilities and its potential for violence, but also more and more cognizant of its multiplicities. My project in South Africa has to do with relationships between health and law, specifically in ways that claims to health are made through the law, often through constitutional recourse.[4] This is a function of the fact that South Africa has a constitutionally enshrined fundamental right to health. I wish in my work to attend ethnographically to the catachrestic manifestations of this rights-based politics. Catachresis, as elaborated by Jacques Derrida, speaks on the one hand to a misuse or "abuse" of a word or concept, especially relevant to thinking the movement of a concept from one context to another (Derrida 1974). This alludes, on the other hand, to the original incompleteness of that word, metaphor, or concept.

Spivak's work further develops a sense of catachresis as a postcolonial political modality, where "misuse" of a concept is precisely its recontextualization: a recontextualization that does not merely "abuse" the meaning of a concept but gives it fresh meaning, in relation to its resituated *political* context.[5] Thus, Spivak emphasizes how catachresis is the *political* resituation of semantic malleability. One sees this well in relation to the idea and ideal of rights. Formally, rights-based constitutionalism is of liberal, Euro-American provenance. Yet in contexts such as the South African one, rights get torqued, most substantially through the Bill of Rights that affords a politically salient place to socioeconomic rights *as* fundamental rights. In other words, "rights," in its Euro-American provenance, out of its Euro-American genealogies, is not a closed concept. It comes to be at stake, both conceptually and politically, in its "global Southern" instantiations.

There is more to say, but this is not the time or book or stage of research to do so, and there are many moving and emergent and unsettled parts to this new research. Suffice to say that attending to the catachrestic functioning of rights as they instantiate in postapartheid South African constitutionalism—which is a historical (and nonhistoricist) as well as a comparative attentiveness—requires ethnographic attunement to a certain ethos of constitutionalism. One that is undoubtedly indebted to Euro-American liberal political ideals and genealogies, but that cannot be reductively assumed to simply derive from them or be an instantiation of them "elsewhere." One that is undoubtedly, deeply, contested today, but not in the same ways that pronounce the death of liberalism from the metropole.

It has been difficult for me to articulate a textured and differentiated relationship to these global Southern liberal political forms in the American university, not just because of the financialized, corporatized imperialist naturalization of a certain liberal universalism as normative, but more proximally because those closest to me intellectually and politically have too often already written its obituary. I remember the sense of utter alienation I felt at a conference in my university, when the speaker, who is a scholar I like and respect, answered a question by saying, "Well, of course, we're all united in our dislike of liberalism!" and the room burst out laughing. "Not me!" I was screaming in my head, though hardly a liberal myself, thinking of how the alternative to liberalism in India has, so quickly, become an intolerant and grotesque *il*liberalism. Thinking most of all of the Eurocentrism attendant to the insensitivity to the possibility that liberalisms elsewhere might be scripted Otherwise; an incomprehension of forms of otherness that, often for very progressive reasons, refuse radical alterity to Western ideals as the horizon of justice, instead inhabiting their inheritances otherwise. A certain universality.

Why did the alternative to Eurocentric liberal hegemony have to be radically other to liberalism itself, I wondered? Even as I recognized the decolonizing impulses of this mode of critique, what stuck in my throat is that in a certain ironic way, the valorization of radical alterity contains its own potential for Eurocentrism, its own inability to recognize the myriad inheritances of a European Enlightenment project gone global, such that the articulation of and insistence upon difference from elsewhere often expresses itself diasporically, full of contradictions, and without the purity of incommensurable otherness. Instead, there are all the impurities of inheritance, often itself patriarchal, occasionally queer, always fractious and at odds with itself. It is often with certain universal aspirations of its own, thoroughly noninnocent but also potentially emancipatory. The easy argument of this book is the one it wages against a phallogocentric disciplinary history and against a corporatizing, financializing metropolitan university. Its more difficult, unresolved, and irresolvable argument is with itself, an argument between its insistence on the partiality of all perspective as a feminist and decolonizing epistemic stance, and the diasporic voicing of a certain ideal of universality Otherwise, a refusal to abandon the liberatory and transformative potential of Enlightenment thought, even (especially?) as enshrined in postcolonial liberal political forms. This is the anguish of recognizing the insufficiency of the establishment of difference for a promise of justice (see chapter 2) and the necessity of contending with the multiplicities of diasporic inheritance, especially as they make their way into both fieldwork encounters and classrooms.

To reiterate, liberalism is legitimately and thoroughly critiqued in South Africa (and India) as well, also for good reason, also from the left. The person who had taken me to the iftaar at BoKaap is herself an anthropologist with complex diasporic itineraries and investments; that evening, she explained to me with patience and clarity the failures of the postapartheid promise of South African constitutionalism, a failure that I had heard about in related ways from a number of my other interlocutors as well. The substance of what I was hearing there was not dissimilar to the progressive Euro-American critiques of liberalism that I encounter in the American university, many of which are vital intellectual and political contributions to our thinking and learning today. Yet its tone was so radically different. It was not a dismissal but a careful, vexed, almost mournful reconsideration; not the repudiation of an ideal itself but a questioning of how ideals can become hollow if they are not substantiated, if their actual itineraries are quite literally immaterial for too many of the people they are supposed to benefit. There are requiems to liberalism being sung everywhere, but their intonations differ. Not every critique of liberalism from South Africa is careful or considered or mournful; there is also immense anger. It is unthinkable for me, however, to imagine that particular kind of laughter that I heard in my university, its certitude, its presumptuousness, which can come only from the unmarked space of centrality.

Staying attuned to the immensely different political meaning that results from these differential atmospheres within and through which critique is voiced matters. Not because one voicing is more authentic than another. Not because the endgame is consensus on what constitutes a good or virtuous politics. Rather, because the decolonial critique of metropolitan ideals and practices runs the risk of reinscribing a metropolitan parochialism that, including in the name of radical alterity or antihegemonic critique, too often fails to hear other kinds of voicings, other tonalities, other stakes, even when they are voiced from within the walls of the metropolitan university itself.

....

This ambivalence, marked by my unequivocal refusal of phallogocentrism alongside a conflicted refusal of a certain repudiation of the inheritances of political modernity (enshrined in the practice of ethnography, the discipline of anthropology, the institution of the contemporary university, but also in the ideals and philosophies of liberal thought), is reflected in some of my key engagements in this book. I reflect on three such engagements: with comparison, with sight, and in my citational practices.

In chapters 1 and 2, I consider comparison alongside scale as somewhat equivalent potential multisituated modalities. While presenting a version of chapter 2 at a conference, "African Ethnographies," at the University of the Western Cape, I was, however, asked, why comparison at all, given the deeply colonial history of comparison as a practice, a colonialism that endures in the ways in which it continues to be used purely as the analyst's framing of the problem, especially in its more sociological renderings? A further provocation, then: why not scale *instead* of comparison, rather than scale alongside comparison?

The question reflects a move to concerns with scale in anthropology over the past two decades, marked in some sense by Anna Tsing's seminal *Friction* (2004) but also engaged with by a range of other anthropologists in the development of their method.[6] It is one that I have thought about considerably since being asked it. My answer can only be provisional, and it betrays what I am about to say subsequently about sight and citation. It speaks to the broader problem of how to deal critically, methodologically, and diasporically, in a multisituated fashion, with the political question of colonial (and liberal) inheritance.

I consider scale alongside comparison in the development of a multisituated modality because that reflects in the method of the ethnographic work that I do. Scaling an analysis and problem, from the nano- to the macro-, in order to think structural political economic questions through the contingency of proximal, intimate ethnographic encounters, is at the heart of my own ethnographic method. At the same time, my work has always been explicitly comparative: between India and the United States for my first two books, and between South Africa and India (and the United States) for the new project that I have embarked upon. It is how I have been taught, it is how I have learned to think ethnographically, and, while acknowledging all the colonial residues of the history of the comparative project in anthropology, I insist upon its epistemic value in shedding light on difference, which has always been at the heart of ethnographic praxis. My stakes therefore lie in *supplementation* rather than supplantation. What would happen if we supplemented the comparative project with the diasporic, multisituated question: comparison *from where*? This is not merely a question of identity but one of autobiography, itinerary, and inheritance (see chapter 3). It is not just the metropole that compares. Immigrants (and diasporic beings of other kinds) compare too, all the time . . . the question is, how do we generate other and Other kinds of comparisons, which might also be potentially better comparisons, which stay attentive to the situations out of which comparisons are made, situations that might potentially radically change figure and ground and undo and remake the comparative project itself (albeit never with purity, innocence, or mere virtue)?

This speaks to a broader stake and method of the book, which is that it is not providing *solutions* to the problem of phallogocentric ethnographic inheritance that endures in the current practice, teaching, and disciplining of ethnography. Rather, each chapter stays with the trouble of elements of ethnographic praxis—scaling, comparison, encounter, and dialogue—in ways that are simultaneously critical of (exploring or probing at their limits) and invested in them. Some ethnographers scale as part of their method; others compare; others provide templates for ethnographic evocation and conceptualization at the scene of the intimate encounter; yet others explicitly generate new dialogic modalities. Some do more than one of these. Some do these in more thoughtful, less phallogocentric ways than others. But—and this is an implicit insistence of the book, and at the heart of its politics—there is no innocence to any of these. Decolonization is not, cannot be, about the virtuous, pure, or morally unimplicated path. I believe it is about the proliferation of new norms and forms of ethnographic practice and narration, including and especially in ways that tread old problem-spaces in newly vigilant ways. I want to stay with the trouble of comparison (and scale, and encounter, and dialogue) because I think there *are* better ways to do each of these practices as part of an ethnographic method. I do not want to adjudicate one of these praxiological modalities over another. I would prefer to think through how to compare Otherwise, rather than (just) thinking Otherwise to comparison.

There is a very similar sense of investment in relation to the question of sight. There is a way in which I privilege sight as the sensory modality of ethnographic practice in this book, especially when I consider ethnography alongside and through photography (chapter 3). Yet again, this is simply in part because sight is what I do. Or, rather, photography is what I do, and it is a practice I have thought about in itself and in relation to ethnography. The question that is at stake is not about photography as a representative practice, but, rather, what modes of attention and attunement are called into account when we see the world through a camera. I believe this is important, on its own terms, for three reasons.

First, this mode of bodily attunement—which goes well beyond just a visual attentiveness—shares skin with the kinds of bodily attunement called for in ethnographic practice. How does thinking with and through one practice allow us to think with and through the other? Especially, second, when the stakes of the matter exceed the representational or sociologically analytical function of ethnography/photography, as I insist they do? The core argument of this part of the book concerns the stakes of ethnography in generating what Gabriele Schwab calls a "literary knowledge" (Schwab 2012): an epistemic and evocative modality that, I suggest, can be thought not just through the novel (as Schwab does) but also through the photograph, albeit in specific and nonidentical ways. Third, however, the photograph, like writing, is not innocent. It is both attached to histories of violence but also (Derrida's insistence in relation to the question of writing) is a fundamentally violent practice. Thinking through the constitutive violence of sight is at the heart of the work of this chapter.

Therefore, as with the question of comparison, my point is not to abandon sight for other, less phallogocentric modalities of bodily and sensorial attunement, but rather to stay with the trouble of sight. This is a faithful insistence on a Derridean deconstructive modality, which is expressed throughout the book and indeed constitutes its politics, learning from the way in which he—and those who follow his method such as Spivak—insists on the constitutive violence of writing while maintaining an intimate attachment to writing as a practice and praxis. This cannot and should not preclude other modes of sensory ethnographic engagement and attunement by others who are more qualified to elaborate those in terms of multimodal ethnographic possibilities.[7]

There is something more fundamentally at stake here, however, and it concerns the foundational influence of Donna Haraway's argument for "situated knowledges," which in many ways structures the argument of this book writ large (Haraway 1988; see also the introduction). On the one hand, the very core of Haraway's argument, in its call for a privileging of partial perspective, is a radical call to go beyond sight (a "view from nowhere" objectivity being, as it were, constitutively wedded to sight). Hence, a serious internalization of Haraway's lesson does necessarily enjoin us to think beyond visual modalities of engaging the world, in order to generate better and more non-phallogocentric modes of knowing. On the other hand, I reiterate the other call at the heart of Haraway's essay, the haunting call that animates the text, at the moment she asks "with whose blood were my eyes crafted" (585)?

This is not simply a diagnostic question that critiques sight as the locus of objective and objectifying knowledge. It is also a reflexive, autobiographical, situating (and, through Schwab, I insist a transferential) question, a question of inheritance. This book is thoroughly, intimately, obsessively, argumentatively concerned with the question of inheritance, which is a question at once of transference (through Schwab), of affect and intimacy (through Berlant), and of deconstruction (through Derrida and Spivak). In other words, what is at stake here, again, is to stay with the trouble—in this case, with the trouble of sight, with all its constitutive violence. To emphasize what I said earlier about comparison, my argument throughout the book is that decolonization cannot be a supplantation of colonial modes of knowing. It has to contend with the inheritances of those epistemic modalities (including as they express or repress in ourselves, as producers of ethnographic knowledge). This is especially important for diasporic ethnographic practitioners (of all sorts), whose inheritances can never claim the virtuous space of pure alterity to the colonizing, masculinist gaze, who are always implicated within and indebted to these modes of seeing and knowing in all manner of ways, but not necessarily in the ways in which such modes of scopic knowledge are canonized in the teaching of disciplinary histories.

Staying with this trouble of inheritance is also at the heart of the citational practices I employ in the book. This is a book that is engaged with and indebted to a range of feminist scholarship: the work and methods of Donna Haraway, Marilyn Strathern, Gayatri Spivak, Gabriele Schwab, Lauren Berlant, Kathleen Stewart, and Shawn Michelle Smith (to name just some) animate my thinking. Yet I also engage considerably with some canonical white male figures, especially Clifford Geertz and Roland Barthes, in shaping my arguments in chapters 2 and 3, respectively (and indeed with Marcus and Fischer, whose work provides the foundational grounds for my analysis). What does that do for the postcolonial vision and diasporic critique of this book?

The politics of citation is one of the most important questions in relation to the decolonization of anthropology (and of thought more generally).[8] At the heart of this politics is not just a question of whom one cites, but also of where one cites them: how are citations emplaced? Who do we read through whom? When I teach undergraduates about anticolonial and postcolonial thought, I often tell them that the real praxis of this class is to think: how might we understand the world differently if we had to read Fanon before Marx and Freud for a change? This question of emplacement is at the heart of curricular debates around decolonizing anthropology in South Africa today; it was also at the heart of pedagogical experiments I have undertaken myself in teaching the canon, both at the University of Chicago (while teaching "Systems" with John Kelly) and earlier at the University of California at Irvine. And yet one does not decolonize by ignoring inheritance. This is not a privileging of the voice of the white male intellectual: it is an acknowledgment of the fact that what we know and how we know it is shaped in some measure by modes of inquiry that have both colonial and masculinist provenance, and we do not exit those epistemic politics by simply not reading them, not citing them.

The decolonial politics of citation sometimes play out in the classroom in intolerant ways: I had mentioned a student dropping my "Multi-si(gh)ted" seminar because we were reading Geertz in it, for example. This was not a principled, intimate, ethical engagement with and critique of Geertz; it was a refusal to read him at all, to engage with him at all, an anti-intellectualism justified on the grounds of identitarian virtue. Mine is not a conservative justification of the white male's right to "speech." It is rather a methodological insistence that critique (especially in its deconstructive ethos) cannot be repudiation; it has to be a form of intimate engagement. That includes (especially) with one's adversaries, with the genealogies of thought and action that one critiques, even perhaps that one loathes, not least because they continue to inhabit us, and disavowing them will not rid us of the inhabitation. Only careful, considered, generous, and generative critique will.

I use Geertz and Barthes in this book in the manner that I do simply because they are important to my thinking of ethnographic praxis in the manner that I articulate. Geertz's insistence on a translational and interpretive modality for thinking the relationship between experience-proximity and experience-distance is, for me, a very important conceptual and methodological move in the history of anthropology, one that at once allows for a certain move away from a Malinowskian romantic authorship wedded to "becoming Other" and that serves as an important condition of possibility for Marcus and Fischer to even think multisited and multilocale ethnography in the manner that they do. Geertz is important to the genealogies of *Anthropology as Cultural Critique*, and genealogies matter. Then there is Geertz's crucial insistence about "reading natives' inner lives . . . as poems," which is an important prelude to thinking beyond the purely representational or sociological function of ethnography, opening up to the possibility of chapter 3 and thinking the evocative function of ethnography as a form of literary knowledge. This does not remove the phallogocentrism at the heart of a Geertzian anthropology. It does, however, make him an important (to me, even obligatory) point of passage in the development of my argument.

Similarly, Barthes has helped me think my photographic practice, even as *Camera Lucida* is a phallogocentric book. My reading of Barthes is through Shawn Michelle Smith, whose critique of Barthes is exemplary because of the empathy that she brings to her reading. This specifically, as I argue, has to do with the empathy for the nonreproductive body. Barthes is important not just for what he says about photography—which is both a part of my inheritance in thinking and doing the practice, and phallogocentric—but for a consideration of the reproductive politics of photographic circulation. This articulates directly to my critique of institutional pedagogy that is confined to concerns with disciplinary reproduction. Barthes (through Smith) allows me to think the possibilities for queering circulation—which does not at all have to attach to a pure or virtuous non-phallogocentric politics in other aspects of his writing (about photography or anything else). As I insist throughout this book (and especially in my reading through Spivak of Tayeb Salih's *Season of Migration to the North* in chapter 2), a decolonizing praxis does not have to be pure and is rarely virtuous.

My insistence on staying with the trouble of comparison and of sight, or of inhabiting the deeply vexed and troubling inheritances of our white male intellectual ancestors, attaches to an absolute intellectual and political investment in keeping open the promise of a certain universality as the horizon of our epistemology, ethics, and politics. An insistence that runs through Derrida's articulation of the spirit of deconstruction, that the ethics of the Enlightenment is unconditional, even as Enlightenment is as yet in *l'avenir*, the future-to-come.[9] I fear that it has become extremely conditional for some strains of decolonial thought. I do not want this book to become a polemic against such expressions of decolonization, but my various insistences and refusals are a manifestation of an insistence in thinking decolonization in ways that are not reducible to identity or alterity as the final grounds of a decolonial politics. Multisituatedness is therefore not about a valorization of the authenticity of radical, identitarian difference. It is about looking elsewhere and elsehow, about allowing for reciprocities of sight and other forms of sensory experience, with other eyes and other bodies that displace and decenter the ways in which, to use Michel-Rolph Trouillot's formulation, "the history of Anthropology is a mirror of the history of the west" (2003: 1). This involves at some level objectifying the West, in thick, comparative, nonreductive, and nonsimplifying ways, such that the Western project that objectifies the Other comes at least to be subverted (if never quite fully inverted).[10] Most of all, it is about a certain diasporic attunement.

This book is at its core an argument for recognizing that ethnography is a diasporic practice. In important ways, this is a reflection of the discipline of anthropology becoming postcolonial. However, the sense in which I use the term "diaspora" is more expansive than this. It speaks to all manner of intersectional movements of ethnographic practitioners (including those not located in anthropology, in the metropolitan university, or even in academic research), especially those whose subjectivities are marked by race, gender, sexuality, and geography, and whose commitments are toward a feminist, postcolonial politics. A project of disciplinary pedagogy that reproduces itself without cognizance of this can never truly decolonize anthropology from its phallogocentric inheritances. At the same time, a pedagogy that *reduces* diaspora to already given identity categories such as race, sex, class, or gender is also not good enough. My insistence on a diasporic sensibility is not a repudiation of a white male anthropology, but a plea for creating the pedagogical and institutional spaces for inhabiting its inheritance Otherwise.

This cannot just be about care—caring for students of different backgrounds and experiences within our disciplinary spaces, for instance— though that is undoubtedly essential. It is also, I insist, epistemic. About the kinds of knowledge that are sanctioned, the kinds that are normed, the kinds that are constantly forced to justify themselves. A diasporic anthropology necessarily involves the reconceptualization of the norms and forms of ethnography itself. Crucially, it must reconsider the constitutive place of the native informant in the generation of ethnographic knowledge, in ways that develop situated knowledges. The insistence on incommensurable ways of knowing, being, and relating is vital to this, but it cannot be its only (or even primary) end. It must also develop dialogic forms of ethnographic praxis that attend to differentially situated and articulated aspirations toward commensuration, even for a certain universality, that nonetheless reject the dominant scripts and hegemonic understandings of center and periphery, foundational and derivative, through which commensuration is too often enforced. This is an ethnographic attunement that itself can never be innocent or objectively diagnostic, that cannot but be haunted by the ethnographer's own autobiographical traces and inheritances.

I am arguing for an ethnographic ethos, and an anthropological signature, whose stakes are not about making the strange familiar or the familiar strange (a commonly used mantra that immediately begs the diasporic question: strange and familiar for whom?). Rather, I argue for one that stays with the trouble of the complex epistemic and institutional relationships between reproduction and kinship, kinship and alterity, alterity and diaspora, and diaspora and reproduction that lie at the heart of ethnographic practice and disciplinary pedagogy. These relationships can only be thought, and taught, through a dialogic praxis of intimate encounters that generate an epistemology of scaling and comparison Otherwise, in differential (and differentially political) ways that deconstruct, dislocate, and decenter phallogocentric modes of knowing. And also, I suggest in conclusion, by keeping alive a certain universality, not of the hegemonic and intolerant kind that obliterates difference, but of that more uncertain and tenuous, substantively cosmopolitan variety, of the kind voiced by the maulvi during his prayer in BoKaap. Not just an elucidation and celebration of difference as an end-in-itself, but a disposition that keeps open possibilities for interlocution and solidarity across difference, including and especially within our most proximal pedagogical spaces.

Notes

Introduction

1 I experienced some of these problems acutely the one year that I co-taught
the introductory "Systems" course in the Anthropology Department at the
University of Chicago in 2013. This course is legendary in departmental and
disciplinary lore. My pedagogical colleague was John Kelly, who accepted my
suggestion that we design a syllabus to teach the disciplinary canon alongside
a postcolonial, feminist counter-canon. The class would meet twice a week.
On Thursdays, we designed a sequence that began with Boas and proceeded
sequentially through twentieth-century metropolitan anthropology. On
Tuesdays, we began with Mahashweta Devi—feminist, postcolonial, non-
anthropological literature about indigeneity—and worked backward. I am
deeply indebted to the enthusiasm and generosity with which Kelly embraced this experiment. Yet it ultimately failed, for various complex reasons,
not least of which was the fact that the subject positions of the teachers
mapped on to the content that we respectively designed, such that the
diasporic anthropologist became the bearer of the counter-canon: the marked
subject taught by a marked subject position. The ways in which this double
marking was received by a cohort that itself was constituted by both metropolitan and diasporic anthropology students, including indigenous students
and students of color, revealed in stark ways the violence and discordance
between canonical inheritances and the ways the discipline is currently being
peopled.

2 In this regard, Christopher Newfield's *Unmaking the Public University* (2011)
is particularly important. Also see Chris Newfield, "As Trump Privatizes

Education, Dumping Identity Studies Is the Worst Possible Advice," Remaking the University, November 25, 2016, http://utotherescue.blogspot.com /2016/11/as-trump-privatizes-education-dumping.html, for a more recent analysis in the wake of Donald Trump's election. Bill Reading's *The University in Ruins* (1996) is a classic that remains relevant.

3 See Lionel Trilling's story "Of This Time, Of That Place," which contains the haunting question, asked by Tertan, a student of modern drama, "Of this time, of that place, of some parentage, what does it matter?" (Trilling 1980: 78). The form of this question, asked within the space of pedagogical interaction in the American university, engendering reflexive questions about the nature of pedagogy and the modern university in a manner that is attentive to history, location, and inheritance, inspires the form of analysis that this book undertakes.

4 For an elaboration of the relationship between an epistemic milieu and histories of social thought in nineteenth- and twentieth-century Germany, see Dominic Boyer's *Spirit and System* (2005). For a postcolonial exploration of intellectual milieus in the thought of Caribbean anticolonial thought, see David Scott's "The Temporality of Generations" (2014).

5 I am thinking of the programmatic importance of *Argonauts of the Western Pacific* (Malinowski [1922] 2014) in structuring a disciplinary imaginary of what fieldwork ought to be.

6 The critical theory mini-seminar, "Multi-si(gh)ted: Pharmocracy, Postcoloniality and Perception," consisted of three lectures delivered at the Critical Theory Institute, University of California at Irvine, March 2018. In the course of writing this manuscript, I came to recognize that it was situation, not sight, that was at the core of the supplementarity to multisited and multilocale ethnography that I was after. Hence, this book is called *Multisituated*, even as the seminar and lectures that gave it form were called "Multi-si(gh)ted."

7 The examples of this are too numerous to cite, but I think especially of the formative importance of the ethnographies facilitated out of Xerox Palo Alto Research Center (PARC) in the 1980s and 1990s, which opened new directions in the anthropology of science and technology even as it proved to be a harbinger of corporate-based ethnography in high-tech worlds for purposes such as user interface studies. For important examples of this earlier work, see Lucy Suchman's *Plans and Situated Actions* (1987) and *Human-Machine Reconfigurations* (2006: especially chapter 1, in which Suchman tells the story of some of her early research at Xerox PARC) and Julian Orr's *Talking about Machines* (1996).

8 Again, there are far too many examples of this to do justice to in a note, but I especially want to mention recent work at the intersection of ethnography and the environmental sciences that has experimented with and expanded possibilities for what one can do ethnographically with environmental data.

See, for instance, Sara Wylie's work in this regard, which intervenes in the generation of environmental health knowledge, with an orientation toward making extractive corporate practices visible, through methods that combine ethnographic research, sociological analysis, design, and the creative arts (see https://sarawylie.com/, last accessed November 15, 2019). This does not preclude the anthropological monograph, as her extraordinary book *Fractivism*, written alongside this collaborative work, testifies (Wylie 2018). This is part of a broader body of work on environmental data justice that is emerging collaboratively, for instance, through the Environmental Data and Governance Initiative, of which Wylie is a founding member along with other historians, sociologists, geographers, philosophers, and STS scholars who adopt an ethnographic approach to visualizing, preserving, and reflecting upon environmental data in the age of Trump (see, for example, Dillon et al. 2017). See also the work of the Disaster STS Network and The Asthma Files, platforms developed by Kim and Mike Fortun and their collaborators, which demonstrates a similar ethnographic ethos that is designed toward a combination of description, conceptualization, advocacy, and accountability (https://disaster-sts-network.org/, https://theasthmafiles.org/, both last accessed November 15, 2019).

9 It is hard and not particularly useful to draw definitional boundaries about who "is" or "is not" an anthropologist. Nonetheless, I wish here to acknowledge STS scholars Donna Haraway and Sheila Jasanoff, philosopher of science Sabina Leonelli, geographer Gail Davies, literary scholars Gabriele Schwab and Lauren Berlant, art historian Winnie Wong, and political scientist Lisa Wedeen. Each of them is an ethnographer who is not trained or located in an Anthropology Department (though most are, to paraphrase Haraway, "anthropologists with a transit visa"), and I have learned enormously about the practice and conceptualization of ethnography from each of them from the examples their work has set and also from personal conversations over the years. I do not engage specifically with all of their work in this book, but each of these scholars has provided significant inspiration for its ethos.

10 The term "concept work" was introduced by Paul Rabinow (2003) and has developed in generative ways through conversations in the Anthropological Research on the Contemporary (ARC) Collaboratory over the past decade and a half (http://anthropos-lab.net/, last accessed July 21, 2018). I prefer the term to "theory," which is often reified as a "thing" rather than as a process with its own praxis and method that can be learned and cultivated.

11 See chapter 1 for an elaboration of the distinction between the research topic and object of study, which is at the heart of ethnographic methods pedagogy developed by Kristin Peterson and Valerie Olson at the University of California at Irvine.

12 I might add, at an earlier iteration of these interfaces than those seen recently in the course of the so-called ontological turn in the human sciences, as seen in the interest that anthropological journals such as *HAU* took in STS. (See the "colloquium" on the ontological turn in *HAU*, edited by John Kelly, in its 2014 summer issue.) This more recent interest constructs a genealogy for STS that derives very much from Michel Callon's and Bruno Latour's actor-network theory to trace its conversations with (especially French philosophical) anthropology. It does not do justice to the multiple other genealogies of STS that have informed anthropological work and ethnographic sensibilities for the prior two decades, especially those that come out of feminism and are in strong conversation with and debt to the "1980s moment" in the human sciences. This genealogy would, for instance, consider Sharon Traweek's *Beamtimes and Lifetimes* (1988) to be equally or more foundational to an STS/anthropology interface than Latour. This speaks to other kinds of long twentieth-century genealogies of the anthropological discipline: Traweek was trained by Gregory Bateson, and the Batesonian methodological echo is strong in this seminal comparative ethnography of high-energy physics communities in the United States and Japan. Yet Latour, in a remarkably ungenerous review, attacked the book as not being the kind of ethnography that STS should do (Latour 1990). Kim Fortun and Michael Fischer, in separate articles in the *HAU* colloquium, argue for a broader historical understanding of the anthropology/STS interface than the ontological turn-obsessed moment allowed, one that especially attended to questions of the political in less masculinist and Eurocentric ways (Fischer 2014; K. Fortun 2014). My own training and investment in the anthropology/STS interface comes out of this *longue durée* genealogy that emerges out of the strong feminist and postcolonial commitments of the 1980s, as this book will explore.

13 See, for instance, Simpson 2007 and Jackson 2010.

14 At Chicago, this led Julie Chu to elaborate the "Methods" curriculum into a two-part sequence (now renamed "Modes of Inquiry"), the second part of which is exclusively dedicated to students doing small practicums using two creative forms that go beyond participant observation. This class has thus far had two iterations: the first taught by Chu and myself; the second by Chu and Mareike Winchell. Students have explored practices such as documentary filmmaking, photography, digital cartography, drawing, poetry, and fiction writing.

15 These critiques span postcolonial, feminist, critical race, and indigenous perspectives, and they are too numerous to cite exhaustively. Two seminal examples that continue to inspire me are Talal Asad's "The Concept of Cultural Translation in British Social Anthropology" (1986), for how power enters into processes of metropolitan cultural translation, and Audra Simpson's "On Ethnographic Refusal" (2007), for a method of writing about the

Mohawk in ways that decenter colonial assumptions of "self" and "other" that structure the legacy of anthropological writing about indigeneity.

16 Bhabha's *Location of Culture* is a seminal postcolonial intervention into thinking the question of postcolonial diaspora along and through postcolonial Black radical thought, especially Fanon's *Black Skin, White Masks* ([1952] 1994). See also Du Bois's *The Souls of Black Folk* ([1903] 2016), where he introduces the important notion of double consciousness.

17 For an articulation of the postcolonial stakes and resonances of translation, see Niranjana 1992 and Sakai 1997.

18 I am grateful to my students in the "Multi-si(gh)ted" seminar for relentlessly pointing this out, in myriad explicit and implicit ways. See also the virtual session "Mother Antihero: Reports from a 21st Century Field," organized for the 2018 Society for Cultural Anthropology meetings by Amber Benezra, Hanna Garth, Ann Kelly, Tina Harris, Dana Powell, Emilia Sanabria, Megan Carney, Cari Maes, Daisy Deomampo, Jessica Hardin, Olga Soodi, Laurie Willis, Rosario Garcia Meza, Clare Chandler, and Emily Yates-Doerr (https://displacements.jhu.edu/mother-antihero-reports-from-a-21st-century -field/, last accessed July 23, 2019).

19 The politics of such refusal is complex and emerges out of political conjunctures. I was at a talk at the University of Cape Town in 2017 that discussed genealogies of English studies in the country; at the end of the talk, a student eloquently responded that we do not need to be reading Shakespeare in this decolonizing moment because he was a white man. Closer to home, I had a student at the University of Chicago drop my seminar on multi-si(gh) ted ethnography because we were reading Clifford Geertz, whose own white masculinity (which does manifest quite strongly at many moments of his writing) was antithetical to her expectations from a seminar concerned with postcolonial and decolonizing politics. My attempt to think ethnography Otherwise is not simply based in an identitarian quest for authorial radical alterity. Having said this, the politics of these identitarian refusals, of course, contains its own genealogies; it is impossible to understand the conversation in Cape Town without situating it within the politics of the student protests there in the aftermath of the #RhodesMustFall campaign. In the context of anthropology, one cannot think of the white male history of the discipline in South Africa without understanding, among other things, the history of anthropology as a racist "science of the people" (*volkenkunde*) that provided epistemic justification for apartheid. There are good reasons to refuse white male authorial histories, at least for some people, some of the time. At the same time, I take seriously Dipesh Chakrabarty's insistence on the importance of understanding postcolonial thought (including the possibility for even thinking the political in the postcolony today) through its European inheritance in ways that do not reduce a decolonizing politics to a quest for what Leela Gandhi has called "postcolonial revenge" (Gandhi

1998; Chakrabarty 2000). In other words, we do not have to like the people we have read or the identities they represent, but we do need to understand their thought to understand the postcolonial worlds we inhabit today. My point here is not to take sides on what constitutes an adequately decolonizing epistemic politics. It is necessary both to remain engaged and invested in imperial genealogies of knowledge production, and also to understand decolonial demands for its absolute repudiation in certain places and times. I am grateful to many friends and colleagues, especially Jean Comaroff, John Comaroff, Thomas Cousins, Colleen Crawford-Cousins, Kelly Gillespie, Stacy Hardy, Julia Hornberger, Charne Lavery, Achille Mbembe, Daniel Moshenberg, Neo Muyanga, Leigh-Ann Naidoo, Michelle Pentecost, and Hylton White, for providing me a range of perspectives on movements to decolonize the South African university.

20 See Centre for Humanities Research, "African Ethnographies," June 6, 2018, http://www.chrflagship.uwc.ac.za/african-ethnographies/.

21 I do not fully explore the genealogy of scalar analysis, either in anthropology or in the human sciences more generally. Anna Tsing's *Friction* (2004) is the seminal meta-methodological reflection that brought the question of scale to prominence for my generation of anthropologists. Yet thinking of scale and scale making in the world, and using scalar analysis as a method, has, of course, been at the heart of the practice of critical geography for decades; this cross-disciplinary influence on ethnographic practice is equally important to consider.

22 This critique can be found throughout Strathern's work. Some of its most radical implications, especially in relation to its consequences for conceptualizations of property and Western/colonial notions of possession (as dependent on the prior ontological purification of persons from things), are to be found in her *Property, Substance, and Effect* (Strathern 1999).

23 See Centre for Humanities Research, "African Ethnographies." Thanks to Kelly Gillespie and Annachiara Jung Forte for this formulation.

24 I think here of John Comaroff's provocations on the "end of Anthropology" (Comaroff 2010).

1. Scale

1 I take this essay as a point of departure because it is where Marcus most clearly articulated his call for multisited ethnography, and because it has come to be the most cited point of reference for multisitedness, especially in graduate student dissertations and grant proposals. Thus, it has become an almost programmatic referent. It is important to recognize that this is not the first or last time or place where Marcus has concerned himself with the concept, and subsequent re-visitations have significantly developed or

revised aspects of his formulation here (see especially Marcus 2005). Marcus is also not the only person to have concerned himself with the problem-space of multisitedness. (See especially Marcus and Fischer's call for "multi-locale ethnography" in *Anthropology as Cultural Critique* [1986] for an example of an earlier iteration of the concept with distinct resonances that one can see developed through Fischer's oeuvre.) For an elaboration of the relationship of the notion of multisituated ethnography to earlier ideas of multisited or multilocale ethnography, see the introduction to this book.

2   Marcus's formulation does not fully abandon the Malinowskian paradigm even as it seeks to go beyond it. Indeed, Marcus points to *Argonauts of the Western Pacific* (Malinowski [1922] 2014) as the exemplary text that provides a method for "following the people." My attempt to think beyond Malinowski is embedded in conceptual, epistemological, and political stakes rather than literally with his method, as explained in the introduction. This will hopefully become further evident as my argument proceeds.

3   In this regard, see also Michael Fischer's essay "Culture and Cultural Analysis as Experimental Systems" (2007).

4   Indeed, an alternative to the interpretive turn in the 1960s was the turn to "cognitive anthropology," a behavioralist form of sociocultural anthropology that invested itself in a more positivist, Galilean imaginary of ethnography, drawing especially on experimental psychology and evolutionary biology. See D'Andrade 1995 for an account of the development of cognitive anthropology.

5   In addition to making a programmatic point, *Anthropology as Cultural Critique* proliferates descriptions of exemplary ethnographic texts. It thus serves as an archival bibliography, in which the examples can be read within the arc of the programmatic ambitions Marcus and Fischer are laying out.

6   I know that I am not the only student of Marcus and Fischer to return to these lines. Both Kim Fortun and Kristin Peterson quote this paragraph in the introductions to their respective books, as structuring the method they have employed (K. Fortun 2001; Peterson 2014).

7   Tsing's ethnography is breathtaking in its scope, and it includes fieldwork or interviews in at least eight countries, in addition to collaboratively developed elements with the Matsutake Worlds Research Group (see https://people.ucsc.edu/~atsing/migrated/matsutake/, last accessed July 19, 2018). For exemplary "world-systems" multisited work from an earlier generation that literally follows the object of study, see Sidney Mintz's *Sweetness and Power* (1985). See also West 2012 and Paxson 2013 for other exemplary works that follow the object, and Appadurai 1986 and Latour 1988 for vital methodological programs along these lines.

8   Just missing my arbitrarily decided time of publication here is Lawrence Cohen's *No Aging in India* (1998), which was published shortly before I began my dissertation and served as a huge inspiration to me in my own work, even

though I find its scale and complexity to be inimitable. Another inspiration was Michael Fischer and Mehdi Abedi's *Debating Muslims* (1990), which I reference in chapter 4.

9 An earlier article version of the book, "The Elegiac Addict," focuses exclusively on Alma's story, which is what I primarily attend to in my discussion here (Garcia 2008).

10 Again, an earlier article version of this book, "The Vertiginous Power of Decisions," provides a useful précis (Steinberg 2016b).

11 To understand this in fuller context, it is important to read *Will to Live* (2009), Biehl's companion ethnography to *Vita*. It is his more explicitly institutional analysis.

12 Elaborating the stakes of this challenge is at the heart of my reading of Gayatri Spivak in chapter 2, in order to consider a multisituated sensibility as postcolonial.

13 See the introduction for my stakes in thinking beyond the monologic form of ethnography, as well as chapters 3 and 4 for an elaboration of its dialogic and trialogic stakes.

14 See Jacques Derrida's *Of Grammatology* ([1967] 1976) for his account of the violence of the scene of writing in Lévi-Strauss's encounter with the Nambikwara chief and also Derrida's *Specters of Marx* (1994) and *Politics of Friendship* (1997) for an elaboration of the work of mourning and the politics of friendship in the development of an ethical relation to an Other. See also Gabriele Schwab's psychoanalytic reading of "The Writing Lesson" in *Imaginary Ethnographies* (2012), which I return to in chapter 3.

15 See chapter 3 for an elaboration of the notion of a desire for a life through an engagement with the work of Lauren Berlant and its importance to a multisituated sensibility.

16 It is also a site of haunting: Biehl wonders, in his account, what conditions allowed for such different trajectories for himself, who also came from a similar background to Catarina, such that he ended up in the privileged space of metropolitan academe rather than being socially abandoned like she was. The encounter generates an autobiographical moment of transferential identification that haunts the text. See chapter 3 for an elaboration of the stakes of haunting and autobiography to a multisituated sensibility.

17 It is worth marking this at a disciplinary moment that bristles with multi-specific, ontological, and anthropocenic turns, all of which try to decenter the human for their own firmly grounded and well-articulated ethical and political reasons.

18 See Hayden 2010, 2011 for a development of the notion of politics of the copy.

19 This, it could be argued, is the method of the historian, one whose stakes came to be particularly prominent with the growth of movements of "micro-

history" and "histories from below." Carlo Ginzburg (1980), whose work is exemplary of such a historiography, elaborated such tracking practice as one that developed in the late nineteenth century in relation to a series of epistemic practices across domains. Ginzburg also showed the noninnocence of such tracking projects and their imbrication in colonial projects of rule (even as tracking methods are an important part of indigenous modes of knowing). The politics of tracking as imported from Western as opposed to indigenous epistemes, and the work of appropriation entailed within the former, is important to note.

20 See also Rabinow 2002, from which Ong and Collier (2005) draw their formulation of the term. I am particularly taken by Ong and Collier's move to think of globalization as a problem-space, not just as process—a more conceptually expansive and ethnographically challenging provocation than their move in the same essay to focus on assemblages, a concept that explicitly privileges process at the expense of structure. This is not the place to enter into an extensive critique of the assemblage concept, but see especially Rabinow 1999 and Marcus and Saka 2005 for developments of and engagements with the concept. The specific philosophical genealogy through which Ong and Collier develop their notion of anthropological problems, through the formulations of Michel Foucault, Hannah Arendt, and Karl Polanyi, is also too Eurocentric for my taste. It does not reflect the panoply of ways in which some of the essays of their *Global Assemblages* volume engage anthropological problems, in ways that develop more interestingly comparative frameworks for analysis. See chapter 2 for a development of my stakes in other kinds of comparison that are adequate for non-Eurocentric modes of posing anthropological problems. I should emphasize at this point, lest I be misread, that "non-Eurocentric" modes do not mean abandoning, or not citing, European theorists. It speaks rather to the figure-ground relationships and assumptions through which problems get posed. Ong herself, in her earlier seminal work *Spirits of Resistance and Capitalist Discipline* (1987), provides an extraordinary example of how to do so.

21 I borrow this distinction between research topic and object of study from Peterson, who structures her own methods pedagogy at UC Irvine through this distinction. To quote from an early iteration of her syllabus:

RESEARCH TOPIC

A Research Topic is a *conceptual description* of your dissertation project. It situates your ethnographic data within larger political events, economic concerns, prevailing societal ideas, affect, discourses, institutional changes or any other macro contexts for which the significance of the project can be located. The Research Topic answers the question: "what is the dissertation project about and why does it matter?"

OBJECT OF STUDY

An Object of Study is your *ethnographic focus*. Examples include: "affective labor," "marine biodiversity prospecting," "digital piracy," "autonomous space," "medical stability operations," "diversity management," "interfaith groups," "productive security." It is simultaneously material and conceptual in that it is something to be studied while at the same time it leads you to answering/analyzing your overarching research questions. Your Object of Study is usually not singular in scale but rather can have multiple layers, identities, iterations, lives, etc. That is, it hitches together all the different concepts and ideas you are grappling with in your Research Topic. The Object of Study answers the question, "what is the dissertation project's ethnographic focus and how does it help you conceptually connect to all of the elements of your Research Topic?"

RELATIONSHIP BETWEEN RESEARCH TOPIC AND OBJECT OF STUDY

The Research Topic and the Object of Study need to be thought of as relational, as having equal weight as if each sit on opposite sides of a balancing scale. *They must actively engage each other; they must be connected.* For example, in first attempts to understand this relationship sometimes students can easily make the Object front and center but the Research Topic is not yet clearly articulated. To help crystalize the Research Topic, you need to make sure that the Object doesn't become lazy. By this we mean that the Object can't simply be "marine bioprospecting," or "autonomous space," or "interfaith groups," etc.—that is, it can't just function as a placeholder.

The object has to become active in a way that makes the aims, stakes, and significance of the project legible. Think of all the anthropology projects that have been concerned with "identity" (or labor or modernity, or markets, or religiosity, etc.). Multiple dissertation projects may take "identity" as an object of study, but the Research Topic that "identity" is linked to varies drastically across projects. It is important to show how the connection between the Object and Research Topic makes the stakes of your own project unique.

Peterson has subsequently developed her "Methods" pedagogy at UC Irvine in collaboration with Valerie Olson. Peterson and Olson are in the process of writing a book that will elaborate these and related distinctions.

22 See chapter 2 for my discussion of planetarity, through a reading of Spivak.

23 Fortun has mentioned to me the importance of Maurice Blanchot's *The Writing of the Disaster* (1980) for her, as she was in the field and grappling with this epistemic impossibility that so easily threatened to turn into ethnographic paralysis.

24 It is well worth reading Joseph Masco's *The Nuclear Borderlands* (2006) alongside this. The book, also a seminal multisituated ethnography of toxicity, considers the contemporary American nuclear state through an ethnography of Los Alamos National Laboratories, which cannot but be a situated ethnography of New Mexico. In a stunning introductory account that has resonances with Fortun's parallel conjunctural situation of "Bhopal" out of the Indian and American/global political moment of 1984, Masco runs a fifty-year history of New Mexico in the aftermath of the establishment of Los Alamos alongside a five-hundred-year history of settler colonialism in the region.

　　Parenthetically, it is worth pointing out that the "New Mexico" that emerges in Masco's account is quite different, empirically and politically, from the one that emerges in Garcia's. Masco's New Mexico is located squarely within the realm of settler colonialism and indigenous dispossession; Garcia's, very much in relation to a "Hispanic" New Mexico, shows the inequities and violence of immigration. Thinking political solidarity across parallel dispossessions is neither obvious nor easy. In Fortun's account, the parallel dispossessions of industrialism in Bhopal and the Gulf Coast are temporally adjunct but spatially disconnected. Masco's and Garcia's accounts trace dispossession in the same place, but theirs are two processes of vastly different *durées*. If the scalar disjunctures of the former are spatial, then those of the latter are temporal.

25 I think here of Stephen Colbert's badgering of Ta-Nehisi Coates for "hope" in the age of Trump's racist America, and his increasing frustration at Coates's refusal to oblige. See *The Late Show with Stephen Colbert*, October 3, 2017, https://www.cbs.com/shows/the-late-show-with-stephen-colbert/video /UQmb_R_o8FyDjmN3v6XfiojIQtf3PSYK/ta-nehisi-coates-trump-is-the -first-white-president/. Much as I admire Colbert, this is a textbook example of the white metropolitan, liberal desire to have those who bear the burden of white metropolitan violence also bear the burden of white metropolitan conscience. I have much more to say about white metropolitan desire in chapter 2, through Spivak.

26 Jill J. Tan, class response to Fortun's *Advocacy after Bhopal*, March 1, 2018.

27 See K. Fortun 2012 for an elaboration of discursive gaps and discursive risks in relation to an anthropology of late industrialism.

28 Again, see chapter 2 for an elaboration of this question of planetarity. I return to the question of collectivity in relation to global environmentalism in chapter 3, when I discuss Tim Choy's *Ecologies of Comparison* (2011).

2. Comparison

1 In all of these examples (with good reason), the entities being compared are across nations, but this is not the only axis across which comparisons might be made. For instance, Marilyn Strathern locates her concerns with comparison in relation to Melanesianist anthropology, specifically the terms through which systems of kinship and exchange are explained through comparisons between "highland" and "lowland" Melanesian societies. I discuss the importance of Strathern's comparative method subsequently.

2 See Marcus and Fischer's preface to the second edition, in which they pull back from the idea(l) of repatriation as a central stake or intervention of the book (Marcus and Fischer 1999).

3 For representative (but no means comprehensive) examples of analyses of neoliberalism, see Melinda Cooper's account of the capitalization and neoliberalization of the life sciences (Cooper 2008); David Harvey's diagnoses of neoliberalism and its relationship to accumulation by dispossession (Harvey 2003, 2007); Neil Brenner, Jamie Peck, and Nik Theodore's analyses of the spatialities of neoliberalism (Brenner, Peck, and Theodore 2010); work by scholars following and developing Michel Foucault's notion of governmentality and applying it to questions of contemporary neoliberal governance (Rose 2006); anthropologists involved in the elucidation of the "global assemblages" of neoliberalism (Ong and Collier 2005); and Foucault's theorization of *homo economicus* as the subject of neoliberalism, elaborated upon by Wendy Brown (Foucault 2008; Brown 2015).

4 In the Indian context, a powerful critique of the Nehruvian modernist project started being voiced from the left in the 1980s (see, for instance, Nandy 1983; Viswanathan 1997; Uberoi 2002). The subaltern studies project showed the hegemony of liberal nationalism and developed into a critique with many shades and degrees of allegiance and nonalliance to liberal political modernity. These shades are too extensive to reference here, but Partha Chatterjee's development of the notion of political society as an empirical counterpoint to, and political critique of, liberal notions of civil society is particularly important in the context of the argument I am developing here (Chatterjee 2004, 2011).

5 Geertz defines "experience-near" and "experience-distant" concepts, drawing on the psychoanalyst Heinz Kohut, as follows: "An experience-near concept is, roughly, one which an individual—a patient, a subject, in our case an informant—might himself naturally and effortlessly use to define what he or his fellows see, feel, think, imagine, and so on, and which he would readily understand when similarly applied by others. An experience-distant concept is one which various types of specialists—an analyst, an experimenter, an ethnographer, even a priest or an ideologist—employ to forward their scientific, philosophical, or practical aims. 'Love' in an experience-near concept; 'object cathexis' is an experience-distant one" (1974: 28). See also Kohut 1978.

6 This is at the heart of Geertz's reading of Malinowski's diaries in "From the Native's Point of View." He refuses to get into the question of Malinowski's ethics as simply a question of his character; the question of ethics for Geertz is an intensely epistemological one.

7 For an exploration of the question of translation from a linguistic anthropological perspective, see Susan Gal's "Politics of Translation" (2015). It is worth noting that cultural translation as an ethnographic ideal has a long lineage, indeed a Malinowskian one. By the time he writes *The Coral Gardens and Their Magic* ([1935] 1978), Malinowski is explicit in his assertion that the task of anthropology is "to translate the native point of view to the European" (ix). The epistemic differences between Geertz and Malinowski then concern the how: *how* does one translate in an epistemologically authoritative manner? The Malinowskian ideology that I am writing against here is one that assumes and inscribes a certain notion of fieldwork—as based in a certain kind of romantic, masculinist authorial presence—as the condition of possibility for such translation to occur. The utterly nondiasporic Eurocentrism—where a differently situated anthropology is not even within the scope of a methodological imaginary—is all too obvious in Malinowski's quote above.

8 Thus, Strathern articulates a problem-space not dissimilar to Marcus and Fischer's in *Anthropology as Cultural Critique*. Though writing contemporaneously, Marcus and Fischer do not cite Strathern. In *Partial Connections*, Strathern cites and critiques *Writing Culture* extensively but primarily engages with Stephen Tyler's essay "Post-Modern Ethnography" (1986) and his argument for the evocative function of ethnography. She does not cite *Anthropology as Cultural Critique* (though she does write about her relationship to cultural critique and deconstruction in *Reproducing the Future* [Strathern 1992b]). I suspect this is simply a function of nonoverlapping conversations, but it makes for an odd failure of dialogue between two works and three scholars who are in many ways concerned with similar issues, albeit from different vantage points and with different stakes. The conversation has been well and truly joined among their progeny, however. I learned to think with Strathern through the uptake of her work by feminist anthropology and STS, especially in California. I was taught Strathern by Donna Haraway; I learned the stakes of thinking with Strathern, and some particularly subtle ways of doing so, thanks to conversations with Cori Hayden and Tim Choy, students of Haraway and Anna Tsing. (Hayden subsequently worked with Strathern as a postdoctoral fellow.) Some of Strathern's students at Cambridge have subsequently become my closest peers, especially Emilia Sanabria, who has taught me to think about questions of pharmaceutical value in ways I could never have managed on my own. Thus, Strathern's work has acquired meaning for me through its own diasporic travels more than it has through its interventions in British social anthropological debates. (Sanabria too does not work

within the confines of those debates but is located in France and performs her ethnographic work explicitly through her diasporic stakes as a French-Colombian anthropologist of Brazil who trained in the United Kingdom. See, for instance, Sanabria 2016.)

9 See the introduction to this book for an elaboration of Haraway's idea of situated knowledges and its epistemological and political importance (Haraway 1988).

10 There are disjunctures between the problem-spaces of feminism and anthropology, and those like Strathern who inhabit both are themselves diasporic scholars, accountable to different communities of practice. It is important to reiterate that diaspora exists across domains of praxis that are not just cross-national, but that rather traverse different kinds of intellectual and political domains. See Strathern's essay "An Awkward Relationship" (1987a) for a development of the way she thinks methodologically about the relationship between anthropology and feminism. See also her engagements with feminism in *The Gender of the Gift* (1988) and *Reproducing the Future* (1992b), for an elaboration of how feminism assumes Western concepts about labor, individuality, and property.

My point here is not to come out on the side of Strathern against some unified "Western" feminism. My own readings of Gayatri Spivak in this chapter, and of psychoanalytic feminist approaches that rely on an idea of individuality as the basis of trans-individual relationality in chapter 3, suggest both the differentiated and often-diasporic constitution of "Western" feminism and the importance of Western ideas of individuality to feminist praxis. As someone who has been formed by debates in Indian feminism, I also recognize the absolute importance of Western concepts and ideas to postcolonial feminist praxis (for which, see especially the introduction to Rajeswari Sunder Rajan's *Scandal of the State* [2003]). Rather, I am signaling here the particular Strathernian relationship to a Western feminist project, which is at once a relationship of solidarity and friction, in ways that have methodological and political stakes and consequences. This is especially so in its articulation of and relationship to incommensurability, as I elaborate next.

11 See Strathern's essay "Out of Context" (1987b) for an elaboration of her relationship to poststructuralism.

12 It is important to note at this point that I am forcing a reading not just across disciplinary anthropological traditions (American and British, though neither Marcus and Fischer nor Strathern are orthodox members of these respective genealogies) but also across political conjunctures. Strathern's work at this time must be situated as a response to Thatcherite Britain, which she does in bluntly unambiguous terms in *Reproducing the Future* (1992b) and *After Nature* (1992a). Specifically, as Ashley Lebner points out,

Strathern is writing against an idea of the individual that becomes weaponized in a Thatcherite politics of individualism (Lebner 2019).

While Reagan's America articulated a similar political configuration, the particular conjunctural situation of Strathern's work and her specific arguments and refusals have to be understood out of a very particular epistemic-intellectual-political configuration of Thatcher / the British university / British social anthropology, which is quite different to the milieu out of which Marcus and Fischer were writing. Many thanks to Emilia Sanabria for emphasizing this point to me.

13 Kim Fortun has thought extensively about multisited ethnography through the problem-space of pedagogy. See, for instance, her essay on pedagogy in *Theory Can Be More Than It Used to Be*, which outlines the development of her pedagogy at Rensselaer Polytechnic Institute (K. Fortun 2015).

14 Relatedly, this reflects continuing *longue durée* Cold War legacies, if it renders value to the security state.

15 For a reading of the place of Bhuvaneswari in "Can the Subaltern Speak?," see R. Sunder Rajan 2010.

16 Strathern's consideration of anthropological (and other kinds of humanistic or social scientific) knowledge production within the contemporary British university's "audit cultures" is worth thinking alongside (Strathern 2000). Audit cultures are not the same as financialization, but both reference processes of the capitalization and corporatization of the metropolitan university.

17 For an elaboration of a manifesto for politics "without guarantees," see Derrida 1994.

18 For an elaboration of this point, see especially Spivak 2000. For a situation of these financialized logics within the history of World Bank structural adjustment programs, see Spivak 1994. For an ethnographic consideration of microfinance in Bangladesh, see Lamia Karim's *Microfinance and Its Discontents* (2011); of microcredit in Egypt in terms of processes of dispossession, analyzing the costs to long-term forms of economic value, see Julia Elyachar's *Markets of Dispossession* (2005). For a contemporary historical account of feminism as investment, through a conceptual genealogy of human capital and situated out of the United States and Bangladesh, see Michelle Murphy's *The Economization of Life* (2017). Thinking a critique of international human rights paradigms as they have developed in the "post–Cold War" world alongside trajectories of financialization over the past quarter century is a vital exercise. Reading Robert Meister's *After Evil* (2011) alongside his *Justice Is an Option* (2021) is a good way to do so.

19 See Spivak's translator's preface to Mahashweta Devi's *Imaginary Maps*, a collection of short stories (Spivak 1991). Spivak's reading of one of these stories, "Pterodactyl," is at the heart of *Death of a Discipline*.

20 It is very important to emphasize what should be an obvious point, which is that deconstruction is not merely a "taking apart" but is always an-Other kind of putting together. The idiotic obituary to Jacques Derrida in the *New York Times* did not understand this. See Jonathan Kandell, "Jacques Derrida, Abstruse Theorist, Dies at 74," *New York Times*, October 10, 2004, https://www.nytimes.com/2004/10/10/obituaries/jacques-derrida-abstruse-theorist-dies-at-74.html.

Also, I have found it particularly difficult to talk about imperialism in America, including to liberals and progressives, many of whom have drunk the Kool-Aid of American exceptionalism such that it is precisely *not* recognized as imperialist. I encountered a terrifying instance of this blindness at a debate I attended at the Art Institute of Chicago in 2016 between Asra Nomani and my former undergraduate student Hoda Katebi, on the politics of the hijab (see Chicago Humanities Festival, "Politics and Clothing: The Hijab," YouTube, June 8, 2016, https://www.youtube.com/watch?v=twqAwtUV2D0). Nomani reiterated her well-established position against the hijab, as reflective of fundamentalist Islamic patriarchy. Katebi, who is a fashion blogger and herself wears the hijab, defended it. The debate largely went along anticipated lines (albeit marred by mutual bad temper), until Katebi reframed the debate. In response to a critique of the authoritarian Iranian state by Nomani, Katebi asked whether we should not be considering the role of American imperialism in the twentieth century in the history toward and of authoritarianism in Iran. The audience, no doubt full of liberals, hissed and booed Katebi; the auditorium in the Art Institute suddenly became a hostile space. Katebi as the hijab-clad face of alterity was fine; Katebi as the diagnostician of American imperialism was intolerable. In the question-and-answer session, another former undergraduate, Shiro Wachira (herself an immigrant from Kenya), got up and asked the audience to reflect upon their own inability to hear Katebi's diagnosis of imperialism. Both Katebi and Wachira had read their Spivak.

21 See Chinua Achebe's "An Image of Africa" (1977) for an important reading of *Heart of Darkness* as a racist text.

22 Thinking with Virginia Woolf beyond *A Room of One's Own*, I cannot but help think of the opening to *Mrs. Dalloway*, "I will just get the flowers myself" (Woolf [1925] 1998). There is something profoundly poignant about the quotidian nature of gender relations and inequities in that sentence. I thank Stephanie Taiber's photography for helping me see this.

23 Elaborating this juxtaposition is beyond the scope of this argument, but in this regard, I want to point to Joseph Masco's thinking of planetarity alongside Spivak's. Masco shows that some of the institutions that have developed the most sophisticated modes of thinking beyond the global to the planetary include the US security state with its logics of preemption

and perpetual war, as developed in the global war on terror, and Big Oil with its scenario planning for a world after climate change. Planetarity is as appropriable as it is necessary. See, for instance, Masco 2010. It is also worth pointing to Dipesh Chakrabarty's development of the notion of planetarity, which he argues, in the context of climate change, represents limits to the possibility of thinking the political (Chakrabarty 2018, 2021). Thus, planetarity is not simply a scale up from the global; it is a worldly imaginary of a different order altogether. Conceptualizing what collectivity means in this regard is an altogether urgent, yet fraught and perhaps even impossible, task. Deconstruction has always concerned itself with the urgency of the impossible promise, as the grounds and task of politics.

24 See, for instance, Spivak's essay "Constitutions and Culture Studies" (1990), which I will discuss shortly. This insistence on the multiplicity of universalisms animates much of Spivak's reading of Devi (in *Death of a Discipline* and elsewhere), even as she recognizes the importance of a strategic essentialism in relation to the politics of indigeneity (for which, see especially her translator's preface to *Imaginary Maps* [Spivak 1991]). It also animates her current research on W. E. B. Du Bois (and the diasporic and postcolonial itinerary of his own thought and work) in the Du Bois archives in Accra, Ghana, which additionally involves reading Du Bois with and through Bhimrao Ambedkar (Spivak 2018).

25 Strathern's method does, however, allow for such description, especially when it is ported into different kinds of situations, histories, and political conjunctures. I think especially of Cori Hayden's current work on generic drugs in Mexico and Argentina, itself a comparative project, which takes the question of how similarity and difference are constituted as the ethnographic object. Thus, she reframes the question of the circulation of generic drugs in terms of what she calls the politics of the copy, showing how frameworks of similarity and difference operate to define whether drugs are "innovative" or not, concomitantly defining the ways in which property relations are configured and their circulations policed (Hayden 2010).

I do not want to posit Hayden as simply "Strathernian" in any reductive sense, though I see a strong Strathernian influence in the ways she thinks about kinship as a problem of relatedness, similarity, and difference. Hayden did train with Strathern as a postdoctoral fellow, after PhD training at the University of California, Santa Cruz, where Strathern's influence is strong. I read Hayden's work as a diasporic manifestation of a Strathernian comparative method.

26 In the essay, Spivak engages with Ackerman's then-unpublished manuscript.

27 In this regard, see Darryl Li's *The Universal Enemy* (2019), which is an ethnography of jihadis in Bosnia that, as the title suggests, insists upon jihad as

itself a universalist philosophy of praxis and not a particular Islamist alternative to a single Euro-American universalism.

28 Ji Yea Hong, class response to Spivak's "History," February 16, 2018.

29 See Bateson et al. 1956 for an elaboration of double bind theory, which speaks to a structure of communication involving two or more conflicting messages, where each negates the other. The ethical and political question of acting within the double bind is central to the praxis of deconstruction. Derrida's use of the term "double bind" itself is complex and does not contain the explicitly psychoanalytic resonances of Gregory Bateson's use. See, for instance, his reference to "*double bande*" in *Glas* (Derrida [1974] 1990). A more direct engagement with an idea of the double bind is to be found in Derrida's engagements with Freud, especially his "To Speculate—on 'Freud'" in *The Post Card* (Derrida 1987).

30 For an elaboration of this point, see Étienne Balibar's discussion of the question of difference in *Equaliberty* (2010). For much of this text, Balibar focuses on the antinomy between the concepts of "*égalité*" and "*liberté*" at the heart of the French revolutionary ideal. There is a haunting moment toward the end of his essay "The Proposition of Equaliberty" when Balibar discusses the question of difference as being at the heart of a feminist revolutionary ideal, and as precisely being *not* equality. Thus, within the antinomy between equality and liberty is inscribed another (silent/silenced) antinomy between equality and difference, as two kinds of ideals of justice that are themselves at odds with one another. See Joan Scott's reading of the French revolutionary Olympe de Gouges in *Only Paradoxes to Offer* (1996), for an exploration of this antinomy within the historical and biographical context of de Gouges's struggle for women's rights in 1890s France, as de Gouges insisted upon French revolutionary ideals even as she contended with the question of women's difference from men. This antinomy between equality and difference is, of course, at the heart of all universalist anticolonial thought, perhaps nowhere more poignantly so than in the writings of Frantz Fanon. It is also to be found in so many postcolonial constitutions that seek simultaneously to preserve universalist conceptions of justice through ideals of equality while emphasizing a politics of difference (race- or caste-based affirmative action policies, for instance, or dialogues between liberal and customary law explicitly articulated within constitutions themselves). The Indian and South African constitutions are examples of postcolonial constitutions where these double binds between equality and difference play out constantly, in consequential ways.

31 I think here of a lovely account of kinship that Strathern provides in *Partial Connections* (1991: 23), which seems as if to be about Melanesia, until she reveals that it is in fact an account of a British village in Essex that she had provided a decade previously in *Kinship at the Core* (1981). Thus, for Strathern

the question of comparison, again, is not reducible to a formal technical program, but reveals how we think and write, such that the British village tends never to be made "Other" the way Melanesianist society does. In hegemonic paradigms of Melanesianist anthropology, British social organization is always ground, and Hagen kinship is always figure—a structuring imaginary of the basis of comparison that contains within itself a Eurocentrism that Strathern critiques and decenters throughout her work. This is precisely what Spivak is calling for in her push to consider "Europe as an Other."

32 See Derrida's *Specters of Marx* (1994) for the relationship between the work of mourning and the promise of justice.

33 The importance of thinking with Derrida's *Politics of Friendship* (1997) here is obvious.

34 For an ethnography that parlays this idea(l) of futurity into an account of the politics of Icelandic genome science, see Mike Fortun's *Promising Genomics* (2008). Future anteriority is also central to Kim Fortun's elaboration of an ethnography of late industrialism (K. Fortun 2012).

35 This is not to say that Spivak refuses all essentialism. See especially her considerations of what she calls "strategic essentialism" and its importance to indigenous politics. Even this, however, is laced with healthy skepticism of "becoming native" and is urgent in its call to vigilance toward the politics of translation that are entailed in metropolitan engagements with strategically essentialist indigenous politics. Spivak's translator's preface to Mahashweta Devi's *Imaginary Maps* is one of the best places to find an elaboration of these concerns (Spivak 1991).

36 This is the praxis at the heart of Derrida's reading of Lévi-Strauss's "writing lesson" in *Tristes Tropiques* and his description of the scene of the encounter between the ethnographer and the Nambikwara chief (Derrida [1967] 1976). Gabriele Schwab revisits and supplements this account in her subsequent reading of that same encounter (Schwab 2012). I turn to a reading of Schwab in the next chapter.

37 See the introduction to Rajeswari Sunder Rajan's *Scandal of the State* (2003), which elaborates this problematic from the perspective of Indian feminism and its relationship to the state and to law.

38 When I say "from the postcolony," I am drawing on Jean and John Comaroff's formulation of "theory from the South" (Comaroff and Comaroff 2012). It is not adequate to write of politics *in* the postcolony, which in itself is an exercise in postcolonial objectification, one that retains the center-periphery relations of colonial objectification. Rather, the Comaroffs provide a method for thinking of a theorization of Western politics through a situated analysis from the "South." Part of the task of taking this call seriously is to acknowledge the investigation of the various locations of the "South," including within metropolitan, "First World" centers.

3. Encounter

1 It is worth noting that a reading of Melanie Klein often mediates Spivak's psychoanalytic turns.

2 What LaCapra does not do that Spivak does beyond this is acknowledge the continuing geopolitical history of imperialism that invariably scripts and animates these relationships in the phallogocentric scene of metropolitan intellectual production.

3 Is this not precisely the structural libidinal misrecognition that allows the white, working-class victims of deindustrialization in both America and Europe to turn their anger upon immigrants rather than upon the corporate power that structurally created their plight? After all, there is a fine line between saving and killing the subaltern, the two sides of the interventionist coin of imperialism, as many important critiques of humanitarianism keep reminding us. This is what Spivak means when she alludes to the "white man saving the brown woman from the brown man" (1998: 296). There is less of a distance between the metropolitan project of giving voice to radical alterity and US military interventions in Afghanistan and Iraq than we might like to acknowledge.

I am grateful to my student Jill J. Tan for a stunning paper that auto-biographically explores this misrecognition. "Notes on the Bicentennial of a F/l/ound/er/ing (2019): Scribbles on Poetic Access to a Moving Object" was written as a term paper for my "Multi-si(gh)ted" seminar. Tan reflects on her own misreading of "History" as being about female subaltern subjectivity in light of her autobiography as a diasporic Singaporean who has been taught not to notice the enduring violence of imperial corporate power in structuring where she comes from. This has resulted, Tan says, "in an entrenched reading of colonial violence as a birthmark rather than a scab," one that has consequences for articulations of Singaporean nationalism and deferral to authoritarian rule. Tan's meditation, in her words, is an "autobiographical para-site." This is part of a broader multimedia performance Tan has developed, available at https://jilljtan.com/post/188012670564/notes-on-the-bicentennial-of-a-floundering (last accessed September 20, 2020). I think about questions of autobiography and the literary function of ethnography as this chapter proceeds, and I discuss para-sites in the next chapter.

4 See Marilyn Strathern's critique of Stephen Tyler's argument for ethnography as evocation in *Partial Connections* (Tyler 1986; Strathern 1991). Strathern's point is that the evocative function that Tyler invokes in his essay "Post-modern Ethnography" is embedded in Western ways of knowing. This is an important diagnosis. Yet precisely by attending to the ways in which evocations themselves operate relationally between text and reader, one can understand something ethnographic about the structure of the reader's (in

this case metropolitan intellectual) desire. This is my critique of Strathern's reading of Tyler: it is exemplary in diagnosing the epistemic violence of the metropolitan gaze and in rescripting an understanding of the Other "society" that is the object of this epistemology. It does not, however, open up the question of metropolitan intellectual desire as an ethnographic question the way that Spivak's work consistently does alongside its diagnosis of epistemic violence. See chapter 2 for my reading of Strathern alongside and against Spivak in this regard.

5   Schwab is, of course, hardly the first person to allude to the importance of the reader, which has a long history of consideration in poststructuralist literary criticism (see, for instance, Umberto Eco's *The Role of the Reader* [1979]). I am interested in the usefulness of thinking with Schwab for developing a consideration of ethnographic method, one that goes beyond a consideration of the semiotics of texts-in-themselves.

6   For an important reading of Conrad's biography into his writing of violence, see Michael Taussig's "Culture of Terror—Space of Death" (1984).

7   More than either of these two texts, it is William Golding's *Lord of the Flies* (1954) that *John Dollar* most self-consciously invokes and rescripts.

8   My student Melissa Itzkowitz, who is also a photographer, said, "For me, this is photography. For me, this is about vulnerability" (Melissa Itzkowitz, class response to Gabriele Schwab, January 29, 2018). In this regard, see Donna Haraway's elaboration of what she calls "encounter value" (Haraway 2007). I discuss Itzkowitz's articulation of and relation to photography subsequently in this chapter.

9   See J. D. Vance's *Hillbilly Elegy* (2017), which was a particularly prominent and popular example of such an analysis. Such a book contributed to the deluge of white liberal sentiment in the aftermath of that election that directly contrasted "economic" issues to "identity politics," blaming the rise of the latter within the Democratic Party for Hillary Clinton's defeat, thus directly equating economic anxiety as a purely "white" (and male) concern and reducing African American concerns with incarceration and police brutality, Latinx concerns with immigration, or women's concerns with reproductive choice, sexual violence, and equal pay to "identitarian" (and implicitly, therefore, not economic) ones.

10 I had assigned a short introduction to a special issue of the journal *Critical Inquiry* on intimacy that Berlant had edited. The essays in this issue were subsequently published as an edited volume (Berlant 2000).

11 Jeanne Lieberman and Nida Paracha, class responses to Lauren Berlant's "Intimacy," February 1, 2018.

12 Ji Yea Hong, class response to Berlant, February 1, 2018 (emphasis in original).

13 See E. Summerson Carr's *Scripting Addiction* (2010) for an important ethnographic elaboration of this latter notion of scripting.

14 See especially Berlant's *Cruel Optimism* (2011). Timothy Choy is developing an analytics of atmosphere to think about environmental politics. See Choy 2011 (especially 139–168), 2012; Choy and Zee 2017. See also Yael Navaro-Yashin's analysis of a spatial melancholia, "an environment or atmosphere which discharges . . . an affect," in her analysis of ruined spaces in northern Cyprus (Navaro-Yashin 2009: 16).

I think here of how this opens up the potential for new kinds of ethnographic methodological imaginings. For example, one of the students in my seminar, Winston Berg, is a political scientist planning an ethnography of white nationalism in America. On reading Berlant, he contemplated a refiguration of his project in ways that attended to atmospheres thus: "In my current project, I return time and time again to the sort of conventional narrative that journalists, public historians and everyone else brings up about the American far right, especially the alt right. The trajectory of inquiry always begins as the question, 'why would these normal white boys *join* the far right?' . . . [A]nd nearly always ends, even when it's the alt-right guys themselves asking and answering the question, with one insipid answer: 'I/they wanted to be a part of a group, I/they wanted to feel like a part of *something*.' But what I think I ought to ask is, under what conditions is this *something*?" (Winston Berg, class response to Berlant, February 1, 2018, emphasis in original).

15 Melissa Itzkowitz and Alexandra Kaul, class responses to Kathleen Stewart's *Ordinary Affects* (February 1, 2018).

16 Alexandra Kaul, class response to Stewart (February 1, 2018). Kaul is also a photographer.

17 I am grateful to Hussein Agrama for helping me think through the idea of conceptual loss.

18 I think this point is a very important one to emphasize in the development of a pedagogy of ethnographic attentiveness. When I taught at the University of California at Irvine, I was advising two students, Asya Anderson and Cortney Aponte, on their dissertation proposals. I suggested that rather than dive into the writing of the proposal—a genre of speculative fiction if there ever was one—they might want to hone their ethnographic sensibilities first. I asked both of them to go to the Ikea in Orange County together but to write field notes of their visit separately. Aponte only noticed people and their raced, gendered, and heteronormative manners of relating (remember, Orange County). All Anderson saw were arrows: as her field notes progressed, one was enveloped in her claustrophobia of a place where the arrows kept leading you in and never led you out. There was something telling in their differential ethnographic attentiveness, which led over the course of their dissertation to very different kinds of ethnographic voice. Howard's provocation has literally materialized in a different kind of collaboration, Berlant and Stewart's *The Hundreds* (2018), which contains dialogic hundred-

word vignettes that the two write together, to each other, developing the kind of voice Stewart displays in *Ordinary Affects* in collaborative fashion.

19 Photographically, I think here of Gregory Halpern's ZZYZX (2016), a photo book about Los Angeles that displaces our conventionally visualized understanding of the megapolis and its environs through stunningly curated images and juxtapositions. As with Stewart's writing, there is poesis to each of Halpern's individual images and to the connections that emerge between them. These connections emerge dynamically in the reading of the book, transferentially: they are not just objects "there" to be seen, but potential relations that emerge in the encounters between photographer and image and subsequently between image and reader.

20 Claude Lévi-Strauss's "writing lesson" in *Tristes Tropiques* ([1955] 1992) is exemplary. This is Lévi-Strauss's account of teaching the Nambikwara chief how to "write," in which the anthropologist's reading of the chief's squiggles as a form of formal mimesis of the act of writing even in the absence of the knowledge of its content is a mode of establishing the latter's authority by establishing his relationship to the former. Jacques Derrida provided a deconstruction of this text as being a quintessential example of the epistemic violence of the scene of writing (Derrida [1967] 1976). Schwab, in *Imaginary Ethnographies* (2012), makes another move. She argues that Lévi-Strauss's account, far from being an "objective" diagnosis of the chief's "motives" in writing, reveals instead his own transferential understanding of the scene of the encounter, one that romantically establishes his own (European, masculinist) authority as the bearer of knowledge and writing, through an act of interpretation that can see the chief's act only as "mere" imitation. Both Derrida (deconstructively) and Schwab (psychoanalytically) show the operation of epistemic violence at the scene of the colonial ethnographic encounter. Stewart provides a method to encounter Otherwise, in a way that is multisituated while refusing phallogocentric romantic authority.

21 I have often encountered responses to Stewart that are of the order of "yes, she is a beautiful writer, but . . . ," as if the value of her work is purely aesthetic. Such a reading presumes that theory ought to be Theory with a capital *T*—declaratory, objectifying, masculinist. My point here is not just to critique the phallogocentrism of such a sentiment, but also to allude to the constraints it poses on ethnographic imaginations of Other modalities of staging and writing the encounter, especially at the dissertation stage, particularly when such a sentiment operates with implicit institutionalized norms of Theory as, precisely, declaratory, objectifying, and masculinist, in a manner that refuses the authorial vulnerability that Stewart insists upon and embodies.

22 In this regard, think back to my discussion in chapter 2 of Gayatri Spivak's concern with what she calls "planetarity" in *Death of a Discipline* (2003).

23 Inspired by Choy's work, I am currently embarked on a collaborative project with the South African writer Stacy Hardy and composer Neo Muyanga, called "Pulmonographies," which investigates the politics of breath as situated out of South Africa, with a focus on the political history of tuberculosis. We seek to develop this collaboration through a series of performance lectures that will be experiments in ethnographic, literary, and musical form. The first performance lecture is available on the CC:World website, https://ccworld.hkw.de/#kaushik-sunder-rajan-stacy-hardy-neo-muyanga (last accessed September 14, 2020), and the description of the larger project is on the Neubauer Collegium for Culture and Society website, https://neubauercollegium.uchicago.edu/pulmonographies/ (last accessed March 9, 2021). See also "The Life of Breath," a collaborative project out of Durham University and the University of Bristol, led by Jane McNaughton and Havi Carel (https://lifeofbreath.org/, last accessed October 6, 2019).

24 I recall sitting in the Café Ara Gurel in Istanbul, looking at Gurel's book of photographs of the city from the past half century. In the introduction to the book, he says something like this: "The magic of photography lies in seizing a moment and transmitting it to future generations." I said to myself, this is it.

This, for me, is photography.

"The moment" is not contingency. The moment is a question of time. Before going to the café, I was in the Museum of Innocence. In the book by the same name, Orhan Pamuk has a chapter on time. He distinguishes time from the present. Time has a linearity: it is about the narratives that we construct for ourselves, narratives that we seek to give our lives, narratives that are given to us to live our lives by. The present punctuates those narratives. The present (presence) punctuates (punctures) those narratives. The present (presence) presents to us punctuation and puncture; it pierces, it pricks; it is the punctum. The evidence of photography, then, is not that of the thing it objectifies, but of a moment of encounter that is transmitted to futures-yet-to-come.

As is hopefully evident, my reading of Barthes is mediated deeply by my own photographic practice and is itself hardly an "objective" reading that adjudicates Barthes's account of the practice. Nor is it one that wishes to set Barthes's description as somehow definitive of all photographic practice. My reading, in other words, is itself a transferential one; it does not (at this point) require me to show my photographs in order to reveal the ways in which my photography is a work of mourning. For more on Barthes and mourning, see Derrida's "The Deaths of Roland Barthes" (1988). I say more about my photographic practice (and my refusal to display it here) later in this chapter.

25 See here again Lévi-Strauss's "writing lesson" alongside the dialogue between Derrida's deconstructive and Schwab's psychoanalytic readings of it (Lévi-Strauss [1955] 1992; Derrida [1967] 1976; Schwab 2012).

26 How this violence manifests is specific to different visual media. See Berger's *Ways of Seeing* (1972) to consider this in relation to art and photography; Laura Mulvey's seminal essay "Visual Pleasure and Narrative Cinema" (1975) for a discussion of the masculinist gaze of film; and Susan Sontag's *On Photography* (1977) for considerations of the representational violence of photography.

27 There are many different elements to this, especially as it relates to the question of pornography, that go far beyond Berger's analysis and beyond the scope of my account here. See especially Paul Preciado's *Pornotopia* (2014), which considers the violence of sight and the appropriation by the male gaze from the perspective of a queer politics that radically decenters Berger's heteronormative perspective.

28 Melissa Itzkowitz, class response to Roland Barthes's *Camera Lucida*, February 8, 2018.

29 The photography of Mona Kuhn is an exemplary demonstration of how to look with "intimacy rather than desire," in the terms that Itzkowitz uses these categories. Kuhn makes sensuous photographs of nudes without ever reducing them to eroticism. She does so without looking elsewhere: these are full-on, direct, explicit photographs, not subtle or merely suggestive, yet never voyeuristic or pornographic. Kuhn spoke of how important the development of long-term intimacy and friendship with the subjects of her work was to achieving this kind of visual attunement (Kuhn 2018). See also Berger's distinction in *Ways of Seeing* (1972) between the nude, as the aestheticized, eroticized, objectified, and commodified object of the (invariably male) gaze, and the naked, as something more vulnerable, tentative and intimate. There is kinship between Berger's notion of nakedness and Stewart's of the ordinary.

30 Melissa Itzkowitz, class response to Barthes, February 8, 2018.

31 The reader/viewer is not the same as "audience." Once reduced to the question of "audience," the reader/viewer is immediately rendered a consumer in a market and hence cannot but be a commodifying and appropriative move.

32 Melissa Itzkowitz, class response to Barthes, February 8, 2018.

33 I have thought often about the relationship of my own ethnographic praxis to my emergent photographic practice. The latter shares skin with and is inspired by Itzkowitz's work, though our specific styles and modalities of photographing are quite different. When I started making photographs a few years ago, I found that the world started looking different when I looked at it through a camera. Indeed, I found myself developing quite a different photographic voice to my rather didactic ethnographic one. I want to keep it that way and to allow each to develop unencumbered by the other (though it is impossible for one not to be touched by the other somehow, as both voices develop alongside one another). Nonetheless, at no point are my photographs an illustration of my ethnographic projects or material.

I thought about whether to show some of my photographs here to illustrate my practice but decided against it. In part, it is because that work is emergent, and this is not the time, place, or medium for its display. I have not reached the stage of the fourth encounter, certainly not for this audience. I do show my work to other photographers, have exhibited in a couple of group shows, and am in the early stages of a photo book project, provisionally titled "Time is caught between breath and mourning," which is in part inspired by and in conversation with the "Pulmonographies" collaboration I am involved in with Stacy Hardy and Neo Muyanga (see note 23 of this chapter). Even as I do not show my photos here, I feel it is important to mention them: as Itzkowitz gently admonished, I cannot write about her practice without revealing some of my own stakes, not just as an ethnographer but also as a photographer. Itzkowitz has, as is surely evident, unintentionally become a native informant in my account of photographic practice here, and this reciprocity is the least I owe her. This account of her practice has been based on mutual conversation and dialogue that has extended beyond the "Multi-si(gh)ted" seminar, and I have incorporated her feedback into earlier drafts. I am grateful for her continuing conversation about ethnographic and photographic matters and for her engaged critique of this account.

Many thanks are owed here also to Sasha Wolf, who has mentored my photography; to Jane Fulton Alt, whose critique groups have helped sustain and develop my practice; and to Stephanie Taiber, who has been my most rigorous and encouraging photo critic and whose own practice has significantly imprinted and inspired my own.

34 Ji Yea Hong, class response to John Berger's *Ways of Seeing*, February 8, 2018.

35 Rachel Howard, class response to Barthes, February 8, 2018.

36 Jeanne Lieberman, class response to Barthes, February 8, 2018.

37 In another register, see Marilyn Strathern's *Partial Connections* (1991) for her reflections on the relationship between singularity and comparison.

38 Alexandra Kaul, class response to Barthes, February 8, 2018.

39 Alexandra Kaul, class response to Barthes, February 8, 2018.

40 To me, this is one of the most difficult, poignant, and brilliant aspects of *Ordinary Affects*. The scenes of Stewart's encounters—often in the heart of white America—are located in places and among people who feel so radically Other to me, within sites that often articulate and represent a politics that I loathe. Yet the book elicits an empathy within me, as a reader *without* identification.

This is very different from the romantic deep South that I encounter, for instance, in Sally Mann's photography. For all its poignancy and beauty, it elicits a kernel of alienation in me as a viewer. For what Mann portrays, in my eyes, is *her* South, one that, in its whiteness and its histories and presents of violence toward bodies of color, so resolutely is not (cannot be) mine. Mann's photography is a work of love, but it is a love that requires prior identification. Stewart's ethnography, however, opens to a love that is more universal. I am grateful to Emilia Sanabria for helping me think love in terms of equanimity.

41 Melissa Itzkowitz, class response to Barthes, February 8, 2018.

42 See Charles Baudelaire's famous description of the flâneur in *The Painter of Modern Life* (Baudelaire [1863] 1964) and Walter Benjamin's equally re-nowned reading of Baudelaire for his account of the flâneur in relation to the alienation of contemporary capitalism (Benjamin 2006). The flâneur is simultaneously a noninnocent and a critical figure. With the flâneur, the man of leisure who strolls the streets of Paris with a wandering eye, there is a bourgeois self-indulgence to his image. At the same time, as Benjamin suggests, there is a mode of attentiveness to the world that the flâneur cul-tivates that is a response to the intensification of the commodity culture of mid-nineteenth-century Paris, one that serves as a potential critique of the alienation that it has wrought.

43 Melissa Itzkowitz, class response to Teju Cole's *Blind Spot*, February 13, 2018. A day after we discussed this book in class, a shooter opened fire at the Marjory Stoneman Douglas High School in Parklands, Florida, killing sev-enteen people. Photography, writing, reading, and ethnography—and their pedagogy—are all inscribed in the future anterior of the mourning that is to come.

44 I know. I like photographing curtains and have photographed many. Only two images are worthwhile.

45 In responding to an earlier draft of this chapter, Itzkowitz had this to add: "Right—the point is that the image is necessarily transferential and that transference undoubtedly produces the feeling of mourning. So while Cole saw this curtain, or better yet, this image of the curtain after he already made it, and connected it to World War II, I saw it and without reading the text felt an undeniable feeling of sadness, likely connecting it, in some way, to some personal or worldly memory (like World War II)" (Melissa Itzkow-itz, personal correspondence, June 29, 2019).

46 Ji Yea Hong, class response to Cole, February 13, 2018.

47 Jeanne Lieberman, class response to Cole, February 13, 2018.

48 Of course, photography is not the only creative medium that works this way. So too does literature, and the structure of relationality that I am de-scribing here through Cole and Barthes is very similar to Gabriele Schwab's treatment of literary knowledge. What particularly interests me with Cole, to reiterate, is that his is in some significant way not *just* a work of photo-graphy; the work of a literary writing (even if it does not take the genre form of the novel) is central. So too is the work of juxtaposition of image to text. Rajeswari Sunder Rajan considers this question of juxtaposition of genres and creative forms, as itself part of an emergent form of the contemporary

novel, in her reading of Orhan Pamuk's *Museum of Innocence* (2008) (R. Sunder Rajan in preparation). This is Pamuk's novel, subsequently built and curated as a museum in Istanbul, with its own attendant genres of writing (the museum catalogue), such that even as the museum "collects" the objects of the novel, the catalogue documents the objects of the museum. Sunder Rajan reads the novel and catalogue in ways that are inscribed by her own visit to the physical museum, a visit engendered itself by a curiosity borne of a prior reading of the novel. The question of the relations between the contingency of objects, locales, encounters, and the transferential relations they engender is as similar—while being utterly different—in Sunder Rajan's encounter with Pamuk's novel/museum/catalogue and in Hong's encounter with Seoul through Cole's photos of "Seoul." See note 24 of this chapter for a brief mention of my own visit to the Museum of Innocence and its influence on how I articulate my photographic practice.

49 Melissa Itzkowitz, class response to Cole, February 13, 2018.

50 Again, in responding to an earlier version of this, Itzkowitz added, "Right. . . . If you're going to photograph people, you as the viewer should care about them. Not necessarily because you *care* specifically about them like my grandfather in the photo of my grandmother, but because they elicit in you unconscious feelings or connections to other people whom you actually do care about. That's why I didn't want to know about the woman in the photograph. I wanted to transferentially care about her. By knowing too much about her life while she doesn't know that I ever saw such a vulnerable image of her feels like voyeurism" (Melissa Itzkowitz, personal correspondence, June 29, 2019).

51 This is a very different relationship to the stranger that is being imagined and conjured to the phallogocentric one that Sara Ahmed describes as "stranger fetishism" (Ahmed 2000), which can be found both in the stranger's expulsion as the origin of danger (e.g., neighborhood watch) or their celebration (in a certain manner, under certain conditions) as the origin of difference (e.g., multiculturalism).

52 I am not moved by a certain kind of photography, quite prevalent in the United States, that valorizes a purely solipsistic idea and ideal of intimacy: the photographer's own self, own family, own space, own lovers, own suffering, to the exclusion of other (and Other) kinds of relational possibilities. Of course, autobiographical traces must matter. What Cole, Stewart, and Choy do so well is to activate them in ways that do not depend on a prior binarization of self and other, where intimacy resides in relation to the former and objectification in relation to the latter. This is their multisituated praxis. Some of the photographers who most inspire me—and Itzkowitz is one of them—manage to capture their selves without depending on this prior, possessive drawing of boundaries. Thus, Itzkowitz's photographs of Brooklyn allow me to inhabit them in my own way and through my own

memories of growing up in Delhi, even though they are of her places, not mine, and even though mine are very different in their objective specifics. Not many photographers make work with an openness and generosity (and, importantly, vulnerability) that allows this.

53 Smith's work, across her oeuvre, explores the entanglements between the history of photography and race in far more elaborated ways than I can manage here. In addition to *At the Edge of Sight*, see her *Photography on the Color Line* (Smith 2004). I engage with *At the Edge of Sight* here to think specifically of the relationship between the racialized and reproductive histories and trajectories of photography and the praxis of multisituatedness.

54 The image can be seen at https://www.flickr.com/photos/kcl_photography _usa_2010/4241010605 (last accessed December 22, 2018).

55 Nida Paracha, class response to Shawn Michelle Smith's *At the Edge of Sight*, February 15, 2018.

4. Dialogue

1 Fischer draws on Donald MacKenzie's *Mechanizing Proof* (2001) as an exemplary text that works through these questions of hype and infrastructure. For accounts of hype in structuring the political economy of biotechnology, see Mike Fortun's *Promising Genomics* (2008) and my *Biocapital* (2006: especially chapter 3). The literature on the anthropology of infrastructures is lively and growing. Brian Larkin's *Signal and Noise* (2008), Stephen Collier's *Post-Soviet Social* (2011), and Michael Fisch's *An Anthropology of the Machine* (2018) are three exemplary ethnographies of infrastructure that have charted paths and demonstrated methods for the study of infrastructure in structurally attuned ways. Christopher Kelty's dissertation and postdissertation work (on telemedicine and free software, respectively) has attended simultaneously to questions of hype and infrastructure (Kelty 1999, 2008).

2 See Joseph Masco's *The Theater of Operations* (2014) for an ethnography of the American security state that methodologically and conceptually develops modes of ethnographic analysis of the scenario, while also elucidating how the scenario is an object of ethnographic interest for the American security state.

3 Fischer has engaged in such work toward the conceptualization of reflexive social institutions, at Harvard-MIT with his involvement in the transdisciplinary Division of Health Science and Technology (HST) and also in Singapore over the past decade. See, for instance, Fischer 2013. See my discussion of Spivak's *Death of a Discipline* in chapter 2 for the importance of understanding our ethnographic (and more generally humanistic) knowledge-producing activities within the context of the globalizing and financializing corporate metropolitan university.

4　This is his argument with Donna Haraway's figure of the cyborg as becoming the exemplary figure to think ethnography with, as Marilyn Strathern argues for. Strathern's *Partial Connections* (1991) takes issue with the trope of the traveler as the imaginary of the ethnographer, preferring that of the cyborg. For Fischer, this would expunge what for him is a necessary focus on life history.

5　Of course, the question of individual ethical agency and struggle is not just one for the immigrant or diasporic intellectual. It ought to be one for the metropolitan intellectual too, for surely the perpetrator must also be haunted, somehow? See Gabriele Schwab's *Haunting Legacies* (2010), which is a searing exploration of post–World War II repression of the Holocaust in Germany, which for Schwab is also an auto-ethnographic self-reckoning of her own generation that grew up with(in) the silence of the generation of perpetrators (see also chapter 3 of this book). I often wonder, seriously and without accusation, why British social anthropology does not thus seem haunted by the legacies of colonialism.

6　Fischer writes this well before the "ontological turn" became fashionable. For a reiteration of this move beyond or elsewhere than ontology, see Fischer 2014. Bruno Latour, one of the vanguard figures of the ontological turn, was one of the other speakers at the presidential plenary at the 2000 Vienna meeting of 4S, which had been curated precisely to consider the role of critical STS thinking within conjunctures such as the rise of the Freedom Party. I do not remember what he said.

7　Let us remember that decolonizing ethnography is not just about critiquing white masculinity, but white *Christian* masculinity. For a non-phallogocentric praxis, it is useful to consider what Derrida, in *Acts of Religion* (2001), has called "globalatinization," a global universalism constructed and shaped as Christian.

8　For a prefiguration of this move, see Fischer's description of the Karbala paradigm and its structuring role in differentiating Shia and Sunni Islamic traditions in *Iran: From Religious Dispute to Revolution* (Fischer 1980).

9　The stakes of what I am about to say are more complex than the terms in which I am about to say it, and elaborating it would be beyond the scope of this book. But I do want to mark this as a point of debate within contemporary anthropological and philosophical critiques of secularism. I especially note *Debating Muslims* as a salutary methodological contrast to Saba Mahmood's *Politics of Piety* (2005), which articulates the praxis of religious Muslim women in Egypt as a counterpoint to liberal secular universalism, which can only code such praxis *as* religious (and hence nonsecular). Mahmood articulates a non-zero-sum interpretation of everyday practice, but the uptake of her work in the metropolitan academy has tended to romanticize the agency of radical alterity (the Islamic woman as female subaltern) in ways that ultimately create a strawman of liberal secular universalism, as if such a complex and variegated set of norms and practices could be singularized as simply homogeneous and homogenizing. The stakes of such an outcome, which I suggest is ultimately an expression of metropolitan intellectual desire for radical alterity, at a historical moment when religious fundamentalisms of all kinds (including and especially in their various anti-Islamic varietals) are caricaturing secularism in precisely such reductive terms, are high. Joan Scott's recent *Sex and Secularism* (2017) is exemplary of such a reductionist understanding of the striations and differentiations of secularism at the altar of a thirst for the agency of radical alterity (see R. Sunder Rajan 2018 for a more rigorous rebuttal of Scott than I can offer here). Anuradha Needham and Rajeswari Sunder Rajan have explored some of the complex politics around critiques of secularism in India in their edited collection *The Crisis of Secularism in India* (2007). Étienne Balibar has addressed and complexified this debate from the empirical situation of French *laïcité*, in ways that constantly critique the fundamentalism of the practice without reducing the complexities of its ethos, genealogies, and conjunctural manifestations in a world of increasing religious fundamentalisms (see especially his recent *Secularism and Cosmopolitanism* [2018]). For a critique of secularism that ethnographically attends to the praxis of dialogue in the *fatwa* and other "Islamic" family law practices, see Hussein Agrama's *Questioning Secularism* (2012). In this, Agrama develops his own dialogic method that is distinct from Fischer's and Abedi's, and he draws on the genealogy of Talal Asad and Alasdair MacIntyre; there is kinship between his investment in showing the ambiguities of secularism and Fischer's and Abedi's in showing religious practice as open-ended and contested, even as their specific philosophical genealogies, ethnographic methods, and argumentative styles are quite different.

10 "Forms of life" is Fischer's reference to socialities of action that contain ethical dilemmas and the face of the Other. Drawing on Ludwig Wittgenstein, Emmanuel Levinas, and Raymond Williams, Fischer's articulation of the term can be reduced neither to the structures and functions of groups preidentified *as* societies nor simply to a study of process or practice without a concomitant structural elucidation (Wittgenstein [1953] 1973: para. 241). Veena Das's work is exemplary of an ethnographic method derived from a Wittgensteinian attentiveness to forms of life (for which, see especially Das 2006), though her ethnography tends to privilege "the everyday" at the expense of the structural.

11 Think this alongside my discussion of the figuration of the woman, the Arab, and the indigenous in Spivak's reading of *Heart of Darkness* through Virginia Woolf, Tayeb Salih, and Mahashweta Devi in *Death of a Discipline* (see chapter 2 of this book).

12 I think here of *Charred Lullabies* (1996), E. Valentine Daniel's ethnography of the sectarian violence in Sri Lanka and its haunting by autobiographical traces. This book also speaks to the question of a diasporic anthropology,

writing about violence in one's "own" society (including and especially for a metropolitan readership). Also see chapter 3 in this book for an elaboration of the place of autobiography in thinking of ethnography as a praxis of encounter.

13 I use the word "design" loosely here, but in fact the question of design in regard to conceptualizing the para-ethnographic has received serious recent consideration. See, for instance, Luke Cantarella, Christine Hegel, and George Marcus's *Ethnography by Design* (2019). Keith Murphy's *Swedish Design* (2015) thinks design as both object and method via an ethnography of Swedish furniture designers. Kim and Mike Fortun explore the importance of software design logics in building their digital platforms The Asthma Files and Platform for Experimental Collaborative Ethnography (https://theasthmafiles.org/ and https://worldpece.org/, both last accessed October 17, 2019). Two anthropology graduate students at the University of Chicago, Alejandra Azuero and Taylor Lowe, curated a yearlong series of conversations on ethnography and design, "De-signing Praxis," which explored some of these themes. There are many para-ethnographic modalities beyond that of the para-site. I describe the para-site as exemplary because it is the one I know best and one that I have experimented with myself.

14 Jill J. Tan, class response to Holmes and Marcus's "Cultures of Expertise," January 25, 2018.

15 A particularly interesting example of this is a para-ethnographic collaboration that Marcus was involved in with Marc Abeles around the World Trade Organization (WTO). This included a dialogue with the then-director of the WTO, Pascal Lamy, and involved curating an exhibition within the WTO that made visible the organization's own interventions in the first two decades of its existence. Thus, even as this was a project involved in studying the WTO, it contained within itself formats for generating self-reflexivity within the organization about its own trajectory and legacies, a function not merely of the creation of objective knowledge but of *curation*: a staging, alongside. See Marcus 2017 for an account of this collaboration.

These interlocutors do not have to be powerful people. They can be activists we have learned to be in solidarity with, but who caricature institutions of power in ways that can be debilitating to their own praxis. My own engagements with activist groups in the course of my research on *Pharmocracy* have been attempts at such critical interlocution, which demands constant accountability and always contains within itself the risk of betrayal (K. Sunder Rajan 2017).

16 Marilyn Strathern has written extensively about the politics of making knowledge applicable and actionable in relation to audit cultures and interdisciplinarity. See, for example, her *Audit Cultures* (2000), "Anthropology and Interdisciplinarity" (2005a), and "Experiments in Interdisciplinarity" (2005b).

17 See the introduction to *Pharmocracy* for my elaboration of the importance of a conjunctural methodology (K. Sunder Rajan 2017).

18 Susan Leigh Star and James Griesemer's notion of boundary objects is relevant to thinking about translational research here, as a provisionally stabilized category that has different meanings for the different actors involved (Star and Griesemer 1989). Eduardo Viveiros de Castro's concept of controlled equivocation also helps us think through this situated provisionality (Viveiros de Castro 2004). The point I wish to elaborate as my account unfolds is how fragile this can be, especially in situations of transnational collaboration across power hierarchies and differential individual investments.

19 The full list of participants and their affiliations at the time of the para-site is as follows: Kaushik Sunder Rajan (associate professor of anthropology, University of California, Irvine; anthropologist of science and technology); Martha Gray (J. W. Kiekhefer Professor of Medical and Electrical Engineering, MIT; director of the HST Division, MIT, from 1995 to 2008); Michael M. J. Fischer (Andrew W. Mellon Professor of Humanities and Professor of Anthropology and Science and Technology Studies, MIT; current research project on the institutionalization of global biomedicine with a focus on Singapore); Mriganka Sur (Sherman Fairchild Professor of Neuroscience and head, Department of Brain and Cognitive Science, MIT; basic research on developmental plasticity and dynamic changes in mature cortical networks during information processing, learning, and memory); Adam Drake (postdoctoral associate in the lab of Jianzhu Chen at MIT; development of humanized mouse models to study immune responses); K. Vijayraghavan (director of the National Centre for Biological Sciences [NCBS], Bangalore; basic research on the developmental neurobiology of animal movement, in particular the formation of muscles in *Drosophila*); Satyajit Mayor (professor in the area of cellular organization and signaling, NCBS, Bangalore; basic research on mechanisms of endocytic trafficking of transmembrane and lipid-anchored proteins); Chetan Chitnis (research scientist in the malaria group at the International Center for Genetic Engineering and Biotechnology, New Delhi; research on erythrocyte invasion by malarial parasites; involved in developing antimalarial vaccines); Sunil Shaunak (professor of infectious diseases, Division of Investigative Science, Imperial College, London; research involves developing drugs against hepatitis C; cofounder of a start-up, PolyTherics); Fiona Murray (Sarofim Family Career Development Professor of Management of Technological Innovation and Entrepreneurship, Sloan School of Management, MIT; studies on science commercialization, the organization of scientific research, and the role of science in national competitiveness); Ganesh Venkataraman (chief scientific officer and senior vice president of research, Momenta Pharmaceuticals, Inc., Cambridge, Massachusetts; research faculty member, Harvard-MIT division of HST); Joe Smith (vice president of emerging technologies,

Corporate Office of Science and Technology, Johnson & Johnson); Nimish Vaccharajani (vice president of pharmaceutical development, Advinus Therapeutics Private Limited, Bangalore; previously, director of clinical development, Bristol Myers Squibb Pharmaceutical Research Institute); Shiladitya Sengupta (assistant professor of medicine and HST, Harvard Medical School, Brigham and Women's Hospital; research on developing engineering and nanotechnology solutions for complex diseases; founder of three start-up companies in the United States, United Kingdom, and India); Mehmet Toner (professor of surgery [biomedical engineering] and HST, Harvard Medical School, Massachusetts General Hospital; research focusing on the physiochemical aspects of freezing cells and engineered tissues); Brian Seed (professor of genetics and HST, Harvard Medical School, Massachusetts General Hospital; research on using new technologies to couple rapid identification of interesting genes with methods to study their consequences in an organismic context); Beth Karlan (director of the Women's Cancer Research Institute, Cedars Sinai Medical Center, Los Angeles, and professor of obstetrics and gynecology, Geffen School of Medicine, University of California, Los Angeles; surgeon and research on the genetic definition and phenotypic determinants of human ovarian carcinomas, molecular biomarker discovery, and inherited cancer susceptibility); Alok Srivastava (professor and head of the Department of Hematology and head of the Centre for Stem Cell Research, Christian Medical College, Vellore; research on and treatment of hemophilia); K. Srinath Reddy (president, Public Health Foundation of India; previously, head of the Cardiology Department, All India Institute of Medical Sciences, New Delhi; clinical cardiologist with a career commitment to preventive cardiology and public health); Uma Chandra Mouli Natchu (Department of Biotechnology Ramalingaswamy Fellow, THSTI; completing a PhD in public health at the Harvard School of Public Health; trained as a pediatrician; research on pediatric malnutrition); Michael Montoya (assistant professor of anthropology and Chicano/Latino studies, University of California, Irvine; medical anthropologist researching the relationship between biomedicine and social indicators such as race and poverty); Gopal Dabade (medical doctor, community health activist, and convener of the All India Drug Action Network, Dharwad, Karnataka; actively involved in public advocacy around access to essential medicines in India); Sarah Kaplan (associate professor of strategic management, Rotman School of Business, University of Toronto; author of the *New York Times* business best-seller *Creative Destruction* [with coauthor Richard Foster], which studies the culture and systems of long-established companies and how that often results in their underperforming in the market over time); Bhaven Sampat (assistant professor in the Department of Health Policy and Management and in the School of International and Public Affairs, Columbia University; research at the intersection of issues in innovation policy and health policy); and Thomas Pogge (Leitner Professor of Philosophy and International Affairs, Yale University; has written extensively on political philosophy and more recently on extreme poverty and global justice; involved in the establishment of Health Impact Fund, which is an attempt to provide an incentive structure through international governments for pharmaceutical companies to provide medicines and treatments for developing countries at an affordable cost).

20 My attempts to perform epistemic equivalence through the curation of the para-site hardly eradicated the enactment of violence. This was not merely the epistemic violence of ignoring certain perspectives. For example, while the funding for the para-site came from a number of different sources, including my own personal research account, its administration was out of MIT. It took over a month for air travel to be reimbursed, which is a fairly normal timeline for reimbursement in the accounting processes of the American university. It was, however, extremely awkward for a community health activist from India, for whom international airfare is not a trivial outlay, to have to wait that long to be reimbursed. This highlights the taken-for-granted assumptions of what, quite literally, is the price of entry into a global conversation at an elite metropolitan university, including to a conversation that purports to be about building biomedical research and health infrastructure for the benefit of "the poor," a bottom-of-the-pyramid rhetoric that was quite commonly espoused as part of the ideals of THSTI, including and especially out of HST.

21 Martha Gray, letter to Indo-US Forum, 2009.

22 See Michael Fischer's "Technoscientific Infrastructures and Emergent Forms of Life" (2005) for an elaboration of what he calls the "peopling of technoscience" and the importance of its ethnographic elucidation. Fischer was a sounding board and interlocutor in the THSTI project, which was developing alongside his own research in biomedical institutional development in Singapore. Fischer himself teaches in the HST program and was a participant and active coconspirator in the para-site I organized at MIT. There was a synchronicity of our ethnographic investments, and my own stakes in thinking of this ethnography as a means to facilitating a dialogic reflexivity in the course of institutional development owe much to lessons learned from him. There were also undoubtedly moments when our specific readings of situations diverged, and there is no question that I developed a more antagonistic perspective on MIT as a hegemonic corporate institution the more time I spent researching this project from the perspective of its Indian interlocutors.

23 See Sheila Jasanoff and Sang-Hyun Kim's *Dreamscapes of Modernity* (2015) and George Marcus's *Technoscientific Imaginaries* (1994) for an elaboration of

how to think "imaginary" in relation to the institutional developments I am describing here.

24 I am grateful to Rajeswari Sunder Rajan for helping me think with and through Rushdie. Sunder Rajan is currently working on a book manuscript, *The Burden of the Nation*, which traces the influence of Rushdie on the contemporary Indian novel in English. My drawing on Rushdie here owes much to her manuscript in progress and to conversations with her about Rushdie.

25 Much as I share solidarity with many contemporary left critiques of nationalism, I refuse to think of nationalism as *only* parochial. I think that the question of nationalism is itself an ethnographic (and often postcolonial and generational) question that intimately attaches the structural to the biographical and the affective. For an elaboration of this, see my debate with Brenna Bhandar at "Dangerous Conjunctures," a conference to celebrate the thirtieth anniversary of the publication of Étienne Balibar and Immanuel Wallerstein's *Race, Nation, Class* (1988), available at HKW 100 Years of Now, "Kaushik Sunder Rajan, Brenna Bhandar: On Nation-Forms and Nation-Forming," YouTube, April 27, 2018, https://www.youtube.com/watch?v=4dbfqqPMomo.

26 THSTI capacity-building conversations often involved HST actors emphasizing their investments in building institutional infrastructures for good science globally, usually in genuinely good faith. They would, however, invariably be met with at least a slightly raised eyebrow. An Indian interlocutor once asked me why it was then that two of MIT's most expensive, ongoing institution-building initiatives at the time involved agreements with the governments of Singapore and Russia: "why are they doing deals with autocrats and oligarchs, then?" This is not a rhetorical question, and it is worth asking what consequences such forms of globalization have for a certain scientific ethos of democratic republicanism (for which, see especially Robert Merton's "The Normative Structure of Science" [1942], Michael Polanyi's "The Republic of Science" [1962], and Alvin Weinberg's "Science and Trans-science" [1972]). The point here is not to make some simply normative argument for science as a democratic institution (though it is a nice enough ideal to aspire to and fight for) or to make moral judgments about MIT's activities (the complexities of which require empirical and structural analysis in its own right) or even to suggest that there is something inappropriate about building collaborations with scientists in authoritarian countries (it could be argued that it is all the more vital to establish and maintain avenues of intellectual exchange with academics in countries where freedom of thought and expression is otherwise curtailed). Rather, it is to suggest how claims of virtue ring especially hollow in collaborations across power differentials when the institutions from which those claims are made are seen quite clearly from the outside (and certainly from the global South) as profit-maximizing corporations that are leveraging brand value in

exchange for financial flows, including from regimes that practice forms of governance that are antithetical to the institution's professed values. What this also shows, again, are the complexities in relations, and perceptions of relations, between HST and MIT. HST actors consistently saw *themselves* acting in good faith, spreading *HST's* ethos. For many Indian actors, HST and MIT were indistinguishable hegemons or at least were institutions whose personae shaded into one another. This contributed to a constant undercurrent of cynicism on the part of a number of Indian actors in the collaboration toward HST's professed (and quite likely genuine) good faith and virtue. Needless to say, these speak to structural institutional issues concerning the globalizing and corporatizing university and are hardly particular to MIT, even if there are particular manifestations of this at MIT as a function of its own history, expertise, and specific brand value.

For a description of the MIT-Russia collaboration, see MIT News, "MIT and Skolkovo Foundation Announce Collaboration," June 18, 2011, http://news.mit.edu/2011/skolkovo-mit-announcement-0618; for the MIT-Singapore collaboration, see MIT News, "MIT Signs Formal Agreement with Singapore University of Technology and Design," January 26, 2010, http://news.mit.edu/2010/sutd-mit.

27 See David Scott's "The Temporality of Generations" (2014) for an ethnographic method that reflects upon the Caribbean postcolonial condition through structured life-history interviews with Caribbean intellectuals in order to explore, hermeneutically, the lived relationships between the lives, thoughts, visions, and situated understandings of intellectuals (when the very question of who, or what, constitutes an intellectual is also very much at stake) and their political investments in and articulations of a modality of politics. His is a certain hermeneutic exploration of postcolonial political modernity. My conversations with Indian scientists would often organically veer toward such directions: there was no way in which my Indian interlocutors in the THSTI project were *not* thinking of themselves as postcolonial actors, even as they often espoused radically different individual politics. However, I did not know enough at the time of my research to turn these conversations into the kinds of semistructured life-history interviews that Scott conducts. I am using the lessons I have learned from these conversations, now supplemented by a reading of Scott's work, in current research that explores constitutionalism as a mode of politics and as a generational question in South Africa, and I am in the initial stages of conducting life-history interviews with lawyers and judges there, in order to use life history to elucidate lived relationships between structure and peopling in the constitution of postcolonial political modernities.

28 Even at my career stage, I benefited greatly from being in the American university, where anthropology departments still have relative autonomy to value long-term research conceptualized at the scale of the monograph,

without a constant pressure to publish journal articles along the way. The ludicrous audit cultures of the British university with their Research Assessment Exercises would have rendered such a project simply impossible. Or they would have forced publication outcomes that would have felt like a betrayal of my accountabilities to my interlocutors.

29 I am grateful to Emilia Sanabria for thinking through some of these issues with me in light of her current work with shamans, healers, and indigenous communities in Brazil around the use and circulation of ayahuasca. As Sanabria follows ayahuasca worlds from forest to lab to market, there is much more at stake for her than following the object. She is also facilitating dialogue with practitioners whose indigenous knowledge is being rapidly appropriated and commodified into global political economies. The ethics of dialogic facilitation in these situations go far beyond procedural instrumental ones, such as informed consent, to actually consider what forms of reflexivity might be generated and how desirable outcomes (and for whom) might be imagined. Her work is funded by the European Research Council, whose audit cultures require stringently mandated forms of ethical engagement that are highly procedural. The challenge for Sanabria is to work within those procedures but also to torque them to ends that go beyond liberal instrumentality in ways that are accountable to her indigenous interlocutors. Leaving things at a diagnosis of incommunicability, as I did with my para-site, is not an ethical option for her. As Sanabria put it to me, "I think we have a ways to go to re-imagine in generative, feminist, decolonial ways the ethics and practices of such events which can be quite violent (even just at the symbolic level)" (Emilia Sanabria, personal correspondence, July 10, 2019).

Conclusion

1 From my field notes. A week previously, the Modi government, in a completely unconstitutional act of executive fiat that was subsequently legislatively rubber-stamped, revoked Article 370, which had granted special status to Kashmir, and proceeded more or less to place Kashmiris under house arrest in their own land, cutting off their communications to the outside world. There was overwhelming support for their action in India.

2 I take this phrasing from Elizabeth Povinelli, whose *Geontologies* (2016) is subtitled *A Requiem to Late Liberalism.*

3 For an important consideration of the inherent ambiguity—and multiplicity—of universalism as a philosophical category, see Étienne Balibar's "Ambiguous Universality" (1995). My ability to give words to my investments in a certain universality, as I am doing here, is deeply indebted to

Balibar's work. Bruce Robbins's work on cosmopolitanism is an important allied influence (for which see, for instance, Robbins 1992, 2002, 2007), as is Rajeswari Sunder Rajan's *Scandal of the State* (2003), which articulates some of these concerns in relation to the question of (Indian) feminism's relationship to the state.

4 See Biehl and Petryna 2011 for their notion of the judicialization of health, as described from Brazil, an example of what Jean and John Comaroff have described from South Africa as a more generalized judicialization of politics (Comaroff and Comaroff 2006). The modes of relation between health, law, and constitutionalism in South Africa cannot be seamlessly or completely captured within the framework of Biehl and Petryna's concept—the conjunctures and empirical specificities of the processes I am tracing speak to something more or other than judicialization—but there is kinship, and comparative work to be done, in thinking the coproductions of health and law in different global Southern contexts together.

5 See especially the ways in which Spivak thinks catachrestically in her *Outside in the Teaching Machine* (1993).

6 Scale, of course, is not in itself innocent, and it has long epistemic provenance in critical geography, also a discipline with both colonial antecedents and well-articulated postcolonial and decolonizing critiques.

7 I cannot provide a comprehensive overview of what is now a lively set of multimodal approaches to ethnography, but I wish to acknowledge the experimental musician Olivia Block, who has helped develop my fieldwork methods pedagogy with her own cultivation of an attentiveness to soundscapes and listening practices. I am also inspired by the ways in which anthropologists such as Deborah Thomas and Joseph Dumit have incorporated dance and performance into their ethnographic practice and pedagogy, in ways that both supplement and supplant visuality. (See, for instance, http://dumit.net/embodying-improvisation/ and http://dumit.net/fascia-lab/, both last accessed July 18, 2019, for some of Dumit's practices. See also Deborah Thomas's films *Bad Friday* [codirected and produced with John L. Jackson and Junior "Gabu" Wedderburn] and *Four Days in May* [with Junior "Gabu" Wedderburn and Deanne M. Bell] and her multimedia installation *Bearing Witness* [Penn Museum, https://www.penn.museum/sites/expedition/bearing-witness/, last accessed January 7, 2021], for examples of Thomas's.) I am grateful to Emilia Sanabria for conversations around the stakes of thinking the sensorial beyond sight. My current collaboration with writer Stacy Hardy and composer Neo Muyanga, "Pulmonographies," is pushing my thinking on these matters forward in rich and as-yet-evolving ways.

8 See Hylton White 2019 for an important reflection on this in the context of curricular developments in South Africa in the wake of movements for decolonizing the university there.

9 See, for instance, Derrida's essay "The 'World' of the Enlightenment to Come (Exception, Calculation, Sovereignty)" (2003). It was one of his last before his death.

10 Think here of Gayatri Spivak's failed attempt to have the 1980 conference on "Europe and Its Others" renamed "Europe as an Other," as described in the "History" chapter of *A Critique of Postcolonial Reason* (1998; see also chapter 2 in this book).

References

Achebe, Chinua. 1977. "An Image of Africa: Racism in Conrad's *Heart of Darkness.*" *Massachusetts Review* 18 (4): 782–794.

Ackerman, Bruce A. 1991. *We the People.* Cambridge, MA: Belknap Press of Harvard University Press.

Agamben, Giorgio. 1998. *Homo Sacer: Sovereign Power and Bare Life.* Stanford, CA: Stanford University Press.

Agrama, Hussein. 2012. *Questioning Secularism: Islam, Sovereignty, and the Rule of Law in Modern Egypt.* Chicago: University of Chicago Press.

Ahmed, Sara. 2000. *Strange Encounters: Embodied Others in Post-coloniality.* New York: Routledge.

Anzaldúa, Gloria. (1987) 2012. *Borderlands/La Frontera: The New Mestiza.* San Francisco: Aunt Lute Books.

Appadurai, Arjun. 1986. *The Social Life of Things: Commodities in Cultural Perspective.* Cambridge: Cambridge University Press.

Asad, Talal. 1986. "The Concept of Cultural Translation in British Social Anthropology." In *Writing Culture: The Poetics and Politics of Ethnography*, edited by James Clifford and George Marcus, 141–164. Berkeley: University of California Press.

Balibar, Étienne. 1995. "Ambiguous Universality." *differences: A Journal of Feminist Cultural Studies* 7 (1): 48–74.

Balibar, Étienne. 2010. *Equaliberty: Political Essays.* Durham, NC: Duke University Press.

Balibar, Étienne. 2018. *Secularism and Cosmopolitanism: Critical Hypotheses on Religion and Politics.* New York: Columbia University Press.

Balibar, Étienne, and Immanuel Wallerstein. 1988. *Race, Nation, Class: Ambiguous Identities*. London: Verso.

Barthes, Roland. 1980. *Camera Lucida: Reflections on Photography*. New York: Hill and Wang.

Bateson, Gregory. (1936) 1958. *Naven: A Survey of the Problems Suggested by a Composite Picture of the Culture of a New Guinea Tribe Drawn from Three Points of View*. Stanford, CA: Stanford University Press.

Bateson, Gregory, Don Jackson, Jay Haley, and John Weakland. 1956. "Towards a Theory of Schizophrenia." *Behavioral Science* 1 (4): 251–254.

Baudelaire, Charles. (1863) 1964. *The Painter of Modern Life and Other Essays*. New York: Columbia University Press.

Benjamin, Walter. 2006. *The Writer of Modern Life: Essays on Charles Baudelaire*. Edited by Michael W. Jennings. Cambridge, MA: Harvard University Press.

Berger, John. 1972. *Ways of Seeing*. New York: Penguin.

Berlant, Lauren. 1998. "Intimacy: A Special Issue." *Critical Inquiry* 24 (2): 281–288.

Berlant, Lauren. 2000. *Intimacy*. Chicago: University of Chicago Press.

Berlant, Lauren. 2011. *Cruel Optimism*. Durham, NC: Duke University Press.

Berlant, Lauren, and Kathleen Stewart. 2018. *The Hundreds*. Durham, NC: Duke University Press.

Bhabha, Homi K. 1990. "Interview with Homi Bhabha: The Third Space." In *Identity: Community, Culture, Difference*, edited by Jonathan Rutherford, 207–221. London: Lawrence and Wishart.

Bhabha, Homi K. 1994. *The Location of Culture*. New York: Routledge.

Biehl, João. 2005. *Vita: Life in a Zone of Social Abandonment*. Princeton, NJ: Princeton University Press.

Biehl, João. 2009. *Will to Live: AIDS Therapies and the Politics of Survival*. Princeton, NJ: Princeton University Press.

Biehl, João, Byron J. Good, and Arthur Kleinman, eds. 2007. *Subjectivity: Ethnographic Investigations*. Berkeley: University of California Press.

Biehl, João, and Adriana Petryna. 2011. "Bodies of Rights and Therapeutic Markets." *Social Research* 78 (2): 359–386.

Blanchot, Maurice. 1980. *The Writing of the Disaster*. Lincoln: University of Nebraska Press.

Boyer, Dominic. 2005. *Spirit and System: Media, Intellectuals, and the Dialectic in Modern German Culture*. Chicago: University of Chicago Press.

Brenner, Neil, Jamie Peck, and Nik Theodore. 2010. "Variegated Neoliberalization: Geographies, Modalities, Pathways." *Global Networks* 10 (2): 182–222.

Brown, Wendy. 2015. *Undoing the Demos: Neoliberalism's Stealth Revolution*. Cambridge, MA: Zone Books.

Cantarella, Luke, Christine Hegel, and George Marcus. 2019. *Ethnography by Design: Scenographic Experiments in Fieldwork*. London: Bloomsbury.

Carr, E. Summerson. 2010. *Scripting Addiction: The Politics of Therapeutic Talk and American Addiction*. Princeton, NJ: Princeton University Press.

Chakrabarty, Dipesh. 2000. *Provincializing Europe: Postcolonial Thought and Historical Difference*. Princeton, NJ: Princeton University Press.

Chakrabarty, Dipesh. 2018. *The Crises of Civilization: Exploring Global and Planetary Histories*. Oxford: Oxford University Press.

Chakrabarty, Dipesh. 2021. *The Climate of History in a Planetary Age*. Chicago: University of Chicago Press.

Chatterjee, Partha. 2004. *The Politics of the Governed: Reflections on Popular Politics in Most of the World*. New York: Columbia University Press.

Chatterjee, Partha. 2011. *Lineages of Political Society: Studies in Postcolonial Democracy*. New York: Columbia University Press.

Choy, Timothy. 2011. *Ecologies of Comparison: An Ethnography of Endangerment in Hong Kong*. Durham, NC: Duke University Press.

Choy, Timothy. 2012. "Air's Substantiations." In *Lively Capital: Biotechnologies, Ethics, and Governance in Global Markets*, edited by Kaushik Sunder Rajan, 121–154. Durham, NC: Duke University Press.

Choy, Timothy. 2018. "Tending to Suspension: Abstraction and Apparatuses of Atmospheric Attunement in Matsutake Worlds." *Social Analysis* 62 (4): 54–77.

Choy, Timothy, and Jerry Zee. 2017. "Condition—Suspension." *Cultural Anthropology* 30 (2): 210–223.

Clifford, James, and George Marcus. 1986. *Writing Culture: The Poetics and Politics of Ethnography*. Berkeley: University of California Press.

Cohen, Lawrence. 1998. *No Aging in India: Alzheimer's, the Bad Family, and Other Modern Things*. Berkeley: University of California Press.

Cole, Teju. 2017. *Blind Spot*. New York: Random House.

Collier, Stephen. 2011. *Post-Soviet Social: Neoliberalism, Social Modernity, Biopolitics*. Princeton, NJ: Princeton University Press.

Comaroff, Jean, and John Comaroff. 2006. "Law and Disorder in the Postcolony: An Introduction." In *Law and Disorder in the Postcolony*, edited by Jean Comaroff and John Comaroff, 1–56. Chicago: University of Chicago Press.

Comaroff, Jean, and John Comaroff. 2012. *Theory from the South: How Euro-America Is Evolving toward Africa*. New York: Routledge.

Comaroff, John. 2010. "The End of Anthropology, Again: On the Future of an In/Discipline." *American Anthropologist* 112 (4): 524–538.

Conrad, Joseph. 1899. *Heart of Darkness*. https://en.wikisource.org/wiki/Heart_of _Darkness.

Cooper, Melinda. 2008. *Life as Surplus: Biotechnology and Capitalism in the Neoliberal Era*. Seattle: University of Washington Press.

D'Andrade, Roy. 1995. *The Development of Cognitive Anthropology*. Cambridge: Cambridge University Press.

Daniel, E. Valentine. 1996. *Charred Lullabies: Chapters in an Anthropography of Violence*. Princeton, NJ: Princeton University Press.

Das, Veena. 2006. *Life and Words: Violence and the Descent into the Ordinary*. Berkeley: University of California Press.

Das, Veena. 2015. *Affliction: Health, Disease, Poverty*. New York: Fordham University Press.

Davidson, Donald. (1984) 2001. *Inquiries into Truth and Interpretation*. London: Clarendon Press.

Derrida, Jacques. (1967) 1976. *Of Grammatology*. Translated by Gayatri Chakravorty Spivak. Baltimore, MD: Johns Hopkins University Press.

Derrida, Jacques. 1974. "White Mythology: Metaphor in the Text of Philosophy." *New Literary History* 6 (1): 5–74.

Derrida, Jacques. (1974) 1990. *Glas*. Translated by John P. Leavey Jr. and Richard Rand. Lincoln: University of Nebraska Press.

Derrida, Jacques. 1978. *Writing and Difference*. Translated by Alan Bass. Chicago: University of Chicago Press.

Derrida, Jacques. 1987. "To Speculate—on 'Freud.'" In *The Post Card: From Socrates to Freud and Beyond*, translated by Alan Bass, 257–258. Chicago: University of Chicago Press.

Derrida, Jacques. 1988. "The Deaths of Roland Barthes." In *Philosophy and Non-philosophy since Merleau-Ponty*, edited by Hugh J. Silverman, 259–296. New York: Routledge.

Derrida, Jacques. 1994. *Specters of Marx: The State of the Debt, the Work of Mourning, and the New International*. Translated by Peggy Kamuf. New York: Routledge.

Derrida, Jacques. 1997. *The Politics of Friendship*. Translated by George Collins. London: Verso.

Derrida, Jacques. 2001. *Acts of Religion*. New York: Routledge.

Derrida, Jacques. 2003. "The 'World' of the Enlightenment to Come (Exception, Calculation, Sovereignty)." *Research in Phenomenology* 33 (1): 9–52.

Devi, Mahashweta. 1991. *Imaginary Maps*. Translated by Gayatri Chakravorty Spivak. New York: Routledge.

Dewey, John. (1938) 2007. *Logic, the Theory of Inquiry*. New York: Saerchinger Press.

Dillon, Lindsey, Dawn Walker, Nicholas Shapiro, Vivian Underhill, Megan Martenyi, Sara Wylie, Rebecca Lave, Michelle Murphy, Phil Brown, and Environmental Data Governance Initiative. 2017. "Environmental Data Justice and the Trump Administration: Reflections from the Environmental Data and Governance Initiative." *Environmental Justice* 10 (6): 186–192.

Du Bois, W. E. B. (1903) 2016. *The Souls of Black Folk*. Scotts Valley, CA: CreateSpace Independent Publishing.

Dumit, Joseph. 2014. "Writing the Implosion: Teaching the World One Thing at a Time." *Cultural Anthropology* 29 (2): 344–362.

Durkheim, Émile. (1912) 2008. *The Elementary Forms of Religious Life*. Translated by Carol Cosman. Oxford: Oxford University Press.

Eco, Umberto. 1979. *The Role of the Reader: Explorations in the Semiotics of Texts.* Bloomington: Indiana University Press.

Elyachar, Julia. 2005. *Markets of Dispossession: NGOs, Economic Development, and the State in Egypt.* Durham, NC: Duke University Press.

Fanon, Frantz. (1952) 1994. *Black Skin, White Masks.* New York: Grove Press.

Faubion, James, and George Marcus, eds. 2009. *Fieldwork Is Not What It Used to Be: Learning Anthropology's Method in a Time of Transition.* Ithaca, NY: Cornell University Press.

Fisch, Michael. 2018. *An Anthropology of the Machine: Tokyo's Commuter Rail Network.* Chicago: University of Chicago Press.

Fischer, Michael M. J. 1980. *Iran: From Religious Dispute to Revolution.* Madison: University of Wisconsin Press.

Fischer, Michael M. J. 2003. *Emergent Forms of Life and the Anthropological Voice.* Durham, NC: Duke University Press.

Fischer, Michael M. J. 2005. "Technoscientific Infrastructures and Emergent Forms of Life: A Commentary." *American Anthropologist* 107 (1): 55–61.

Fischer, Michael M. J. 2007. "Culture and Cultural Analysis as Experimental Systems." *Cultural Anthropology* 22 (1): 1–64.

Fischer, Michael M. J. 2009. *Anthropological Futures.* Durham, NC: Duke University Press.

Fischer, Michael M. J. 2013. "Biopolis: Asian Science in the Global Circuitry." *Science, Technology and Society* 18 (3): 379–404.

Fischer, Michael M. J. 2014. "The Lightness of Existence and the Origami of 'French' Anthropology: Latour, Descola, Viveiros de Castro, Meillassoux, and Their So-Called Ontological Turn." *HAU: Journal of Ethnographic Theory* 4 (1): 331–355.

Fischer, Michael M. J. 2018. *Anthropology in the Meantime: Experimental Ethnography, Theory, and Method for the Twenty-First Century.* Durham, NC: Duke University Press.

Fischer, Michael M. J., and Mehdi Abedi. 1990. *Debating Muslims: Cultural Dialogues in Postmodernity and Tradition.* Madison: University of Wisconsin Press.

Fortun, Kim. 2001. *Advocacy after Bhopal: Environmentalism, Disaster, New Global Orders.* Chicago: University of Chicago Press.

Fortun, Kim. 2006. "Post-structuralism, Technoscience, and the Promise of Public Anthropology." *India Review* 5 (3–4): 294–317.

Fortun, Kim. 2012. "Ethnography in Late Industrialism." *Cultural Anthropology* 27 (3): 446–464.

Fortun, Kim. 2014. "From Latour to Late Industrialism." *HAU: Journal of Ethnographic Theory* 4 (1): 309–329.

Fortun, Kim. 2015. "Figuring Out Theory: Ethnographic Sketches." In *Theory Can Be More Than It Used to Be: Learning Anthropology's Method in a Time of*

Transition, edited by Dominic Boyer, James Faubion, and George Marcus, 147–168. Ithaca, NY: Cornell University Press.

Fortun, Michael. 2008. *Promising Genomics: Iceland and deCODE Genetics in a World of Speculation*. Berkeley: University of California Press.

Foucault, Michel. 2008. *The Birth of Biopolitics: Lectures at the Collège de France, 1978–1979*. London: Picador.

Fukuyama, Francis. (1991) 2006. *The End of History and the Last Man*. New York: Free Press.

Gal, Susan. 2015. "Politics of Translation." *Annual Review of Anthropology* 44: 225–240.

Gandhi, Leela. 1998. *Postcolonial Theory: A Critical Introduction*. New York: Columbia University Press.

Gaonkar, Dilip, ed. 2001. *Alternative Modernities*. Durham, NC: Duke University Press.

Garcia, Angela. 2008. "The Elegiac Addict: History, Chronicity, and the Melancholic Subject." *Cultural Anthropology* 23 (4): 718–746.

Garcia, Angela. 2010. *The Pastoral Clinic: Addiction and Dispossession along the Rio Grande*. Berkeley: University of California Press.

Geertz, Clifford. 1973. *The Interpretation of Cultures*. New York: Basic Books.

Geertz, Clifford. 1974. "From the Native's Point of View: On the Nature of Anthropological Understanding." *Bulletin of the American Academy of Arts and Sciences* 28 (1): 26–45.

Ginzburg, Carlo. 1980. "Morelli, Freud and Sherlock Holmes: Clues and Scientific Method." *History Workshop* 9: 5–36.

Golding, William. 1954. *Lord of the Flies*. London: Faber and Faber.

Good, Byron. 1994. *Medicine, Rationality and Experience: An Anthropological Perspective*. Cambridge: Cambridge University Press.

Good, Byron. 2012. "Theorizing the 'Subject' of Medical and Psychiatric Anthropology." *Journal of the Royal Anthropological Institute* 18 (3): 515–535.

Good, Byron, and Mary-Jo DelVecchio Good. 2000. "Fiction and Historicity in Doctors' Stories: Social and Narrative Dimensions of Learning Medicine." In *Narrative and the Cultural Construction of Illness and Healing*, edited by Cheryl Mattingly and Linda C. Garro, 50–69. Berkeley: University of California Press.

Gramsci, Antonio. (1926) 2000. "Some Aspects of the Southern Question." In *The Antonio Gramsci Reader: Selected Writings 1916–1935*, edited by David Forgacs, 171–185. New York: New York University Press.

Grant, Philip. 2011. "Collaborative Performances: Agency, Gender and Californian-Iranian Women's Activists." PhD diss., University of California at Irvine.

Griesemer, James. 2011. "Modeling Scientific Knowledge and Values." Paper presented at the "Knowledge/Value" conference, University of Chicago.

Grossberg, Lawrence. 1996. "On Postmodernism and Articulation: An Interview with Stuart Hall." In *Stuart Hall: Critical Dialogues in Cultural Studies*, edited by David Morley and Kuan-Hsing Chen, 131–150. New York: Routledge.

Gupta, Akhil, and James Ferguson. 1998. *Anthropological Locations: Boundaries and Grounds of a Field Science*. Berkeley: University of California Press.

Halpern, Gregory. 2016. ZZYZX. London: MACK Books.

Haraway, Donna. 1988. "Situated Knowledges: The Science Question in Feminism, and the Privilege of Partial Perspective." *Feminist Studies* 14 (3): 575–599.

Haraway, Donna. 2007. *When Species Meet*. Minneapolis: University of Minnesota Press.

Harvey, David. 2003. *The New Imperialism*. Oxford: Oxford University Press.

Harvey, David. 2007. *A Brief History of Neoliberalism*. Oxford: Oxford University Press.

Hayden, Cori. 2010. "The Proper Copy: The Insides and Outsides of Domains Made Public." *Journal of Cultural Economy* 3 (1): 85–102.

Hayden, Cori. 2011. "No Patent, No Generic: Pharmaceutical Access and the Politics of the Copy." In *Making and Unmaking Intellectual Property: Creative Production in Legal and Cultural Perspective*, edited by Mario Biagioli, Peter Jaszi, and Martha Woodmansee, 285–304. Chicago: University of Chicago Press.

Holmes, Douglas, and George Marcus. 2005. "Cultures of Expertise and the Management of Globalization: Toward the Re-functioning of Ethnography." In *Global Assemblages: Technology, Politics, and Ethics as Anthropological Problems*, edited by Aihwa Ong and Stephen Collier, 235–252. Oxford: Blackwell.

Irvine, Judith T., and Susan Gal. 2000. "Language Ideology and Linguistic Differentiation." In *Regimes of Language: Ideologies, Polities, Identities*, edited by Paul V. Kroskrity, 35–84. Santa Fe, NM: School of American Research Press.

Jackson, John L. 2010. "On Ethnographic Sincerity." *Current Anthropology* 51 (s2): S279–S287.

Jain, S. Lochlann. 2013. *Malignant: How Cancer Becomes Us*. Berkeley: University of California Press.

Jakobson, Roman. 1962. "On the Linguistic Approach to the Problem of Consciousness and the Unconsciousness." In *Selected Writings VII*, 148–162. Berlin: Mouton.

Jasanoff, Sheila. 2005. *Designs on Nature: Science and Democracy in Europe and the United States*. Princeton, NJ: Princeton University Press.

Jasanoff, Sheila, and Sang-Hyun Kim, eds. 2015. *Dreamscapes of Modernity: Sociotechnical Imaginaries and the Fabrication of Power*. Chicago: University of Chicago Press.

Karim, Lamia. 2011. *Microfinance and Its Discontents: Women in Debt in Bangladesh*. Minneapolis: University of Minnesota Press.

Kelty, Christopher. 1999. "Scale and Convention: Programmed Language in a Regulated America." PhD diss., Massachusetts Institute of Technology.

Kelty, Christopher. 2008. *Two Bits: Free Software and the Social Imagination after the Internet*. Durham, NC: Duke University Press.

Kleinman, Arthur. 1989. *The Illness Narratives: Suffering, Healing, and the Human Condition*. New York: Basic Books.

Kleinman, Arthur, Veena Das, and Margaret Lock, eds. 1997. *Social Suffering*. Berkeley: University of California Press.

Kohut, Heinz. 1978. "The Psychoanalyst in the Community of Scholars." In *The Search for the Self: Selected Writings of Heinz Kohut: 1950–1978*, vol. 2, edited by P. H. Ornstein, 685–724. New York: International Universities Press.

Kuhn, Mona. 2018. Keynote lecture at Filter Photo Festival, Chicago.

LaCapra, Dominick. 1983. *Rethinking Intellectual History: Texts, Contexts, Language*. Ithaca, NY: Cornell University Press.

Larkin, Brian. 2008. *Signal and Noise: Media, Infrastructure, and Urban Culture in Nigeria*. Durham, NC: Duke University Press.

Latour, Bruno. 1988. *The Pasteurization of France*. Cambridge, MA: Harvard University Press.

Latour, Bruno. 1990. "Postmodern? No, Simply Amodern! Steps towards an Anthropology of Science." *Studies in the History and Philosophy of Science* 21: 145–171.

Latour, Bruno. 1993. *We Have Never Been Modern*. Cambridge, MA: Harvard University Press.

Lebner, Ashley. 2019. "No Such Thing as *a* Concept: A Radical Tradition from Malinowski to Asad and Strathern." *Anthropological Theory* 20 (1): 1–26. https://doi.org/10.1177/1463499618805916.

Lévi-Strauss, Claude. (1955) 1992. *Tristes Tropiques*. New York: Penguin.

Lévi-Strauss, Claude. 1974. *Structural Anthropology*. New York: Basic Books.

Li, Darryl. 2019. *The Universal Enemy: Jihad, Empire, and the Challenge of Solidarity*. Stanford, CA: Stanford University Press.

MacKenzie, Donald. 2001. *Mechanizing Proof: Computing, Risk, and Trust*. Cambridge, MA: MIT Press.

Mahmood, Saba. 2005. *Politics of Piety: The Islamic Revival and the Feminist Subject*. Princeton, NJ: Princeton University Press.

Malinowski, Bronislaw. (1922) 2014. *Argonauts of the Western Pacific*. New York: Routledge.

Malinowski, Bronislaw. (1935) 1978. *Coral Gardens and Their Magic*. Garden City, NY: Dover.

Marcus, George, ed. 1994. *Technoscientific Imaginaries: Conversations, Profiles, Memoirs*. Chicago: University of Chicago Press.

Marcus, George. 1995. "Ethnography in/of the World System: The Emergence of Multi-sited Ethnography." *Annual Review of Anthropology* 24: 95–117.

Marcus, George. 2005. "Multi-sited Ethnography: Five or Six Things I Know about It Now." Paper presented at workshop on "Problems and Possibilities of Multi-sited Ethnography," University of Sussex, June 27.

Marcus, George. 2011. "Alongside. . . ." Paper presented at the "Knowledge/ Value" conference, University of Chicago.

Marcus, George. 2017. "Art (and Anthropology) at the World Trade Organization: Chronicle of an Intervention." *Ethnos* 82 (5): 907–924.

Marcus, George, and Michael M. J. Fischer. 1986. *Anthropology as Cultural Critique: An Experimental Moment in the Human Sciences*. Chicago: University of Chicago Press.

Marcus, George, and Michael M. J. Fischer. 1999. "Preface to Second Edition." In *Anthropology as Cultural Critique: An Experimental Moment in the Human Sciences*, xv–xxxiv. Chicago: University of Chicago Press.

Marcus, George E., and Erkan Saka. 2005. "Assemblages." *Theory, Culture and Society* 23 (2–3): 107–108.

Marx, Karl. (1852) 1977. *The Eighteenth Brumaire of Louis Bonaparte*. Moscow: Progress.

Marx, Karl. (1871) 2009. *The Civil War in France*. Moscow: Dodo Press.

Masco, Joseph. 2006. *The Nuclear Borderlands: The Manhattan Project in Post–Cold War New Mexico*. Princeton, NJ: Princeton University Press.

Masco, Joseph. 2010. "Bad Weather: On Planetary Crisis." *Social Studies of Science* 40 (1): 7–40.

Masco, Joseph. 2014. *The Theater of Operations: National Security Affect from the Cold War to the War on Terror*. Durham, NC: Duke University Press.

Mead, Margaret. (1928) 2017. *Coming of Age in Samoa: A Psychological Study of Primitive Youth for Western Civilization*. New York: Andesite Press.

Meister, Robert. 2011. *After Evil: A Politics of Human Rights*. New York: Columbia University Press.

Meister, Robert. 2021. *Justice Is an Option: A Democratic Theory of Finance for the Twenty-First Century*. Chicago: University of Chicago Press.

Merton, Robert. 1942. "The Normative Structure of Science." In *The Sociology of Science*, 267–278. Chicago: University of Chicago Press.

Mezzadra, Sandro, and Brett Nielsen. 2013. *Border as Method, or, the Multiplication of Labor*. Durham, NC: Duke University Press.

Mintz, Sidney. 1985. *Sweetness and Power: The Place of Sugar in Modern History*. New York: Penguin.

Mulvey, Laura. 1975. "Visual Pleasure and Narrative Cinema." *Screen* 16 (3): 6–18.

Murphy, Keith. 2015. *Swedish Design: An Ethnography*. Ithaca, NY: Cornell University Press.

Murphy, Michelle. 2017. *The Economization of Life*. Durham, NC: Duke University Press.

Naficy, Nahal. 2009. "The Dracula Ballet: A Tale of Fieldwork in Politics." In *Fieldwork Is Not What It Used to Be: Learning Anthropology's Method in a Time of Transition*, edited by James Faubion and George Marcus, 113–128. Ithaca, NY: Cornell University Press.

Nandy, Ashis. 1983. *The Intimate Enemy: Loss and Recovery of Self under Colonialism.* New Delhi: Oxford University Press.

Navaro-Yashin, Yael. 2009. "Affective Spaces, Melancholic Objects: Ruination and the Production of Anthropological Knowledge." *Journal of the Royal Anthropological Institute* 15: 1–18.

Needham, Anuradha, and Rajeswari Sunder Rajan, eds. 2007. *The Crisis of Secularism in India.* Durham, NC: Duke University Press.

Newfield, Christopher. 2011. *Unmaking the Public University: The Forty-Year Assault on the Middle Class.* Cambridge, MA: Harvard University Press.

Niranjana, Tejaswini. 1992. *Siting Translation: History, Post-structuralism, and the Colonial Context.* Berkeley: University of California Press.

Nixon, Rob. 2011. *Slow Violence and the Environmentalism of the Poor.* Cambridge, MA: Harvard University Press.

Ong, Aihwa. 1987. *Spirits of Resistance and Capitalist Discipline.* Binghamton: State University of New York Press.

Ong, Aihwa, and Stephen Collier. 2005. *Global Assemblages: Technology, Politics, and Ethics as Anthropological Problems.* Oxford: Blackwell.

Orr, Julian. 1996. *Talking about Machines: An Ethnography of a Modern Job.* Ithaca, NY: ILR Press.

Ortner, Sherry. 1995. "Resistance and the Problem of Ethnographic Refusal." *Comparative Studies in Society and History* 37 (1): 173–193.

Pamuk, Orhan. 2008. *The Museum of Innocence.* New York: Vintage.

Paxson, Heather. 2013. *The Life of Cheese: Crafting Food and Value in America.* Berkeley: University of California Press.

Peterson, Kristin. 2014. *Speculative Markets: Drug Circuits and Derivative Life in Nigeria.* Durham, NC: Duke University Press.

Pickering, Andrew. 1995. *The Mangle of Practice: Time, Agency, and Science.* Chicago: University of Chicago Press.

Polanyi, Michael. 1962. "The Republic of Science, Its Political and Economic Theory." Lecture delivered at Roosevelt University, January 11.

Povinelli, Elizabeth. 2001. "Radical Worlds: The Anthropology of Incommensurability and Inconceivability." *Annual Review of Anthropology* 30: 319–334.

Povinelli, Elizabeth A. 2016. *Geontologies: A Requiem to Late Liberalism.* Durham, NC: Duke University Press.

Pratt, Mary Louise. 1994. *Imperial Eyes: Travel Writing and Transculturation.* New York: Routledge.

Preciado, Paul. 2014. *Pornotopia: An Essay on Playboy's Architecture and Biopolitics.* Cambridge, MA: MIT Press.

Quine, William van Orman. 1960. *Word and Object.* Cambridge, MA: MIT Press.

Rabinow, Paul. 1995. *Making PCR: A Story of Biotechnology*. Chicago: University of Chicago Press.

Rabinow, Paul. 1999. *French DNA: Trouble in Purgatory*. Chicago: University of Chicago Press.

Rabinow, Paul. 2002. "Midst Anthropology's Problems." *Cultural Anthropology* 17 (2): 135–149.

Rabinow, Paul. 2003. *Anthropos Today: Reflections on Modern Equipment*. Princeton, NJ: Princeton University Press.

Ramanujan, A. K. 1973. "Annayya's Anthropology." Papers, Box 45, Folder 6–7, Special Collections Research Center, University of Chicago Library.

Reading, Bill. 1996. *The University in Ruins*. Cambridge, MA: Harvard University Press.

Rheinberger, Hans-Jörg. 1997. *Toward a History of Epistemic Things: Synthesizing Proteins in the Test Tube*. Stanford, CA: Stanford University Press.

Robbins, Bruce. 1992. "Comparative Cosmopolitanism." *Social Text* 31/32: 169–186.

Robbins, Bruce. 2002. "What's Left of Cosmopolitanism?" *Radical Philosophy* 116: 30–37.

Robbins, Bruce. 2007. "Cosmopolitanism, New and Newer." *Boundary 2* 34 (3): 47–60.

Rose, Nikolas. 2006. *The Politics of Life Itself: Biomedicine, Power, and Subjectivity in the Twenty-First Century*. Princeton, NJ: Princeton University Press.

Rushdie, Salman. 1980. *Midnight's Children*. New York: Modern Library.

Rushdie, Salman. (1983) 2008. *Shame*. New York: Random House.

Sakai, Naoki. 1997. *Translation and Subjectivity: On "Japan" and Cultural Nationalism*. Minneapolis: University of Minnesota Press.

Salih, Tayeb. (1966) 2009. *Season of Migration to the North*. New York: New York Review Books Classics.

Sanabria, Emilia. 2016. *Plastic Bodies: Sex Hormones and Menstrual Suppression in Brazil*. Durham, NC: Duke University Press.

Sapir, Edward. 1949. "The Unconscious Patterning of Behavior in Society." In *Selected Writings in Language, Culture, and Personality*, edited by David G. Mandelbaum, 544–559. Berkeley: University of California Press.

Scheper-Hughes, Nancy. 1992. *Death without Weeping: The Violence of Everyday Life in Brazil*. Berkeley: University of California Press.

Schwab, Gabriele. 2010. *Haunting Legacies: Violent Histories and Transgenerational Trauma*. New York: Columbia University Press.

Schwab, Gabriele. 2012. *Imaginary Ethnographies: Literature, Culture, and Subjectivity*. New York: Columbia University Press.

Scott, David. 2014. "The Temporality of Generations: Dialogue, Tradition, Criticism." *New Literary History* 45 (2): 157–181.

Scott, Joan. 1996. *Only Paradoxes to Offer: French Feminists and the Rights of Man*. Cambridge, MA: Harvard University Press.

Scott, Joan. 2017. *Sex and Secularism*. Princeton, NJ: Princeton University Press.

Silverstein, Michael. 1979. "Language Structure and Linguistic Ideology." In *The Elements: A Parasession on Linguistic Units and Levels*, edited by Paul R. Clyne and William F. Hanks, 193–247. Chicago Linguistic Society, University of Chicago.

Silverstein, Michael, and Greg Urban, eds. 1996. *Natural Histories of Discourse*. Chicago: University of Chicago Press.

Simpson, Audra. 2007. "On Ethnographic Refusal: Indigeneity, 'Voice,' and Colonial Citizenship." *Junctures* 9: 67–80.

Smith, Shawn Michelle. 2004. *Photography on the Color Line*. Durham, NC: Duke University Press.

Smith, Shawn Michelle. 2013. *At the Edge of Sight: Photography and the Unseen*. Durham, NC: Duke University Press.

Sontag, Susan. 1977. *On Photography*. New York: Farrar, Straus and Giroux.

Spivak, Gayatri Chakravorty. 1985. "The Rani of Sirmur: An Essay in Reading the Archives." *History and Theory* 24 (3): 247–272.

Spivak, Gayatri Chakravorty. 1988. "Can the Subaltern Speak?" In *Marxism and the Interpretation of Cultures*, edited by Cary Nelson and Lawrence Grossberg, 271–313. Basingstoke, UK: Macmillan Education.

Spivak, Gayatri Chakravorty. 1990. "Constitutions and Culture Studies." *Yale Journal of Law and the Humanities* 2 (1): 133–147.

Spivak, Gayatri Chakravorty. 1991. "Translator's Preface." In *Imaginary Maps*, by Mahashweta Devi, xxiii–xxx. New York: Routledge.

Spivak, Gayatri Chakravorty. 1993. *Outside in the Teaching Machine*. New York: Routledge.

Spivak, Gayatri Chakravorty. 1994. "Responsibility." *Boundary 2* 21 (3): 19–64.

Spivak, Gayatri Chakravorty. 1998. *A Critique of Postcolonial Reason: Toward a History of the Vanishing Present*. Cambridge, MA: Harvard University Press.

Spivak, Gayatri Chakravorty. 2000. "Claiming Transformation: Travel Notes with Pictures." In *Transformations: Thinking through Feminism*, edited by Sara Ahmed, Jane Kilby, Celia Lury, Maureen MacNeil, and Beverly Skeggs, 119–130. New York: Routledge.

Spivak, Gayatri Chakravorty. 2003. *Death of a Discipline*. New York: Columbia University Press.

Spivak, Gayatri Chakravorty. 2018. "DuBois in the World: Pan-Africanism and Decolonization." *Boundary 2*. https://www.boundary2.org/2018/12/spivakondubois/.

Star, Susan Leigh, and James Griesemer. 1989. "Institutional Ecology, 'Translations,' and Boundary Objects: Amateurs and Professionals in Berkeley's Museum of Vertebrate Zoology, 1907–39." *Social Studies of Science* 19 (3): 387–420.

Steinberg, Jonny. 2008. *Three-Letter Plague: A Young Man's Journey through a Great Epidemic*. New York: Vintage.

Steinberg, Jonny. 2016a. *A Man of Good Hope*. New York: Vintage.

Steinberg, Jonny. 2016b. "The Vertiginous Power of Decisions: Working through a Paradox about Forced Migration." *Public Culture* 28 (1): 139–160.

Stewart, Kathleen. 2007. *Ordinary Affects*. Durham, NC: Duke University Press.

Strathern, Marilyn. 1981. *Kinship at the Core: An Anthropology of Elmdon, a Village in North-West Essex*. Cambridge: Cambridge University Press.

Strathern, Marilyn. 1987a. "An Awkward Relationship: The Case of Feminism and Anthropology." *Signs: Journal of Women in Culture and Society* 12 (2): 276–292.

Strathern, Marilyn. 1987b. "Out of Context: The Persuasive Fictions of Anthropology." *Current Anthropology* 28 (3): 251–281.

Strathern, Marilyn. 1988. *The Gender of the Gift*. Berkeley: University of California Press.

Strathern, Marilyn. 1991. *Partial Connections*. Lanham, MD: AltaMira Press.

Strathern, Marilyn. 1992a. *After Nature: English Kinship in the Late Twentieth Century*. Cambridge: Cambridge University Press.

Strathern, Marilyn. 1992b. *Reproducing the Future: Essays on Anthropology, Kinship, and the New Reproductive Technologies*. New York: Routledge.

Strathern, Marilyn. 1999. *Property, Substance, and Effect: Anthropological Essays on Persons and Things*. Oxford, UK: Athlone Press.

Strathern, Marilyn. 2000. *Audit Cultures: Anthropological Studies in Accountability, Ethics and the Academy*. New York: Routledge.

Strathern, Marilyn. 2005a. "Anthropology and Interdisciplinarity." *Arts and Humanities in Higher Education* 4 (2): 125–135.

Strathern, Marilyn. 2005b. "Experiments in Interdisciplinarity." *Social Anthropology* 13 (1): 75–90.

Suchman, Lucy. 1987. *Plans and Situated Actions: The Problem of Human-Machine Communication*. Cambridge: Cambridge University Press.

Suchman, Lucy. 2006. *Human-Machine Reconfigurations: Plans and Situated Actions*. Cambridge: Cambridge University Press.

Sunder Rajan, Kaushik. 2006. *Biocapital: The Constitution of Postgenomic Life*. Durham, NC: Duke University Press.

Sunder Rajan, Kaushik. 2011. "Translating Biocapital: The Nature (and Cultures) of Global Biomedical Collaborations." Paper presented at the "Knowledge/Value" conference, University of Chicago.

Sunder Rajan, Kaushik. 2015. "Trans-formations of Biology and of Theory." In *Theory Can Be More Than It Used to Be: Learning Anthropology's Method in a Time of Transition*, edited by Dominic Boyer, James Faubion, and George Marcus, 104–146. Ithaca, NY: Cornell University Press.

Sunder Rajan, Kaushik. 2017. *Pharmocracy: Value, Politics, and Knowledge in Global Biomedicine*. Durham, NC: Duke University Press.

Sunder Rajan, Rajeswari. 2003. *The Scandal of the State: Women, Law, and Citizenship in Postcolonial India*. Durham, NC: Duke University Press.

Sunder Rajan, Rajeswari. 2010. "Death and the Subaltern." In *Can the Subaltern Speak? Reflections on the History of an Idea*, edited by Rosalind Morris, 117–138. New York: Columbia University Press.

Sunder Rajan, Rajeswari. 2018. "Shifting the Blame: An Unlikely Argument about Islamophobia." *Times Literary Supplement*, May 11. https://www.the-tls.co.uk/articles/islamaphobia-west-sex-secularism/.

Sunder Rajan, Rajeswari. In preparation. "A Novel and Its Museum: Orhan Pamuk's 'Museum of Innocence.'"

Tan, Jill J. 2019. "Notes on the Bicentennial of a F/l/ound/er/ing (2019): Scribbles on Poetic Access to a Moving Object." Term paper, University of Chicago.

Taussig, Michael. 1984. "Culture of Terror—Space of Death: Roger Casement's Putamayo Report and the Explanation of Torture." *Comparative Studies in Society and History* 26 (3): 467–497.

Traweek, Sharon. 1988. *Beamtimes and Lifetimes: The World of High Energy Physicists*. Cambridge, MA: Harvard University Press.

Trilling, Lionel. 1980. *Of This Time, Of That Place, and Other Stories*. New York: Harcourt.

Trouillot, Michel-Rolph. 2003. *Global Transformations: Anthropology and the Modern World*. London: Palgrave Macmillan.

Tsing, Anna Lowenhaupt. 2004. *Friction: An Ethnography of Global Connection*. Princeton, NJ: Princeton University Press.

Tsing, Anna Lowenhaupt. 2015. *The Mushroom at the End of the World: On the Possibility of Life in Capitalist Ruins*. Princeton, NJ: Princeton University Press.

Tyler, Stephen. 1986. "Post-modern Ethnography: From Document of the Occult to Occult Document." In *Writing Culture: The Poetics and Politics of Ethnography*, edited by James Clifford and George Marcus, 141–164. Berkeley: University of California Press.

Uberoi, J. P. S. 2002. *The European Modernity: Science, Truth and Method*. New Delhi: Oxford University Press.

Vance, J. D. 2017. *Hillbilly Elegy: A Memoir of a Family and Culture in Crisis*. New York: HarperCollins.

Viswanathan, Shiv. 1997. *A Carnival for Science: Essays on Science, Technology and Development*. New Delhi: Oxford University Press.

Viveiros de Castro, Eduardo. 2004. "Perspectival Anthropology and the Method of Controlled Equivocation." *Tipiti: Journal of the Society for the Anthropology of Lowland South America* 2 (1): 3–22.

Wally, Christine. 2013. *Exit Zero: Family and Class in Postindustrial Chicago*. Chicago: University of Chicago Press.

Weinberg, Alvin M. 1972. "Science and Trans-science." *Science* 177 (4045): 211.

West, Paige. 2012. *From Modern Production to Imagined Primitive: The Social Life of Coffee from Papua New Guinea*. Durham, NC: Duke University Press.

Westbrook, David. 2008. *Navigators of the Contemporary: Why Ethnography Matters*. Chicago: University of Chicago Press.

White, Hayden. 1973. *Metahistory: The Historical Imagination in Nineteenth Century Europe*. Baltimore, MD: Johns Hopkins University Press.

White, Hylton. 2019. "What Is Anthropology That Decolonising Scholarship Should Be Mindful of It?" *Anthropology Southern Africa* 42 (2): 149–160.

Wiggins, Marianne. 1988. *John Dollar*. New York: Simon and Schuster.

Williams, Raymond. 1978. *Marxism and Literature*. Oxford: Oxford University Press.

Wittgenstein, Ludwig. (1953) 1973. *Philosophical Investigations*. Translated by G. E. M. Anscombe. London: Pearson.

Wong, Winnie. 2013. *Van Gogh on Demand: China and the Readymade*. Chicago: University of Chicago Press.

Woolf, Virginia. (1925) 1998. *Mrs. Dalloway*. Ware, Hertfordshire, UK: Wordsworth Editions.

Woolf, Virginia. (1929) 2012. *A Room of One's Own*. Eastford, CT: Martino Fine Books.

Wylie, Sara. 2018. *Fractivism: Corporate Bodies and Chemical Bonds*. Durham, NC: Duke University Press.

Index

activism/activist, 14–15, 21, 53, 107, 141,
  145–146, 149–153, 164, 220n15, 222n19,
  223n20
advocacy, 53–55, 79, 164, 172, 191n8, 222n19
Advocacy after Bhopal, 38–39, 47, 50, 52–55,
  108, 199n26
affect(s)/affective, 27, 46, 69, 78, 95, 97,
  108, 111, 116–118, 126–127, 155, 159–160,
  171, 183, 197–198n21, 210n14, 224n25
"Afterimages: Abu Ghraib," 132–133
alterity, 24, 62, 64, 66–69, 81–83, 86–90,
  106, 138, 176, 178, 180, 183, 186–187,
  193n19, 204n20, 208n3, 218–219n9
America. *See* United States
American academe/university, 7, 14, 22,
  39, 70, 83, 153, 156, 158, 174, 177, 179,
  190n3, 223n20, 225n28
American exceptionalism, 104, 132, 134,
  204n20
"Annayya's Anthropology," 3
anthropological problem(s), 51–52, 54, 57,
  106, 136, 197n20
Anthropology as Cultural Critique, 6, 9, 19,
  25, 27, 31–34, 36, 38–39, 41, 60, 65, 69,
  141, 157, 159, 185, 195n1, 195n5, 201n8
anthropology of science and technology,
  19, 190n7

anticolonial, 21, 81, 184, 190n4, 206n30
antiracism/antiracist, 16, 175
apartheid, 40, 169–173, 178–179, 193n19
appropriated/appropriation/appropria-
  tive, 8, 23, 25, 27, 42–43, 55, 65, 73–75,
  79–81, 101, 113–116, 119–120, 122, 126,
  142–144, 152, 166, 175, 177, 197n19,
  205n23, 213n27, 213n31, 226n29
archive(s), 71–72, 91–96, 112, 205n24
area studies, 3–4, 71, 73, 84, 87, 119
atmosphere(s), 103, 105, 118, 179, 210n14
At the Edge of Sight, 129–132, 217n53, 217n55
audit culture(s), 15, 75, 147, 166, 203n16,
  220n16, 226nn28–29
authoritarian(ism), 4, 7–8, 11, 61, 83, 142–
  143, 162, 174, 204n20, 208n3, 224n26
autobiographical/autobiography, 3, 7–9, 13,
  84, 89–90, 94–95, 98–101, 104, 110, 115–116,
  123, 137–138, 141, 144, 161, 174, 181, 183,
  187, 196n16, 208n3, 216n52, 219–220n12

Balibar, Étienne, 145, 206n30, 219n9,
  224n25, 226–227n3
Barthes, Roland, 25, 109–114, 117–119,
  128–132, 184–185, 212n24, 213n28, 213n30,
  213n32, 214nn35–36, 214nn38–39, 215n41,
  215n48

Bateson, Gregory, 7–9, 58, 192n12, 206n29

Beamtimes and Lifetimes, 58–59, 192n12

Berger, John, 112–113, 116, 213nn26–27, 213n29, 214n34

Berlant, Lauren, 25, 27, 102–103, 105, 113, 117–119, 183, 191n9, 196n15, 209nn10–12, 210n14, 210n18

Bhabha, Homi, 22, 82, 94–95, 193n16

Bhopal, 52–55, 79, 164, 199n24

Bhuvaneswari Bhaduri, 72–73, 76, 81, 91, 203n15

Biehl, João, 38–44, 46, 53, 196n11, 196n16, 227n4

Biocapital, 30, 59–60, 217n1

biographical/biography, 4–6, 9, 12–13, 16, 21, 25, 31, 46, 58, 75, 137, 142, 144, 146, 152, 156–157, 161–162, 171, 206n30, 209n6, 224n25

Blind Spot, 119–127, 215n43

breather(s), 105, 108

British social anthropology, 82, 192n15, 201n8, 203n12, 205n25, 218n5

Camera Lucida, 109, 114, 116, 128–130, 185, 213n28

canon/canonical, 9, 19, 71, 73, 111, 134, 174, 183–184, 189n1

"Can the Subaltern Speak?," 71–72, 89, 93, 133, 203n15

capital/capitalism/capitalization, 6–7, 22, 31, 47–48, 53–54, 60–62, 68–75, 80–82, 97, 113, 149, 152–155, 158, 200n3, 203n16, 203n18, 215n42

cartographer/cartographic/cartography, 69, 81, 120, 123, 192n14

catachresis/catachrestic, 177–178, 227n5

Chakrabarty, Dipesh, 80–82, 193–194n19, 205n23

Choy, Timothy, 101, 105–108, 119–120, 199n28, 201n8, 210n14, 212n23, 216n52

circulation, 48, 131–132, 134, 185, 205n25, 226n29

citation, 13, 180, 183–184

Cole, Teju, 119–128, 215n43, 215nn45–47, 215–216n48, 216n49, 216n52

collaboration/collaborator, 34, 140–141, 147, 150–151, 153–154, 156–161, 163, 166, 191n8, 198n21, 210n18, 212n23, 214n33, 220n15, 221n18, 224–225n26, 227n7

collectivities/collectivity, 8, 55, 76–80, 107–108, 119, 123, 127, 129, 199n28, 205n23

colonial(ism), 1–2, 5, 11–12, 19, 22–28, 32, 44, 62, 69–73, 75–78, 81, 83, 86–87, 93, 97–98, 101, 105, 120, 122, 131, 134, 155, 160, 175, 180–181, 183–184, 193n15, 194n22, 197n19, 207n38, 208n3, 211n20, 218n5, 227n6

Comaroff, Jean, 53, 194n19, 207n38, 227n4

Comaroff, John, 53, 194n19, 194n24, 207n38, 227n4

commensurability/commensuration, 63, 66, 68–70, 80–81, 89, 187

commodified/commodifying, 74, 132, 213n29, 213n31, 226n29

communities of practice, 1, 4, 14–15, 134, 165, 202n10

comparative literature, 71, 73–74, 76, 119

comparison, 6–8, 24–27, 31, 52, 56–63, 66–70, 73–74, 76–77, 79–84, 86–88, 91, 125, 135, 153, 165, 180–183, 185–187, 192n12, 197n20, 200n1, 207n31, 214n37, 227n4

conceptual topology, 25, 31, 47, 53–55, 64, 80, 90, 122

concept work, 18, 80, 176, 191n10

conjunctural/conjuncture, 4, 7, 10–11, 26, 52, 60, 70, 73, 95, 147, 156, 160, 174, 193n19, 199n24, 202–203n12, 205n25, 218n6, 219n9, 221n17, 227n4

Conrad, Joseph, 76–80, 97, 131, 209n6

constitutional(ism), 59, 83, 173, 176–179, 225n27, 227n4

"Constitutions and Culture Studies," 83, 205n24

contingency, 63, 85, 104, 108–110, 112, 117, 145, 155–156, 158, 161, 180, 212n24, 216n48

corporate university, 151, 153–156, 158, 223n22, 225n26

cosmopolitan(ism), 7, 16, 74, 87, 89, 105, 137–138, 156, 162, 187, 227n3

crisis of representation, 2, 10, 68

Critique of Postcolonial Reason, A, 70–71, 91, 93, 228n10
cultural critique, 30, 60, 66, 86, 94, 153, 201n8
"Cultures of Expertise and the Management of Globalization," 140, 142, 220n14
curation, 104–105, 150, 220n15, 223n20

Death of a Discipline, 70–71, 73–74, 76, 97, 119, 203n19, 205n24, 211n22, 217n3, 219n11
Debating Muslims, 138, 196n8, 218n9
decolonial/decolonization, 2, 4–5, 7, 10–11, 16, 20, 23–24, 26, 28, 33, 65, 70–71, 78, 81–82, 132, 166, 174–176, 178–181, 183–186, 193–194n19, 218n7, 226n29, 227n6, 227n8
deconstruction/deconstructive, 7, 12, 24, 27, 52, 57, 70, 72–73, 75, 81, 83, 85–86, 88–90, 92, 101–102, 104, 106, 113, 119, 122, 128, 135, 174–175, 182–184, 186–187, 201n8, 204n20, 205n23, 206n29, 211n20, 212n25
Derrida, Jacques, 10, 12, 67, 86, 88, 106, 108, 110, 112–113, 118, 122, 128, 170, 177, 182–183, 186, 196n14, 203n17, 204n20, 206n29, 207nn32–33, 207n36, 211n20, 212nn24–25, 218n7, 228n9
design, 145, 191n8, 220n13
Designs on Nature, 58–59, 62
desire, 2, 77–78, 81, 83, 87–88, 90, 94, 96–98, 102, 109–110, 112–113, 115, 118–119, 126, 139, 143, 156, 158, 162, 164, 166, 199n25, 213n29
desire(s) for a life, 41, 43, 45, 102, 105, 110, 196n15
Devi, Mahashweta, 75–80, 131, 189n1, 203n19, 205n24, 207n35, 219n11
Dewey, John, 8–9
dialogic/dialogue, 6, 9, 12–13, 15, 21, 24–27, 34, 38, 42–45, 65, 67, 79, 84, 88, 90, 101, 106–107, 116, 123, 129, 136, 138–142, 146, 149, 164–166, 181, 187, 196n13, 201n8, 206n30, 210n18, 212n25, 214n33, 219n9, 220n15, 223n22, 226n29

diaspora/diasporic, 1, 3–5, 7, 10–11, 14, 16, 21–24, 60–62, 78, 83, 87, 89–90, 94, 97, 103, 123, 134–135, 137–138, 142–144, 156, 159–162, 164, 167, 169–171, 177–181, 183–184, 186–187, 189n1, 193n16, 201–202n8, 202n10, 205n24, 208n3, 218n5, 219n12
différance, 85–86, 110, 128
difference, 5, 62, 66, 69, 79, 82–83, 85–87, 123, 128, 139, 146, 151, 159–160, 174–176, 178–179, 181, 186–187, 205n25, 206n30, 216n51
disciplinary reproduction, 1–2, 7, 10, 16, 105, 134–135, 140, 165, 167, 185–186
discursive gaps, 54, 143, 199n27
discursive risks, 54, 143, 199n27
Division of Health Science and Technology (HST), 147, 149–155, 157–164, 217n3, 221–223n19, 223n22, 224–225n26
double bind, 11, 85, 142, 153, 155, 206nn29–30
double consciousness, 22, 193n16
"Dracula Ballet, The," 142–143
dual relativization, 61, 66, 70, 81, 86
Dumit, Joseph, 11, 51, 227n7

Ecologies of Comparison, 101, 105, 108–110, 199n28
encounter, 2, 5–7, 17–18, 24–27, 32, 37, 40, 42, 44–46, 58–59, 63, 87, 89–91, 94–95, 97–99, 101–120, 123, 128–129, 134, 138, 140–141, 143–146, 149, 163, 165, 175, 179–181, 187, 196n14, 196n16, 207n36, 209n8, 211nn19–21, 212n24, 214n33, 214n40, 216n48, 220n12
Enlightenment, 7–8, 22, 61, 74, 81, 93, 178–179, 186, 228n9
epistemic violence, 19, 43, 62, 71, 89, 92, 209n4, 211n20, 223n20
"Ethnography in/of the World System," 9, 31
Eurocentric/Eurocentrism, 57, 82, 85–87, 178, 192n12, 197n20, 201n7, 207n31
Europe/European, 5, 80, 82–83, 86, 93, 122, 170, 177–179, 193n19, 201n7, 207n31, 208n3, 211n20, 228n10

evocation/evocative, 19–20, 25, 28,
95–98, 100–101, 108–109, 119–120, 123,
126, 128, 130, 134–135, 181–182, 185, 201n8,
208n4
exchange, 49, 73–74, 200n1
Exit Zero, 99–100
experience-distance/experience-distant,
25, 32, 37, 63, 66, 185, 200n5
experience-near/experience-proximal,
1–2, 24–25, 31–32, 36–37, 48–49, 63, 66,
101, 108, 185, 200n5
experiment/experimental/experimenta-
tion, 2, 7, 11, 13, 15, 19, 28, 35, 83, 108, 140,
165, 167, 174, 184, 189n1, 190n8, 212n23,
220n13

Fanon, Frantz, 22, 78, 170, 184, 193n16,
206n30
feminism/feminist, 4–6, 8, 11, 13, 19–21,
26, 32, 67, 73–75, 78, 80, 84–85, 143, 164,
166, 179, 183, 186, 189n1, 192n12, 192n15,
201n8, 202n10, 203n18, 206n30, 207n37,
226n29, 227n3
figuration/figure, 24, 44, 46–47, 51, 57,
66, 72, 74, 77–79, 84, 88, 97–98, 108,
113, 116, 122, 130, 142–146, 181, 197n20,
207n31, 215n42, 218n4, 219n11
financial capital/financialization, 7, 11, 28,
31, 70, 73–75, 99, 174, 178–179, 203n16,
203n18, 217n3, 225n26
Fischer, Michael, 2, 6, 9, 19–20, 26–27,
29–31, 33–35, 37, 65, 68–69, 75, 80,
89, 94, 136–139, 146, 157, 159, 161, 166,
184–185, 192n12, 195n1, 195n3, 195nn5–6,
196n8, 200n2, 201n8, 202–203n12,
217n1, 217n3, 218n4, 218n6, 218n8,
219nn9–10, 221n19, 223n22
forms of life, 40, 139, 155, 219n10, 223n22
Fortun, Kim, 31, 38–39, 47, 52–55, 108,
143, 191n8, 192n12, 195n6, 199nn23–24,
199nn26–27, 203n13, 207n34,
220n13
fractal, 69–70, 125
"From the Native's Point of View,"
63–64, 201n6
future anterior, 88, 207n34, 215n43

Garcia, Angela, 38–42, 45–46, 53, 196n9,
199n24
Geertz, Clifford, 25, 27, 32, 63–69, 75–76,
80, 88, 92, 101, 176, 184–185, 193n19,
200n5, 201nn6–7
generation/generational, 2, 5, 99–100,
146, 162–164, 171–173, 218n5, 224n25,
225n27
geopolitics/geopolitical, 53, 142, 144,
208n2
global(ization), 1–2, 6–8, 10, 14, 20, 22, 25,
30–32, 36, 38, 41, 47–50, 52–54, 61–62,
69–70, 73–77, 87, 94, 100, 105, 107, 132,
136–137, 140, 142, 144, 149, 151, 153–156,
158–165, 178, 197n20, 199n24, 199n28,
200n3, 204–205n23, 217n3, 218n7,
223n20, 224–225n26, 226n29
Gramsci, Antonio, 8–9

Haraway, Donna, 5, 8–9, 67, 128, 183,
191n9, 201n8, 202n9, 209n8, 218n4
haunting, 8, 45–46, 53, 55, 79, 85, 94, 99,
104, 110–112, 123, 130, 144, 173, 183, 187,
196n16, 218n5, 219n12
Haunting Legacies, 99–100, 218n5
Heart of Darkness, 76–78, 80, 97–98, 131,
204n21, 219n11
hegemonic/hegemony, 62, 70, 73–74,
81, 142, 144, 152, 154, 176–178, 180, 187,
200n4, 207n31, 223n22, 225n26
"History," 70–72, 76, 81, 83–87, 89, 91–93,
95–96, 112, 133, 206n28, 208n3, 228n10
Holmes, Douglas, 26, 139–142, 144, 146,
164, 220n14
HST. *See* Division of Health Science and
Technology

identitarian/identity, 4–5, 13, 24, 65,
76–78, 80, 88, 131, 139, 169–170, 175–176,
181, 184, 186, 193–194n19, 198n21, 209n9
Imaginary Ethnographies, 96–97, 196n14,
211n20
imperial(ism), 7, 53, 62, 69–73, 75, 77,
81–84, 93–94, 132–134, 157–158, 163, 178,
194n19, 204n20, 208nn2–3
implosion, 49–52, 54

incommensurable/incommensurability, 59, 63, 66–68, 80, 82–83, 86–87, 89, 137, 139, 156, 178, 187, 202n10

incongruence/incongruent, 59, 61, 66, 73, 76–77, 79–80, 156

India, 3–4, 14, 21, 26, 29–30, 52–53, 59–62, 72, 74, 79, 83, 139, 146–164, 166, 170–173, 178–179, 181, 199n24, 200n4, 202n10, 206n30, 207n37, 219n9, 223n20, 223n22, 224n24, 224–225n26, 225n27, 226n1, 227n3

Indian university, 4, 74, 154

indigeneity/indigenous, 4, 61, 74–75, 77–80, 189n1, 192–193n15, 197n19, 199n24, 205n24, 207n35, 219n11, 226n29

informed consent, 6, 20, 64, 175, 226n29

inheritance(s), 1–3, 5, 7–8, 10, 16, 20, 22–24, 26–28, 32, 69–70, 82–84, 89–90, 94, 98–99, 112, 116, 118, 122, 137, 141, 144, 162, 171, 174, 176–181, 183–187, 189n1, 190n3, 193n19

intellectual desire, 65, 72, 78, 90, 92–94, 130, 133, 143, 209n4, 219n9

interdisciplinarity/interdisciplinary, 15, 137, 220n16

interpretive anthropology/interpretive ethnography/interpretive turn, 35–36, 38, 64–66, 68–69, 117, 139, 185, 195n4

intimacy, 6, 25, 44, 87, 95, 99–106, 109–116, 118–120, 126–128, 131, 155, 180–184, 187, 209nn10–11, 213n29, 216n52

Jain, Lochlann, 99–100

Jasanoff, Sheila, 58–59, 62, 191n9, 223n23

John Dollar, 97–98, 209n7

juxtaposition, 7, 54, 59, 71, 73, 76–77, 79–80, 103, 105, 119–120, 125–126, 204n23, 211n19, 215n48

kinship, 66–67, 80, 82, 119, 131, 162, 187, 200n1, 205n25, 206–207n31, 213n29, 219n9, 227n4

late industrialism, 54, 100, 199n27, 207n34

Latour, Bruno, 61, 192n12, 195n7, 218n6

l'avenir, 88, 112, 115, 127, 137, 186

Levinas, Emmanuel, 126, 128, 138, 219n10

Lévi-Strauss, Claude, 38, 43–44, 116, 196n14, 207n36, 211n20, 212n25

liberal(ism), 20, 41, 45, 61–62, 69, 79, 83, 88, 90, 152, 160, 174–180, 199n25, 200n4, 204n20, 206n30, 209n9, 218n9, 226n29, 226n2

life history, 38–43, 146, 172, 218n4, 225n27

linguistic ideologies, 68–69

literary/literature, 25–28, 34–36, 69, 73–74, 76–77, 79, 84, 88, 90–93, 95–96, 98, 105, 112, 134, 208n3, 209n5, 212n23, 215n48

literary knowledge, 27, 95–97, 99, 105, 110, 117, 182, 185, 215n48

logofratrocentrism, 77, 80

Malignant, 99–100

Malinowski, Bronislaw, 9, 16, 23–24, 26–27, 33, 38, 42, 55–56, 95, 100, 185, 190n5, 195n2, 201nn6–7

Man of Good Hope, A, 38, 40–41, 44

Marcus, George, 6, 9, 17, 19–20, 26–27, 30–35, 37, 42, 59, 65, 68–69, 75, 80, 88–89, 139–142, 144–146, 157, 164, 184–185, 194–195n1, 195n2, 195nn5–6, 197n20, 200n2, 201n8, 202–203n12, 220nn13–15, 223n23

Marx, Karl, 7–9, 108, 184

masculinity/masculinist, 11–13, 23–26, 42, 57, 62, 77–78, 105, 112, 132, 146, 183–184, 192n12, 201n7, 211nn20–21, 213n26

Massachusetts Institute of Technology (MIT), 137, 147–151, 154–155, 157–160, 162–163, 165, 223n20, 223n22, 224–225n26

Melanesia/Melanesian/Melanesianist, 69, 200n1, 206–207n31

metropolitan academy, discipline, intellectual (production), (research) university, 1–5, 7, 11, 14–15, 22–24, 60, 74–75, 83, 88, 106, 134, 137, 146, 158, 164–165, 167, 174, 176, 179–180, 186, 189n1, 196n16, 203n16, 208n2, 217n3, 218n5, 218n9, 223n20

MIT. *See* Massachusetts Institute of Technology
modernity, 10, 61–62, 79, 82–83, 90, 180, 198n21, 200n4, 225n27
mourning (work of), 41, 43, 87, 100, 109–112, 115–116, 120, 127, 130, 173, 176, 179, 196n14, 207n32, 212n24, 214n33, 215n43, 215n45
multidisciplinarity/multidisciplinary, 153–154, 159
multilocale ethnography, 5, 9–10, 20, 33, 122, 185, 190n6, 195n1
multimodal(ity), 21, 96, 100, 182, 227n7
"Multi-si(gh)ted," 11, 13, 83, 102, 114, 184, 190n6, 193nn18–19, 208n3, 214n33
multisited ethnography, 5–6, 9–10, 13, 20–21, 25, 30–33, 36–38, 42, 49–50, 52, 59, 88, 120, 123, 141, 185, 190n6, 194–195n1, 195n7, 203n13

Naficy, Nahal, 142–145
Nambikwara, 43, 116, 196n14, 207n36, 211n20
nationalism/nationalist, 72, 79, 81, 84, 162–163, 171, 200n4, 208n3, 210n14, 224n25
native informant, 2, 6, 24–28, 32, 43–45, 56, 62–64, 72–73, 76, 81, 84–85, 87–88, 91, 93, 99–101, 105, 114, 134, 140–141, 143, 166, 175, 187, 214n33
neoliberal(ism), 7, 11, 61, 69, 149, 152, 158, 164, 170, 200n3

objectification/objectify(ing), 1–2, 6, 8, 19, 34, 38, 40–42, 46, 50–51, 62, 73, 84, 87, 89–90, 103–104, 113, 115–116, 118–120, 128–130, 138, 140–141, 145, 175, 183, 186, 207n38, 211n21, 212n24, 213n29, 216n52
objective/objectivity, 8–9, 12, 66, 89, 92–95, 105, 109, 117, 123, 126, 131, 159, 183, 187, 211n20, 212n24, 217n52, 220n15
object(s) of analysis/ethnography/study, 49–53, 55, 62, 82, 86, 88, 93–94, 98, 102, 138–139, 142, 175, 191n11, 197–198n21
ontological turn, 192n12, 196n17, 218n6

Ordinary Affects, 101, 103–105, 108–110, 210n15, 211n18, 214n40
Ortner, Sherry, 64–65, 101

para-ethnography, 26, 28, 139–143, 145–146, 149–150, 160, 164–166, 220n13, 220n15
para-site(s), 26, 145–146, 149–151, 164–167, 208n3, 220n13, 221n19, 223n20, 223n22, 226n29
Partial Connections, 25, 66, 88, 201n8, 206n31, 208n4, 214n37, 218n4
partial connections, 67, 69–70, 88, 125, 177
partial perspective, 8, 13, 82, 179, 183. *See also* situated knowledges/perspective
participant observation, 17–18, 24, 47, 141, 192n14
particular(ity), 1, 37, 60, 63, 156–157, 160, 162
Pastoral Clinic, The, 38–39, 41
pedagogical/pedagogy, 1–6, 9–14, 18–23, 28, 33, 48, 51, 55, 70, 73, 96, 102, 105, 127, 129, 135, 139–141, 146, 156, 158, 167, 170, 175, 184–187, 189n1, 190n3, 191n11, 197–198n21, 203n13, 210n18, 215n43, 227n7
peopling, 146, 155, 157–159, 164, 189n1, 223n22, 225n27
personhood, 6, 9, 25, 27, 31, 33, 38–39, 41, 50, 66, 69, 100, 120, 157, 159
Peterson, Kristin, 38–39, 47–50, 52, 108, 191n11, 195n6, 197–198n21
phallogocentrism, 12, 18, 20, 23, 26–27, 38, 43, 54, 57, 59, 63, 65, 67–69, 72, 77, 80, 88–90, 93, 95, 98, 100–101, 104–106, 117, 119–120, 123, 128, 130–131, 135, 138, 174–176, 179–183, 185–187, 208n2, 211nn20–21, 216n51, 218n7
Pharmocracy, 62, 152, 165, 220n15, 221n17
photography/photographer, 13, 19, 25–26, 28, 90, 95, 101, 103–104, 109–123, 127–132, 134, 182, 185, 192n14, 204n22, 209n8, 210n16, 211n19, 212n24, 213n26, 213n29, 213–214n33, 214–215n40, 215nn43–44,

215–216n48, 216n50, 216–217n52, 217nn53–54

planetarity, 52, 55, 74–75, 77, 79–80, 119, 199n22, 199n28, 204–205n23, 211n22

poesis, 101, 107, 211n19

political economy, 2, 6, 11, 14, 17, 25, 31–32, 36–39, 41, 47–50, 52, 54, 69–70, 87, 97, 99–100, 142, 146, 155, 157, 159, 164–165, 180, 217n1, 226n29

postcolonial/postcolony, 2–6, 19, 21, 23, 26, 32, 51, 61, 63, 65, 70, 73, 78–80, 82–83, 89–90, 94, 105, 112, 132, 143, 149, 152, 154–156, 160–162, 164, 174, 177, 179, 184, 186, 189n1, 190n4, 190n6, 192n12, 192n15, 193nn16–17, 193–194n19, 196n12, 202n10, 205n24, 206n30, 207n38, 224n25, 225n27, 227n6

poststructuralism/poststructuralist, 68, 92, 202n11, 209n5

Povinelli, Elizabeth, 67–68, 226n2

power, 47, 53–55, 60, 62, 67, 72–74, 79–80, 85, 88–89, 92–94, 139–140, 143–144, 146, 151, 153–155, 159–160, 163, 165–166, 175, 192n15, 208n3, 220n15, 221n18, 224n26

procedural ethics, 6, 64, 115–116, 175, 226n29

promise of justice, 85–86, 88, 128, 169, 177, 179, 207n32

property, 66, 69, 79, 194n22, 202n10, 205n25

psychoanalysis/psychoanalytic, 27, 92–93, 95, 196n14, 200n5, 202n10, 206n29, 208n1, 211n20, 212n25

"Pterodactyl," 76, 78–79, 203n19

punctum, 109–111, 114, 117–118, 128–131, 212n24

queer (politics)/queering/queerness, 129–131, 134–135, 178, 185, 213n27

racism/racist, 13, 62, 76–78, 101, 116, 129–132, 175, 193n19, 199n25, 204n21

Rani of Sirmur, 71–73, 76, 91–94, 112

reader, 12, 26–28, 44, 78, 84, 87, 92–93, 96–98, 100–101, 104–105, 115–116, 118–119, 125, 129–131, 134, 144, 170, 208n4, 209n5, 211n19, 213n31, 214n40, 220n12

reflexivity, 8, 15, 17, 51, 62, 88, 98, 129, 138–140, 146, 151, 164, 166, 183, 190n3, 217n3, 220n15, 223n22, 226n29

refusal(s), 8, 20, 43–45, 53, 64–65, 71, 75, 81–82, 92, 104, 106–107, 118–119, 130, 137–138, 141–145, 175–176, 178–180, 184, 186, 193n19, 203n12, 211n20, 212n24

relationality, 63–67, 70, 76, 80, 88, 94, 98, 102, 104–105, 108–117, 122–123, 125–128, 140–142, 146–147, 153–159, 177, 196n14, 202n10, 208n4, 211n19, 215n48, 216n48, 216nn51–52

relativism/relativist, 8, 66, 81, 151, 153–154, 159, 165

representation, 2, 6, 10, 19, 25–26, 32–33, 35, 37, 43, 68, 88–89, 94, 101, 105, 107, 110–111, 113, 119–120, 122, 126–128, 130, 134, 144, 152, 170, 182, 185, 213n26

reproduction, 131–132, 134, 185, 187, 209n9, 217n53

research design, 21, 23, 25, 28, 38, 53–55, 59, 64, 79

research topic, 51, 191n11, 197–198n21

research university, 4, 10, 20, 164

romantic authority/authorship, 24, 27, 33, 56, 95, 98, 100, 105, 165–166, 185, 211n20

Room of One's Own, A, 76, 204n22

Rushdie, Salman, 161–162, 224n24

Salih, Tayib, 76–79, 131, 185, 219n11

scale, 1, 6, 21, 24–27, 29, 31–33, 37–38, 48–55, 64, 108, 135, 155, 165, 176, 180–181, 187, 194n21, 196n8, 198n21, 199n24, 205n23, 227n6

scene of writing, 43, 95, 113, 196n14, 211n20

Schwab, Gabriele, 25, 27, 96–100, 105, 110, 117, 182–183, 191n9, 196n14, 207n36, 209n5, 209n8, 211n20, 212n25, 215n48, 218n5

science and technology studies (STS), 14–16, 19, 21, 33, 58, 137, 191nn8–9, 192n12, 201n8, 218n6

Season of Migration to the North, 76, 78, 132, 185

secular(ism), 83, 145–146, 218–219n9
seminar, 11–13, 83, 102, 114, 184, 190n6, 193nn18–19, 208n3, 210n14, 214n33
settler colonialism, 83, 199n24
sexism/sexist, 78, 101, 116
sight, 113–114, 116, 128, 131, 180, 182–183, 185–186, 190n6, 213n27, 227n7
singularity, 42, 46, 87, 104, 109–110, 112, 114, 118, 144, 214n37
situated knowledges/perspective, 5, 8, 21–22, 40–41, 48, 100, 183, 187, 202n9. *See also* partial perspective
situation(s), 7–10, 13, 15, 41–44, 54, 68, 83, 89, 94, 131, 137, 141, 154, 173–174, 177, 181, 183, 190n6, 199n24, 203n12, 203n18, 219n9, 223n22
Smith, Shawn Michelle, 129–133, 183, 185, 217n53, 217n55
sociological/sociotechnical imaginary, 148–149, 152, 155–156, 160
South Africa, 4–5, 26, 40–41, 45, 59, 169–171, 176–179, 181, 184, 193n19, 194n19, 206n30, 212n23, 225n27, 227n4, 227n8
Speculative Markets, 38, 47–50, 108
Spivak, Gayatri, 21–22, 25, 27, 68, 70–95, 97, 103, 108, 112, 119, 125, 131, 133, 139, 141, 176–177, 182–183, 185, 196n12, 199n22, 199n25, 202n10, 203nn18–19, 204n20, 204n23, 205n24, 205n26, 206n28, 207n31, 207n35, 208nn1–3, 209n4, 211n22, 217n3, 219n11, 227n5, 228n10
staging, 105, 145–146, 149–150, 211n21, 220n15
Steinberg, Jonny, 38–42, 44, 46, 53, 196n10
Stewart, Kathleen, 101, 103–105, 107–108, 119–120, 122, 183, 210nn15–16, 210–211n18, 211nn19–21, 213n29, 214–215n40, 216n52
Strathern, Marilyn, 21–22, 25, 27, 61–62, 66–70, 74, 80–82, 86–89, 104–105, 125, 128, 139, 176, 183, 194n22, 200n1, 201n8, 202nn10–11, 202–203n12, 203n16, 205n25, 206–207n31, 208–209n4, 214n37, 218n4, 220n16
structuralism/structuralist, 34, 102
studium, 109, 129–130

subaltern, 32, 42, 45, 71–75, 77, 87–89, 93–94, 96, 101, 107, 116, 133–134, 146, 208n3, 218n9
subaltern school/subaltern studies, 72, 200n4
subjective/subjectivity, 22, 25, 31, 33, 37–38, 40, 42–43, 50, 53, 64–65, 78, 89, 93–94, 97–98, 103, 109–110, 113, 116–117, 123, 129, 131, 142–144, 186, 208n3
Sunder Rajan, Rajeswari, 73, 202n10, 203n15, 207n37, 215–216n48, 219n9, 224n24, 227n3
supplement/supplementarity/supplementation, 10, 71, 73, 89, 93, 119–120, 139, 181, 190n6, 207n36, 227n7
syllabus, 11–12, 17, 189n1, 197n21
"Systems," 17, 184, 189n1

technoscientific imaginary. *See* sociological/sociotechnical imaginary
theory from the South, 53, 106, 207n38
third space(s), 26, 94–95, 115, 117, 145, 159–160, 164
Three-Letter Plague, 38–41
THSTI. *See* Translational Health Science and Technology Institute of India
toxicity, 52, 58, 199n24
trace(s), 65, 72–73, 85, 94–95, 98–99, 110, 112, 115–116, 123, 138, 142, 144, 187, 216n52, 219n12
tracking, 47, 50, 52, 65, 197n19
transcultural identification, 63–64, 75
transference/transferential, 8, 27, 65, 87, 90, 93–96, 98, 101, 104–105, 113, 116–117, 122–123, 125–131, 134–135, 171, 173, 183, 196n16, 211nn19–20, 212n24, 215n45, 216n48, 216n50
translation, 22, 33–34, 37, 55, 65–66, 68, 75, 95, 142, 161, 185, 192n15, 193n17, 201n7, 207n35
Translational Health Science and Technology Institute of India (THSTI), 139, 146, 148–164, 166–167, 223n20, 223n22, 224n26, 225n27
translational research, 26, 139, 146–150, 152–158, 160, 164, 221n18

Traweek, Sharon, 58–60, 192n12
trialogue/trialogic, 27, 116, 123, 196n13
Tsing, Anna Lowenhaupt, 38, 180, 194n21,
    195n7, 201n8

United States, 3–4, 14, 21, 30, 40–41, 45,
    52–53, 58, 103–104, 109, 119, 122–123,
    132–134, 138, 142, 144, 149, 161–163, 170–
    172, 177–179, 181, 192n12, 199nn24–25,
    203n12, 203n18, 204n20, 208n3, 210n14,
    214n40, 216n52, 217n2
universal/universalism/universality, 37,
    60, 77–79, 81–83, 108, 163, 169–172,
    176–179, 185, 187, 205n24, 206n27,
    215n40, 218n7, 218n9, 226n3
University of California at Irvine, 4, 11,
    17, 39, 145, 184, 190n6, 191n11, 197–
    198n21, 210n18
University of Chicago, 3, 11, 17, 19,
    134, 174, 184, 189n1, 192n14, 193n19,
    220n13

University of the Western Cape (UWC),
    26, 28, 180

Van Gogh on Demand, 38, 47–48, 50, 108
viewer, 26, 101, 109–110, 113, 115–120, 122–123,
    125–126, 128–132, 213n31, 214n40, 216n50
Vita, 38–39, 41–44, 196n11

Wally, Christine, 99–100
Ways of Seeing, 112–113, 212n13, 213n26,
    213n29, 214n34
white masculinity/patriarchy ("white
    male"), 5, 24, 65, 97, 128–131, 133–134,
    170, 176, 184–186, 193n19, 208n3, 209n9,
    210n14, 211n20, 218n7
Wong, Winnie, 38–39, 47–48, 50, 52, 108,
    191n9
Woolf, Virginia, 76–79, 131, 204n22, 219n11
Writing Culture, 19, 88–89, 96, 201n8
"Writing Lesson, The," 44, 196n14,
    207n36, 211n20, 212n25